AFTER THE FACT

❧ ❧ ❦ ❦

Volume I

AFTER THE FACT

❧ ❧ ❦ ❦

The Art of Historical Detection

Fourth Edition

Volume I

James West Davidson

Mark Hamilton Lytle
Bard College

Boston Burr Ridge, IL Dubuque, IA Madison, WI
New York San Francisco St. Louis
Bangkok Bogotá Caracas Lisbon London Madrid Mexico City
Milan New Delhi Seoul Singapore Sydney Taipei Toronto

McGraw-Hill Higher Education

*A Division of The **McGraw-Hill** Companies*

AFTER THE FACT: THE ART OF HISTORICAL DETECTION, VOLUME I, FOURTH EDITION

2 3 4 5 6 7 8 9 0 DOC/DOC 0 9 8 7 6 5 4 3 2 1 0

ISBN 0–07–229427–2

Editorial director: *Jane E. Vaicunas*
Senior sponsoring editor: *Lyn Uhl*
Developmental editor: *Kristen Mellitt*
Marketing manager: *Janise A. Fry*
Senior project manager: *Gloria G. Schiesl*
Senior production supervisor: *Sandra Hahn*
Coordinator of freelance design: *Michelle D. Whitaker*
Photo research coordinator: *John C. Leland*
Senior supplement coordinator: *Candy M. Kuster*
Compositor: *ElectraGraphics, Inc.*
Typeface: *10½/12 Janson*
Printer: *R. R. Donnelley & Sons Company/Crawfordsville, IN*

Freelance interior designer: *Kathy Theis*
Freelance cover designer: *Diane Beasley*
Cover images: *Dutch title,* © *Niemeyer Tabaksmuseum; Magnifying glass,* © *Chris Thomaidis, Tony Stone*
Photo research: *Photosearch, Inc., N.Y.*

Library of Congress has cataloged the complete version as follows:

Davidson, James West.
    After the fact : the art of historical detection / James West
Davidson, Mark Hamilton Lytle.—4th ed.
        p.   cm.
    Includes bibliographical references and index.
    ISBN 0–07–229426–4 (complete version)
    1. United States—Historiography.   2. United States—History.
I. Lytle, Mark H. II. Title.
E175.D38   2000
973.07'2—dc21   99–16991
                                                                    CIP

www.mhhe.com

ABOUT THE AUTHORS

✤ ✤ ✦ ✦

James West Davidson received his Ph.D. from Yale University. A historian who has pursued a full-time writing career, he is the author of numerous books, among them *The Logic of Millennial Thought: Eighteenth-Century New England* and *Great Heart: The History of a Labrador Adventure* (with John Rugge). He has also worked with Mark Lytle (and other coauthors) on *Nation of Nations: A Narrative History of the American Republic*.

Mark H. Lytle, who received his Ph.D. from Yale University, is Professor of History and Environmental Studies and Chair of the American Studies Program at Bard College. He is also Director of the Master of Arts in Teaching Program at Bard. His publications include *The Origins of the Iranian-American Alliance, 1941–1953* and, most recently, "An Environmental Approach to American Diplomatic History," in *Diplomatic History*. He is at work on *The Uncivil War: America in the Vietnam Era*.

CONTENTS

❧ ❧ ❦ ❦

PREFACE

We began this book twenty years ago by asserting that history is not some inert body of knowledge "out there" in the past, but a continual act of construction whose end product is being reshaped and made anew every time someone ventures into the archives. With rueful countenance, we can now reiterate this proposition merely by detailing some of the changes our book has undergone since the previous edition went to press in 1992. If history were not such a moving target, our labors would have been a good deal less strenuous.

Yet good history continues to be written; the historical landscape continues to change; and so must *After the Fact*. For those scholars who have used this book in the past, a summary of the fourth edition's most significant alterations is in order.

In Chapter 1, "Serving Time in Virginia," the discussion of Captain John Smith and Pocahontas raises the possibility, based on the speculations of anthropologists, that Smith's near execution may have been part of an Indian initiation rite. Recent research into Powhatan's confederation has made his political perspectives more evident. Our discussion of the rise of slavery in Virginia also incorporates new scholarship.

One might be forgiven for thinking, after the appearance of pathbreaking studies by Paul Boyer and Stephen Nissenbaum, Chadwick Hansen, Carol Karlsen, and John Demos, that little remained to be discovered regarding the Salem witch trials. But Chapter 2, "The Visible and Invisible Worlds of Salem," reevaluates the psychodynamics of the witchcraft accusations in light of new analysis suggesting that some of the accused were consciously faking their symptoms. (This finding is a kind of historiography come full circle.) In terms of the episode's social dynamics, we contrast the commercial hypothesis, which views the outbreak as a defensive response to a rising market economy in Salem Town, with alternative social explanations, including tensions arising from Quaker neighbors and the threat of Indian attacks.

Historians have long concentrated on intellectual history and textual analysis in their efforts to explicate the Declaration of Independence, and so have we. But in the final section of our revised Chapter 3, "Declaring Independence," we have taken advantage of recent scholarship to focus on slavery, not only as Jefferson and members of the Continental Congress viewed it, but also in terms of the ironic way in which enslaved African Americans themselves, through direct and indirect resistance to their own bondage, affected the outlook of the Declaration's authors.

Over the past decades few fields have been as active as western American history. In Chapter 4, "Jackson's Frontier—and Turner's," we have added a final section, "Jackson and the New Western History," that incorporates the perspectives of that surging field of scholarship. From this point of view, Jackson's frontier of the Old Southwest can be seen as a remarkably multicultural middle ground wherein Indians, white settlers, and African Americans all mixed.

Chapters 5, 6, 7, and 9 have smaller alterations. In "The Invisible Pioneers," we have incorporated research showing that the demise of the bison on the Great Plains was affected not only by white hunters and the commercial demand for hides, but also by a rise in Indian population and the consequent increased hunting pressure. Chapter 6, "The Madness of John Brown," has been rewritten to reflect the devaluation of Sigmund Freud's theories over the past decade, though we make the case that psychological analysis remains important to historians. Chapter 7, "The View from the Bottom Rail," now includes a discussion of the pitfalls of rendering African-American dialect in the slave narrative collections, especially since few of the oral interviews in the collections were tape recorded.

In addition to the alterations themselves, for the first time *After the Fact* is accompanied by an Instructor's Manual, prepared by Juan Garcia of the College of Saint Mary. The manual provides a variety of resources for each chapter, including a summary, discussion questions, suggested activities, and a list of relevant print, web, and multimedia sources. Instructors can also take advantage of a message board located on the book's web site (www.mhhe.com/davidsonatf) to exchange ideas about and share strategies for using *After the Fact* in their courses.

As we survey these changes in the historical landscape, one thing becomes clear. History is a work in progress and so, therefore, is this book. We look forward to more changes in future editions and to the comments and suggestions of our readers, which will certainly help make these stories richer.

Meantime, our debt is not small to those who helped with revisions to the present edition. For comments on one or more chapters, we would like to thank Linda Alkana, California State Unversity–Long Beach; Robert Bain, University of Michigan; George Blakey, Indiana University East; Jamie Bronstein, New Mexico State University; William R. Cario, Concordia College, Wisconsin; Raymond J. Cunningham, Fordham University; Amelia Dees-Killette, Coastal Carolina Community College; Stewart Dippel, University of the Ozarks; Harriet E. Amos Doss, University of Alabama at Birmingham; Laurie Zittrain Eisenberg, Carnegie Mellon University; Juan Garcia, College of Saint Mary; Michael K. Green, Eastern Washington University; Michael Grossberg, Indiana University–Bloomington; David C. Hanson, Virginia Western Community College; Craig Hendricks, California State University–Long Beach; Jerrold Hirsch, Truman State University; Andrew Holman, Bridgewater State College; Chris Kimball, Augsburg College; John D. Krugler, Marquette University; David Rich Lewis, Utah State University; Dane Morrison, Salem State College; Elsa Nystrom, Kennesaw

State University; David B. Parker, Kennesaw State University; Mario A. Perez, Crafton Hills College; Susan Sessions Rugh, Brigham Young University; Michael Schaller, University of Arizona; Thomas A. Scott, Kennesaw State University; Rebecca Shoemaker, Indiana State University; John H. Wigger, University of Missouri; Robert S. Wolff, Central Connecticut State University; and Julian Zelizer, State University of New York at Albany.

Larry Foster, Georgia Institute of Technology, was particularly unstinting with his time and his valuable observations. In addition, our friends and family offered their usual frank, unvarnished, and constructive advice: Michael Stoff, John Rugge, Bill Gienapp, Tom Stoenner, and Gretchen Lytle. Mark Lytle is also indebted to those Bard College students who spent a semester exploring presidential tapes, especially Irma Dedic, Ted Hudson, Timend Bates, Aaron Brokaw, Alex Dezen, Jill Frank, Marco Gruelle, Molly Heekins, Diogo Marzo, Lara Alacantrel, Kwami Davis, Logan Germich, and Zach Mizroch. Finally, we received generous and patient support from our editorial team at McGraw-Hill: Lyn Uhl, Kristen Mellitt, and in production, Gloria Schiesl.

INTRODUCTION

This book began as an attempt to bring more life to the reading and learning of history. As practicing historians, we have been troubled by a growing disinterest in or even animosity toward the study of the past. How is it that when we and other historians have found so much that excites curiosity, other people find history irrelevant and boring? Perhaps, we thought, if lay readers and students understood better how historians go about their work—how they examine evidence, how they pose questions, and how they reach answers—history would engage them as it does us.

As often happens, it took a mundane event to focus and clarify our preoccupations. One day while working on another project, we went outside to watch a neighboring farmer cut down a large old hemlock that had become diseased. As his saw cut deeper into the tree, we joked that it had now bit into history as far back as the Depression. *"Depression?"* grunted our friend. "I thought you fellas were historians. I'm deep enough now, so's Hoover wasn't even a gleam in his father's eye."

With the tree down, the three of us examined the stump. Our woodcutter surprised us with what he saw.

"Here's when my folks moved into this place," he said, pointing to a ring. "1922."

"How do you know without counting the rings?" we asked.

"Oh, *well*," he said, as if the answer were obvious. "Look at the core, here. The rings are all bunched up tight. I bet there's sixty or seventy—and all within a couple inches. Those came when the place was still forest. Then, you notice, the rings start getting fatter all of a sudden. That's when my dad cleared behind the house—in '22—and the tree started getting a lot more light. And look further out, here—see how the rings set together again for a couple years? That's from loopers."

"Loopers?" we asked cautiously.

"Sure—*loopers*. You know. The ones with only front legs and back." His hand imitated a looping, hopping crawl across the log. "Inchworms. They damn near killed the tree. That was sometime after the war—'49 or '50." As his fingers traced back and forth among the concentric circles, he spoke of other events from years gone by. Before we returned home, we had learned a good deal about past doings in the area.

Now it occurs to us that our neighbor had a pretty good knack for putting together history. The evidence of the past, like the tree rings, comes easily enough to hand. But we still need to be taught how to see it, read it,

want to engage students

Are None historians view history

and explain it before it can be turned into a story. Even more to the point, the explanations and interpretations *behind* the story often turn out to be as interesting as the story itself. After all, the fascination in our neighbor's account came from the way he traced his tale out of those silent tree rings.

Unfortunately, most readers first encounter history in school textbooks, and these omit the explanations and interpretations—the detective work, if you will. Textbooks, by their nature, seek to summarize knowledge. They have little space for looking at how that knowledge was gained. Yet the challenge of doing history, not just reading it, is what attracts so many historians. Couldn't some of that challenge be communicated in a concrete way? That was our first goal.

We also felt that the writing of history has suffered in recent years because some historians have been overly eager to convert their discipline into an unadulterated social science. Undeniably, history would lose much of its claim to contemporary relevance without the methods and theories it has borrowed from anthropology, psychology, political science, economics, sociology, and other fields. Indeed, such theories make an important contribution to these pages. Yet history is rooted in the narrative tradition. As much as it seeks to generalize from past events, as do the sciences, it also remains dedicated to capturing the uniqueness of a situation. When historians neglect the literary aspect of their discipline—when they forget that good history begins with a good story—they risk losing that wider audience that all great historians have addressed. They end up, sadly, talking to themselves.

Our second goal, then, was to discuss the methods of American historians in a way that would give proper due to both the humanistic and scientific sides of history. In taking this approach, we have tried to examine many of the methodologies that allow historians to unearth new evidence or to shed new light on old issues. At the same time, we selected topics that we felt were inherently interesting as stories.

Thus our book employs what might be called an apprentice approach to history rather than the synthetic approach of textbooks. A text strives to be comprehensive and broad. It presents its findings in as rational and programmatic a manner as possible. By contrast, apprentices are much less likely to receive such a formal presentation. They learn their profession from artisans who take their daily trade as it comes through the front door. A pewter pot is ordered? Very well, the pot is fashioned. Along the way, an apprentice is shown how to pour the mold. An engraving is needed? Then the apprentice receives a first lesson in etching. The apprentice method of teaching communicates a broad range of knowledge over the long run by focusing on specific situations.

So also this book. Our discussion of methods is set in the context of specific problems historians have encountered over the years. In piecing the individual stories together, we try to pause as an artisan might and point out problems of evidence, historical perspective, or logical inference. Sometimes we focus on problems that all historians must face, whatever their subjects. These problems include such matters as the selection of evidence, historical perspective, the analysis of a document, and the use of broader historical theory. In other cases, we explore problems not encountered by all historians, but characteristic of specific historical fields. These problems include the use of pictorial evidence, questions of psychohistory, problems encountered analyzing oral interviews, the value of decision-making models in political history, and so on. In each case, we have tried to provide the reader with some sense of vicarious participation—the savor of doing history as well as of reading it.

Given our approach, the ultimate success of this book can be best measured in functional terms—how well it works for the apprentices and artisans. We hope that the artisans, our fellow historians, will find the volume's implicit as well as explicit definitions of good history worth considering. In choosing our examples, we have naturally gravitated toward the work of those historians we most respect. At the same time we have drawn upon our own original research in many of the topics discussed; we hope those findings also may be of use to scholars.

As for the apprentices, we admit to being only modest proselytizers. We recognize that, of all the people who read this book, only a few will go on to become professional historians. We do hope, however, that even casual readers will come to appreciate the complexity and excitement that go into the study of the past. History is not something that is simply brought out of the archives, dusted off, and displayed as "the way things really were." It is a painstaking construction, held together only with the help of assumptions, hypotheses, and inferences. Readers of history who push dutifully onward, unaware of all the backstage work, miss the essence of the discipline. They miss the opportunity to question and to judge their reading critically. Most of all, they miss the chance to learn how enjoyable it can be to go out and do a bit of digging themselves.

❧   ❧   ❦   ❦

The Strange Death of Silas Deane

The writing of history is one of the most familiar ways of organizing human knowledge. And yet, if familiarity has not always bred contempt, it has at least encouraged a good deal of misunderstanding. All of us meet history long before we have heard of any of the social science disciplines, at a tender age when tales of the past easily blend with heroic myths of the culture. In Golden Books, Abe Lincoln looms every bit as large as Paul Bunyan, while George Washington's cherry tree gets chopped down yearly with almost as much ritual as St. Nick's Christmas tree goes up. Despite this long familiarity, or perhaps because of it, most students absorb the required facts about the past without any real conception of what history is. Even worse, most think they do know and never get around to discovering what they missed.

"History is what happened in the past." That statement is the everyday view of the matter. It supposes that historians must return to the past through the surviving records and bring it back to the present to display as "what really happened." The everyday view recognizes that this task is often difficult. But historians are said to succeed if they bring back the facts without distorting them or forcing a new perspective on them. In effect, historians are seen as couriers between the past and present. Like all good couriers, they are expected simply to deliver messages without adding to them.

This everyday view of history is profoundly misleading. In order to demonstrate how it is misleading, we would like to examine in detail an event that "happened in the past"—the death of Silas Deane. Deane does not appear in most American history texts, and rightly so. He served as a distinctly second-rate diplomat for the United States during the years of the American Revolution. Yet the story of Deane's death is an excellent example of an event that cannot be understood merely by transporting it, courier-like, to the present. In short, it illustrates the important difference between "what happened in the past" and what history really is.

[handwritten margin notes: "Most people simply learn facts"; "Historians present facts"]

AN UNTIMELY DEATH

Silas Deane's career began with one of those rags-to-riches stories so much appreciated in American folklore. In fact, Deane might have made a lasting place for himself in the history texts, except that his career ended with an equally dramatic riches-to-rags story.

He began life as the son of a humble blacksmith in Groton, Connecticut. The blacksmith had aspirations for his boy and sent him to Yale College, where Silas was quick to take advantage of his opportunities. After studying law, Deane opened a practice near Hartford; he then continued his climb up the social ladder by marrying a well-to-do widow, whose inheritance included the business of her late husband, a merchant. Conveniently, Deane became a merchant. After his first wife died, he married the granddaughter of a former governor of Connecticut.

Not content to remain a prospering businessman, Deane entered politics. He served on Connecticut's Committee of Correspondence and later as a delegate to the first and second Continental Congresses, where he attracted the attention of prominent leaders, including Benjamin Franklin, Robert Morris, and John Jay. In 1776 Congress sent Deane to France as the first American to represent the united colonies abroad. His mission was to purchase badly needed military supplies for the Revolutionary cause. A few months later Benjamin Franklin and Arthur Lee joined him in an attempt to arrange a formal treaty of alliance with France. The American commissioners concluded the alliance in March 1778.

Deane worked hard to progress from the son of a blacksmith all the way to Minister Plenipotentiary from the United States to the Court of France. Most observers described him as ambitious: someone who thoroughly enjoyed fame, honor, and wealth. "You know his ambition—" wrote John Adams to one correspondent, "his desire of making a Fortune. . . . You also know his Art and Enterprise. Such Characters are often useful, altho always to be carefully watched and contracted, specially in such a government as ours." One man in particular suspected Deane enough to watch him: Arthur Lee, the third member of the American mission. Lee accused Deane of taking unfair advantage of his official position to make a private fortune—as much as £50,000, some said. Deane stoutly denied the accusations, and Congress engaged in a heated debate over his conduct. In 1778 it voted to recall its Minister Plenipotentiary, although none of the charges had been conclusively proved.

Deane embroiled himself in further controversy in 1781, having written friends to recommend that America sue for peace and patch up the quarrel with England. His letters were intercepted, and copies of them turned up in a New York Tory newspaper just after Cornwallis surrendered to Washington at Yorktown. For Deane, the timing could not have been worse. With American victory complete, anyone advocating that the United States rejoin Britain was considered as much a traitor as Benedict Arnold. So Deane suddenly found himself adrift. He could not return to America, for no one would have him. Nor could he go to England without confirming his reputation as a traitor. And he could not stay in France, where he had injudiciously accused Louis XVI of aiding the Americans for purely selfish reasons. Rejected on all sides, Deane took refuge in Flanders.

The next few years of his life were spent unhappily. Without friends and with little money, he continued in Flanders until 1783, when the controversy had died down enough for him to move to England. There he lived in obscurity, took to drink, and wound up boarding at the house of an unsavory prostitute. The only friend who remained faithful to him was Edward Bancroft, another Connecticut Yankee who, as a boy, had been Deane's pupil and

"You know his ambition—his desire of making a Fortune. . . . You also know his Art and Enterprise. Such Characters are often useful, altho always to be carefully watched and contracted, specially in such a government as ours."—John Adams on Silas Deane (Photo: Library of Congress)

later his personal secretary during the Paris negotiations for the alliance. Although Bancroft's position as a secretary seemed innocent enough, members of the Continental Congress knew that Bancroft was also acting as a spy for the Americans, using his connections in England to secure information about the British ministry's war plans. With the war concluded, Bancroft was back in London. Out of kindness, he provided Deane with living money from time to time.

Finally, Deane decided he could no longer live in London and in 1789 booked passage on a ship sailing for the United States. When Thomas Jefferson heard the news, he wrote his friend James Madison: "Silas Deane is coming over to finish his days in America, not having one *sou* to subsist on elsewhere. He is a wretched monument of the consequences of a departure from right."

The rest of the sad story could be gotten from the obituaries. Deane boarded the *Boston Packet* in mid-September, and it sailed out of London down the estuary of the Thames. A storm came up, however, and on September 19 the ship lost both its anchors and beat a course for safer shelter, where it could wait out the storm. On September 22, while walking the quarter deck with the ship's captain, Deane suddenly "complain'd of a dizziness in his head, and an oppression at his stomach." The captain immediately put him to bed. Deane's condition worsened; twice he tried to say something, but no one was able to make out his words. A "drowsiness and insensibility continually incroached upon his faculties," and only four hours after the first signs of illness he breathed his last.

Such, in outline, was the rise and fall of the ambitious Silas Deane. The story itself seems pretty clear, although certainly people might interpret it in different ways. Thomas Jefferson thought Deane's unhappy career demonstrated "the consequences of a departure from right," whereas one English newspaper more sympathetically attributed his downfall to the mistake of "placing confidence in his [American] Compatriots, and doing them service before he had got his compensation, of which no well-bred Politician was before him ever guilty." Yet either way, the basic story remains the same—the same, that is, until the historian begins putting together a more complete account of Deane's life. Then some of the basic facts become clouded.

For example, a researcher familiar with the correspondence of Americans in Europe during 1789 would realize that a rumor had been making its way around London in the weeks following Deane's death. According to certain people, Deane had become depressed by his poverty, ill health, and low reputation, and consequently had committed suicide. John Cutting, a New England merchant and friend of Jefferson, wrote of the rumor that Deane "had predetermin'd to take a sufficient quantity of Laudanum [a form of opium] to ensure his dissolution" before the boat could sail for America. John Quincy Adams heard that "every probability" of the situation suggested Deane's death was "voluntary and self-administered." And Tom Paine, the famous pamphleteer, also reported the gossip: "Cutting told me he took poison."

At this point we face a substantial problem. Obviously, historians cannot rest content with the facts that come most easily to hand. They must search the odd corners of libraries and letter collections in order to put together a complete story. But how do historians know when their research is "complete"? How do they know to search one collection of letters rather than another? These questions point up the misconception at the heart of the everyday view of history. History is not "what happened in the past"; rather, it is *the act of selecting, analyzing, and writing about the past.* It is something that is done, that is constructed, rather than an inert body of data that lies scattered through the archives.

The distinction is important. It allows us to recognize the confusion in the question of whether a history of something is "complete." If history were merely "what happened in the past," there would never be a "complete" history of Silas Deane—or even a complete history of the last day of his life. The past holds an infinite number of facts about those last days, and they could never all be included in a historical account.

The truth is, no historian would want to include all the facts. Here, for example, is a list of items from the past that might form part of a history of Silas Deane. Which ones should be included?

Deane is sent to Paris to help conclude a treaty of alliance.
Arthur Lee accuses him of cheating his country to make a private profit.
Deane writes letters which make him unpopular in America.
He goes into exile and nearly starves.
Helped out by a gentleman friend, he buys passage on a ship for America as his last chance to redeem himself.
He takes ill and dies before the ship can leave; rumors suggest he may have committed suicide.

* * *

Ben Franklin and Arthur Lee are members of the delegation to Paris.
Edward Bancroft is Deane's private secretary and an American spy.
Men who know Deane say he is talented but ambitious and ought to be watched.

* * *

Before Deane leaves, he visits an American artist, John Trumbull.
The *Boston Packet* is delayed for several days by a storm.
On the last day of his life, Deane gets out of bed in the morning.
He puts on his clothes and buckles his shoes.
He eats breakfast.
When he takes ill, he tries to speak twice.
He is buried several days later.

Even this short list demonstrates the impossibility of including all the facts. For behind each one lie hundreds more. You might mention that

Deane put on his clothes and ate breakfast, but consider also: What color were his clothes? When did he get up that morning? What did he have for breakfast? When did he leave the table? All these things "happened in the past," but only a comparatively small number of them can appear in a history of Silas Deane.

Readers may object that we are placing too much emphasis on this process of selection. Surely, a certain amount of good judgment will suggest which facts are important. Who needs to know what color Deane's clothes were or when he got up from the breakfast table?

Admittedly this objection has some merit, as the list of facts about Deane demonstrates. The list is divided into three groups, roughly according to the way common sense might rank them in importance. The first group contains facts which every historian would be likely to include. The second group contains less important information, which could either be included or left out. (It might be useful, for instance, to know who Arthur Lee and Edward Bancroft were, but not essential.) The last group contains information that appears either too detailed or else unnecessary. Deane may have visited John Trumbull, but then, he surely visited other people as well—why include any of that? Knowing that the *Boston Packet* was delayed by a storm reveals little about Silas Deane. And readers will assume without being told that Deane rose in the morning, put on his clothes, and had breakfast.

But if common sense helps select evidence, it also produces a good deal of pedestrian history. The fact is, the straightforward account of Silas Deane we have just presented has actually managed to miss the most fascinating parts of the story.

Fortunately, one enterprising historian named Julian Boyd was not satisfied with the traditional account of the matter. He examined the known facts of Deane's career and put them together in ways that common sense had not suggested. Take, for example, two items on our list: (1) Deane was down on his luck and left in desperation for America; and (2) he visited John Trumbull. One fact is from the "important" items on the list and the other from items that seem incidental. How do they fit together?

To answer that, we have to know the source of information about the visit to Trumbull's, which is the letter from John Cutting informing Jefferson of Deane's rumored suicide.

> A subscription had been made here chiefly by Americans to defray the expense of getting [Deane] out of this country. . . . Dr. Bancroft with great humanity and equal discretion undertook the management of the *man* and his *business*. Accordingly his passage was engaged, comfortable cloaths and stores for his voyage were laid in, and apparently without much reluctance he embarked. . . . I happen'd to see him a few days since at the lodging of Mr. Trumbull and thought I had never seen him look better.

We are now in a better position to see how our two items fit together. And as Julian Boyd has pointed out, they don't fit. According to the first, Deane was depressed, dejected, almost starving. According to the second, he had "never looked better." Alert historians begin to get nervous when they see contradictions like that, so they hunt around a little more. And Julian Boyd found, among the collection of papers published by the Connecticut and New York historical societies, that Deane had been writing letters of his own.

One went to his brother-in-law in America, who had agreed to help pay Deane's transportation over and to receive him when he arrived—something that nobody had been willing to do for years. Other letters reveal that Deane had plans for what he would do when he finally returned home. He had seen models in England of the new steam engines, which he hoped might operate gristmills in America. He had talked to friends about getting a canal built from Lake Champlain in New York to the St. Lawrence River in order to promote trade. These were not offhand dreams. As early as 1785, Deane had been at work drumming up support for his canal project. He had even laboriously calculated the cost of the canal's construction ("Suppose a labourer to dig and remove six feet deep and eight feet square in one day. . . . 2,933 days of labour will dig one mile in length, twenty feet wide and eight feet deep.") Obviously, Deane looked forward to a promising future.

Lastly, Deane appeared to believe that the controversy surrounding his French mission had finally abated. As he wrote an American friend,

> It is now almost ten years since I have solicited for an impartial inquiry [into the dispute over my conduct]. . . . that justice might be done to my fortune and my character. . . . You can sufficiently imagine, without my attempting to describe, what I must have suffered on every account during so long a period of anxiety and distress. I hope that it is now drawing to a close.

Other letters went to George Washington and John Jay, reiterating Deane's innocence.

All this information makes the two items on our list even more puzzling. If Deane was depressed and discouraged, why was he so enthusiastic about coming back to build canals and gristmills? If he really believed that his time of "anxiety and distress" was "drawing to a close," why did he commit suicide? Of course, Deane might have been subject to dramatic shifts in mood. Perhaps hope for the future alternated with despair about his chances for success. Perhaps a sudden fit of depression caused him to take his life.

But another piece of "unimportant" information, way down on our third list, makes this hypothesis difficult to accept. After Deane's ship left London, it was delayed offshore for more than a week. Suppose Deane did decide to commit suicide by taking an overdose of laudanum. Where did he get the drug? Surely not by walking up to the ship's surgeon and asking for it. He must have purchased it in London, before he left. Yet he remained on shipboard for more than a week. If Deane bought the laudanum during a temporary "fit" of depression, why did he wait a week before taking it? And if his depression was not just a sudden fit, how do we explain the optimistic letters to America?

This close look at three apparently unrelated facts indicates that perhaps Deane's story has more to it than meets the eye. It would be well, then, to reserve judgment about our first reconstruction of Silas Deane's career and try to find as much information about the man as possible—regardless of whether it seems relevant at first. That means investigating not only Deane himself but also his friends and associates, like Ben Franklin, Arthur Lee, and Edward Bancroft. Since it is impossible in this prologue to look closely at all of Deane's acquaintances, for purpose of example we will take only one: his friend Bancroft.

SILAS DEANE'S FRIEND

Edward Bancroft was born in Westfield, Massachusetts, where his stepfather presided over a respectable tavern, the *Bunch of Grapes*. Bancroft was a clever fellow, and his father soon apprenticed him to a physician. Like many boys before him, Edward did not fancy his position and so ran away to sea. Unlike many boys, he managed to make the most of his situation. His ship landed in the Barbadoes, and there Bancroft signed on as the surgeon for a plantation in Surinam. The plantation owner, Paul Wentworth, liked the young man and let him use his private library for study. In addition, Bancroft met another doctor who taught him much about the area's exotic tropical plants and animals. When Bancroft returned to New England in 1766 and continued on to London the following year, he knew enough about Surinam's wildlife to publish a book entitled *An Essay on the Natural History of Guiana in South America*. It was well received by knowledgeable scholars and among other things, established that an electric eel's shock was caused by electricity, a fact not previously recognized.

A young American bright enough to publish a book at age twenty-five and to experiment with electric eels attracted the attention of another electrical experimenter then in London, Ben Franklin. Franklin befriended Bancroft and introduced him to many influential colleagues, not only learned philosophers but also the politicians with whom Franklin worked as colonial agent for Pennsylvania. A second trip to Surinam produced more research on plants used in making color dyes; research so successful that Bancroft soon found himself elected to the prestigious Royal Society of Medicine. At the same time, Franklin led Bancroft into the political arena, both public and private. On the public side, Bancroft published a favorable review of Thomas Jefferson's pamphlet, *A Summary View of the Rights of British America*; privately, he joined Franklin and other investors in an attempt to gain a charter for land along the banks of the Ohio River.

Up to this point it has been possible to sketch Bancroft's career without once mentioning the name of Silas Deane. Common sense would suggest that the information about Bancroft's early travels, his scientific studies, his friends in Surinam, tell us little about Deane, and that the story ought to begin with a certain letter Bancroft received from Deane in June 1776. (Common sense is again wrong, but we must wait a little to discover why.)

The letter, which came to Bancroft in 1776, informed him that his old friend Silas Deane was coming to France as a merchant engaged in private business. Would Bancroft be interested in crossing over from England to meet Deane at Calais to catch up on news for old time's sake? An invitation like that would very likely have attracted Bancroft's curiosity. He did know Deane, who had been his teacher in 1758, but not very well. Why would Deane now write and suggest a meeting? Bancroft may have guessed the rest, or he may have known it from other contacts; in any case, he wrote his "old friend" that he would make all possible haste for Calais.

The truth of the matter, as we know, was that Deane had come to France to secure military supplies for the colonies. Franklin, who was back in Philadelphia, had suggested to Congress's Committee of Secret Correspondence that Deane contact Bancroft as a good source of information about British war plans. Bancroft could easily continue his friendship with English officials, because he did not have the reputation of being a hotheaded American patriot. So Deane met Bancroft at Calais in July and the two concluded their arrangements. Bancroft would be Deane's "private secretary" when needed in Paris and a spy for the Americans when in England.

It turned out that Deane's arrangement worked well—perhaps a little too well. Legally, Deane was permitted to collect a commission on all the supplies he purchased for Congress, but he went beyond that. He and Bancroft used their official connections in France to conduct a highly profitable private trade of their own. Deane, for instance, sometimes sent ships from France without declaring whether they were loaded with private or public goods. Then if the ships arrived safely, he would declare that the cargo was private, his own. But if the English navy captured the goods on the high seas, he labeled it government merchandise and the public absorbed the loss.

Deane used Bancroft to take advantage of his official position in other ways. Both men speculated in the London insurance markets, which were the eighteenth-century equivalent of gambling parlors. Anyone who wished could take out "insurance" against a particular event that might happen in the future. An insurer, for example, might quote odds on the chances of France going to war with England within the year. The insured would pay whatever premium he wished, say £1,000, and if France did go to war, and the odds had been five-to-one against it, the insured would receive £5,000. Wagers were made on almost any public event: which armies would win which battles, which politicians would fall from power, and even on whether a particular lord would die before the year was out.

Obviously, someone who had access to inside information—someone who knew in advance, for instance, that France was going to war with England—could win a fortune. That was exactly what Bancroft and Deane decided to do. Deane was in charge of concluding the French alliance, and he knew that if he succeeded Britain would be forced to declare war on France. Bancroft hurried across to London as soon as the treaty had been concluded and took out the proper insurance before the news went public. The profits shared by the two men from this and other similar ventures amounted to approximately £10,000. Like most gamblers, however, Deane also lost wagers. In the end, he netted little for his troubles.

Historians know these facts because they now have access to the papers of Deane, Bancroft, and others. Acquaintances of the two men lacked this advantage, but they suspected shady dealings anyway. Arthur Lee publicly accused Deane and Bancroft of playing the London insurance game. (Deane shot back that Lee was doing the same thing.) And the moralistic John Adams found Bancroft's conduct distasteful. Bancroft, according to Adams, was

> a meddler in stocks as well as reviews, and frequently went into the alley, and into the deepest and darkest retirements and recesses of the brokers and jobbers . . . and found amusement as well, perhaps, as profit, by listening to all the news and anecdotes, true or false, that were there whispered or more boldly pronounced. . . . This man had with him in France, a woman with whom he lives, and who by the French was called La Femme de Monsieur Bancroft. At tables he would season his foods with such enormous quantities of cayenne pepper which assisted by generous burgundy would set his tongue a running in the most licentious way both at table and after dinner. . . .

Yet for all Bancroft's dubious habits, and for all the suspicions of men like Lee and Adams, there was one thing that almost no one at the time suspected, and that not even historians discovered until the records of certain British officials were opened to the public more than a century later. Edward Bancroft was a double agent.

At the end of July 1776, after he had arranged to be Deane's secretary, Bancroft returned to England and met with Paul Wentworth, his friend from Surinam, who was then working in London for Britain's intelligence organization. Immediately Wentworth realized how valuable Bancroft would be as a spy and introduced him to two secretaries of state. They in turn persuaded Bancroft to submit reports on the American negotiations in France. For his services, he received a lifetime pension of £200 a year—a figure the British were only too happy to pay for such good information. So quick was Bancroft's reporting that the secretaries of state knew about the American mission to France even before the United States Congress could confirm that Deane had arrived safely!

Eventually, Bancroft discovered that he could pass his information directly to the British ambassador at the French court. To do so, he wrote innocent letters on the subject of "gallantry" and signed them "B. Edwards." On the same paper would go another note written in invisible ink, to appear only when the letter was dipped in a special developer held by Lord Stormont, the British ambassador. Bancroft left his letters every Tuesday morning in a sealed bottle in a hole near the trunk of a tree on the south terrace of the Tuileries, the royal palace. Lord Stormont's secretary would put any return information near another tree on the same terrace. With this system in operation Stormont could receive intelligence without having to wait for it to filter back from England.

Did any Americans suspect Bancroft of double dealing? Arthur Lee once claimed he had evidence to charge Bancroft with treason, but he never produced it. In any case, Lee had a reputation for suspecting everybody of everything. Franklin, for his part, shared lodgings with Deane and Bancroft during their stays in Paris. He had reason to guess that someone close to the American mission was leaking secrets—especially when Lord Stormont and the British newspapers made embarrassingly accurate accusations about French aid. The French wished to keep their assistance secret in order to avoid war with England as long as possible, but of course Franklin knew America would fare better with France fighting, so he did little to stop the leaks. "If I was sure," he remarked, "that my *valet de place* was a spy, as he probably is, I think I should not discharge him for that, if in other respects I liked him." So the French would tell Franklin he *really* ought to guard his papers more closely, and Franklin would say yes, yes, he really would have to do something about that; and the secrets continued to leak. Perhaps Franklin suspected Deane and Bancroft of playing the London insurance markets, but there is no evidence that he knew Bancroft was a double agent.

What about Deane, who was closer to Bancroft than anyone else? We have no proof that he shared the double agent's secret, but his alliance with Bancroft in other intrigues tells against him. Furthermore, one published

The Tuileries, much as it appeared when Bancroft and Lord Stormont used the south terrace as a drop for their secret correspondence. The royal palace overlooks a magnificent formal garden that, as a modern observer has noted, "seems so large, so full of surprising hidden corners and unexpected stairways, that its strict ground plan—sixteen carefully spaced and shaped gardens of trees, separated by arrow-straight walks—is not immediately discernable."

leak pointed to a source so close to the American commissioners that Franklin began to investigate. As Julian Boyd has pointed out, Deane immediately directed suspicion toward a man he knew perfectly well was not a spy. We can only conclude he did so to help throw suspicion away from Bancroft. Very likely, if Bancroft was willing to help Deane play his games with the London insurers, Deane was willing to assist Bancroft in his game with British intelligence.

Of the two, Bancroft seems to have made out better. While Deane suffered reproach and exile for his conduct, Bancroft returned to England still respected by both the Americans and the British. Not that he had been without narrow escapes. Some of the British minstry (the king especially) did not trust him, and he once came close to being hung for treason when his superiors rightly suspected that he had associated with John the Painter, an unbalanced fanatic who tried to set England's navy ablaze. But Bancroft left for Paris at the first opportunity, waited until the storm blew over, and returned to London at the end of the war with his lifetime pension raised to £1,000 a year. At the time of Deane's death, he was doing more of his scientific experiments, in hopes that Parliament would grant him a profitable monopoly on a new process for making dyes.

DEANE'S DEATH: A SECOND LOOK

So we finally arrive, the long way around, back where the story began: September 1789 and Deane's death. But now we have at hand a much larger store of information out of which to construct a narrative. Since writing history involves the acts of analyzing and selecting, let us review the results of our investigation.

We know that Deane was indeed engaged in dubious private ventures; ventures Congress would have condemned as unethical. We also have reason to suspect that Deane knew Bancroft was a spy for the British. Combining that evidence with what we already know about Deane's death, we might theorize that Deane committed suicide because, underneath all his claims to innocence, he knew he was guilty as Congress charged. The additional evidence, in other words, reveals a possible new motive for Deane's suicide.

Yet this theory presents definite problems. In the first place, Deane never admitted any wrongdoing to anyone—not in all the letters he wrote, not in any of his surviving papers. That does not mean he was innocent, nor even that he believed himself innocent. But often it is easier for a person to lie to himself than to his friends. Perhaps Deane actually convinced himself that he was blameless; that he had a right to make a little extra money from his influential position; that he did no more than anyone would in his situation. Certainly his personal papers point to that conclusion. And if Deane believed himself innocent—correctly or not—would he have any obvious motive for suicide? Furthermore, the theory does not explain the puzzle that started this investigation. If Deane felt guilty enough about his conduct to commit suicide, why did that guilt increase ten years after the fact? If he did feel suddenly guilty, why wait a week aboard ship before taking the fatal dose of laudanum? For that matter, why go up and chat with the captain when death was about to strike?

No, things still do not set quite right, so we must question the theory. What proof do we have that Deane committed suicide? Rumors about London. Tom Paine heard it from Cutting, the merchant. And Cutting reports in his letter to Jefferson that Deane's suicide was "the suspicion of Dr. Bancroft." How do we know the circumstances of Deane's death? The captain made a report, but for some reason it was not preserved. The one account that did survive was written by Bancroft, at the request of a friend. Then there were the anonymous obituaries in the newspapers. Who wrote them? Very likely Bancroft composed at least one; certainly, he was known as Silas Deane's closest friend and would have been consulted by any interested parties. There are a lot of strings here, which, when pulled hard enough, all run back to the affable Dr. Bancroft. What do we know about *his* situation in 1789?

We know Bancroft is dependent upon a pension of £1,000 a year, given him for his faithful service as a British spy. We know he is hoping Parliament will grant him a monopoly for making color dyes. Suddenly his old associate Deane, who has been leading a dissolute life in London, decides to return to America, vindicate himself to his former friends, and start a new life. Put yourself in Bancroft's place. Would you be just a little nervous about that idea? Here is a man down on his luck, now picking up and going to America to clear his reputation. What would Deane do to clear it? Tell everything he knew about his life in Paris? Submit his record books to Congress, as he had been asked to do so many years before? If Deane knew Bancroft was a double agent, would he say so? And if Deane's records mentioned the affair of John the Painter (as indeed they did), what would happen if knowledge of Bancroft's role in the plot reached England? Ten years earlier, Bancroft would have been hanged. True, memories had faded, but even if he were spared death, would Parliament grant a monopoly on color dyes to a known traitor? Would Parliament continue the £1,000 pension? It was one thing to have Deane living in London, where Bancroft could watch him; it would be quite another to have him all the way across the Atlantic Ocean, ready to tell—who knows what?

Admit it: if you were Bancroft, wouldn't you be just a little nervous?

We are forced to consider, however reluctantly, that Deane was not expecting to die as he walked the deck of the *Boston Packet.* Yet if Bancroft did murder Deane, how? He was not aboard ship when death came and had not seen Deane for more than a week. That is a good alibi, but then, Bancroft was a clever man. We know (once again from the letters of John Cutting) that Bancroft was the person who "with great humanity and equal discretion undertook the management of the *man* and the *business*" of getting Deane ready to leave for America. Bancroft himself wrote Jefferson that he had been visiting Deane often "to assist him with advice, medicins, and money for his subsistence." If Deane were a laudanum addict, as Bancroft hinted to

Cutting, might not the good doctor who helped with "medicins" also have procured the laudanum? And having done that, might he not easily slip some other deadly chemical into the mixture, knowing full well that Deane would not use it until he was on shipboard and safely off to America? That conclusion is only conjecture. We have no direct evidence to suggest that this scenario is what really happened.

But we do know one other fact for sure; and in light of our latest theory, it is an interesting one. Undeniably, Edward Bancroft was an expert on poisons.

He did not advertise that knowledge, of course; few people in London at the time of Deane's death would have been likely to remember the fact. But twenty years earlier, the historian may recall, Bancroft wrote a book on the natural history of Guiana. At that time, he not only investigated electric eels and color dyes, but also the poisons of the area, particularly curare (or "Woowara" as Bancroft called it). He investigated it so well, in fact, that when he returned to England he brought samples of curare with him, which (he announced in the book) he had deposited with the publishers so that any gentleman of "unimpeachable" character might use the samples for scientific study.

Furthermore, Bancroft seemed to be a remarkably good observer not only of the poisons but also of those who used them. His book described in ample detail the natives' ability to prepare poisons that,

> given in the smallest quantities, produce a very slow but inevitable death, particularly a composition which resembles wheat-flour, which they sometimes use to revenge past injuries, that have been long neglected, and are thought forgotten. On these occasions they always feign an insensibility of the injury which they intend to revenge, and even repay it with services and acts of friendship, until they have destroyed all distrust and apprehension of danger in the destined victim of the vengeance. When this is effected, they meet at some festival, and engage him to drink with them, drinking first themselves to obviate suspicion, and afterwards secretly dropping the poison, ready concealed under their nails, which are usually long, into the drink.

Twenty years later Bancroft was busy at work with the color dyes he had brought back from Surinam. Had he, by any chance, also held onto any of those poisons?

> * As the Author has brought a confiderable quantity of this Poifon to *England*, any Gentleman, whofe genius may incline him to profecute thefe experiments, and whofe character will warrant us to confide in his hands a preparation, capable of perpetrating the moft fecret and fatal villainy, may be fupplied with a fufficient quantity of the *Woorara*, by applying to Mr. *Becket*, in the *Strand*.

An excerpt from An Essay on the Natural History of Guiana in South America by Edward Bancroft. (Library of Congress)

Unless new evidence comes to light, we will probably never know for sure. Historians are generally forced to deal with probabilities, not certainties, and we leave you to draw your own conclusions about the death of Silas Deane.

What does seem certain is that whatever "really happened" to Deane 200 years ago cannot be determined today without the active participation of the historian. Being courier to the past is not enough. For better or worse, historians inescapably leave an imprint as they go about their business: asking interesting questions about apparently dull facts, seeing connections between subjects that had not seemed related before, shifting and rearranging evidence until it assumes a coherent pattern. The past is not history; only the raw material of it. How those raw materials come to be fashioned and shaped is the central concern of the rest of this book.

❧ ❧ ❧ ADDITIONAL READING ❧ ❧ ❧

The historian responsible for the brilliant detective work exposing the possibility of foul play on the *Boston Packet* is Julian Boyd. He makes his case, in much greater detail than can be summarized here, in a series of three articles entitled "Silas Deane: Death by a Kindly Teacher of Treason?" *William and Mary Quarterly*, 3d ser., 16 (1959): 165–87, 319–42, and 515–50. For additional background on Silas Deane, see the entry in the *Dictionary of American Biography* (New York, 1946). (The *DAB*, incidentally, is a good starting point for historians who seek biographical details of American figures. It provides short sketches as well as further bibliographical references.) For details on additional intrigue surrounding the American mission to France, see Samuel F. Bemis, "The British Secret Service and the French-American Alliance," *American Historical Review* 29 (1923–1924): 474–95.

Interested readers who wish to examine some of the primary documents in the case may do so easily enough. Much of Deane's correspondence is available in *The Deane Papers*, published as part of the New-York Historical Society's *Collections* 19–23 (New York, 1887–1891) and in *The Deane Papers: Correspondence between Silas Deane, His Brothers . . . 1771–1795*, Connecticut Historical Society *Collections* 23 (Hartford, Conn., 1930). These volumes shed helpful light on Deane's state of mind during his London years. The London obituary notices are reprinted in the *American Mercury* (Hartford, Conn., 28 December 1789), the *Gazette of the United States* (Philadelphia, Pa., 12 December 1789), and other newspapers in New York and Boston. See also the *Gentleman's Magazine* of London 59, pt. 2 (September 1789): 866. American colonial newspapers are available in many libraries on microprint, published by the Readex Microprint Corporation in conjunction with the American Antiquarian Society.

Edward Bancroft's role as double agent was not established conclusively until the private papers of William Eden (Lord Auckland) were made public in the 1890s. As director of the British Secret Service during the Revolution,

Eden and his right-hand man, Paul Wentworth, were in close touch with Bancroft. The details of the Bancroft-Wentworth-Eden connection are spelled out in Paul L. Ford, *Edward Bancroft's Narrative of the Objects and Proceedings of Silas Deane* (Brooklyn, N.Y., 1891). Further information on Bancroft may be found in Sir Arthur S. MacNalty, "Edward Bancroft, M.D., F.R.S. and the War of American Independence," Royal Society of Medicine *Proceedings* 38 (1944): 7–15. The Historical Society of Pennsylvania, in Philadelphia, has a collection of Bancroft's papers. And further background may be gained, of course, from the good doctor's own writings, chief among them the *Essay on the Natural History of Guiana in South America . . .* (London, 1769).

We have pointed out that no evidence in the historical record conclusively links Edward Bancroft with Silas Deane's death. In an eminently fair-minded manner, we left you to draw your own conclusions. Yet, as the lesson of this chapter makes clear, every historical narrative is bound to select facts in shaping its story—including this narrative. Given our limitations of space, we chose to concentrate on the evidence and arguments that illuminated Boyd's hypothesis most forcibly. So we suspect that most readers, if left to draw their "own" conclusions, will tend to find Bancroft guilty as charged.

Boyd's case strikes us as impressive too, but it certainly can be questioned. How sound, for instance, is the hypothesis about Deane's depression (or lack of it)? Many people who have contemplated suicide, it could be argued, do so over an extended period of time, and their moods of depression may alternate with happier periods. Perhaps Deane toyed with the idea, put it away, then returned to it in the gloomy confines of the *Boston Packet*. If Deane were a laudanum addict and had a large quantity of the drug on hand, might he not easily take an overdose during a sudden return of severe depression? For that matter, if he were a careless addict, might he not have taken an *accidental* overdose?

In another area, William Stinchcombe has suggested that, contrary to Julian Boyd's suggestion, Deane did not face any really hopeful prospects for success in America. If Deane continued to be destitute and down on his luck when he departed for America, then the suicide theory again becomes more probable. Stinchcombe's article, "A Note on Silas Deane's Death," may be found in the *William and Mary Quarterly*, 3d ser., 32 (1975): 619–24.

We can also report with pleasure that the first edition of this book sparked an interesting counter to Boyd's thesis. Dr. Guido Gianfranceschi, a surgeon from Danbury, Connecticut, read our prologue in a course on historical methods he was taking at Western Connecticut State College. He points out to us that a check of the standard medical reference, *Goodman and Gilman's Pharmacological Basis of Therapeutics* (6th ed., New York, 1980), reveals that Deane was not likely done in by curare. Though quite toxic when entering the bloodstream, curare is "poorly and irregularly absorbed from the gastrointestinal tract. d-Tubocurarine is inactive after oral administration, unless huge doses are ingested; this fact was well known to the South American Indians, who ate with impunity the flesh of game killed with curare-poisoned arrows." (It was also known to Bancroft, who notes in his own work that, "when received by the alimentary passage," the poison "is subdued by the action of the digestive organs.")

Of course, curare was only one of many poisons Bancroft learned about from the natives of Guiana. "I have spent many days in a dangerous and almost fruitless endeavor to investigate the nature and quantities of these plants," he reported in 1769, "and by handling, smelling, tasting, etc. I have frequently found, at different times, almost all the several senses, and their organs either disordered or violently affected." Could it have been another one of those deadly substances that Deane ingested? Perhaps; Boyd makes no guess what the poison might have been. But while Bancroft indicated he had brought home snake specimens, curare is the only poison he specifically mentions having in London. Furthermore, Dr. Gianfranceschi points out that the symptoms of opium overdose are similar to those Deane is said to have experienced prior to his death. Finally, for a third opinion, consult D. K. Anderson and G. T. Anderson, "The Death of Silas Deane," *New England Quarterly* 62 (1984): 98–105. The Andersons surveyed several medical authorities and concluded that Deane may well have suffered from chronic tuberculosis and died from a stroke or some other acute attack.

Murder, suicide, stroke, or accidental overdose? We eagerly await new evidence that our readers may turn up.

⇜ ⇜ ONE ⇝ ⇝

Serving Time in Virginia

As has become clear, the historian's simple act of selection irrevocably separates "history" from "the past." The reconstruction of an event is quite clearly different from the event itself. Yet selection is only one in a series of interpretive acts that historians perform as they proceed about their business. Even during the preliminary stages of research, when the historian is still gathering information, interpretation and analysis are necessary. That is because the significance of any piece of evidence is seldom apparent at first glance. The historian quickly learns that the words *evidence* and *evident* rarely amount to the same thing.

For historians attempting to reconstruct an accurate picture of the first English settlements in Virginia, the difficulty of taking any document at face value becomes quickly apparent. The early Virginians were, by and large, an enterprising lot. They gave America its first representative assembly, gave England a new and fashionable vice (tobacco), and helped establish slavery as a labor system in North America. These actions raise perplexing and important questions for historians, and yet the answers to them cannot be found in the surviving source materials without a good deal of work.

The difficulty does not arise entirely from lack of information. Indeed, some Virginians were enterprising enough to write history as well as make it, not the least of them being Captain John Smith. Captain Smith wrote an account of the young colony entitled *A Generall Historie of Virginia*, published in 1624. Much of his history is based on eyewitness, firsthand knowledge. At a vigorous age twenty-seven, he joined the expedition to Virginia in 1606 sent by the Virginia Company of London and played a crucial role in directing the affairs of the inexperienced Jamestown colony.

Yet Smith's evidence cannot be accepted without making some basic interpretive judgments. Simplest and most obvious—is he telling the truth? If we are to believe his own accounts, the young captain led a remarkably swashbuckling life. Before joining the Virginia expedition, he had plunged as a soldier of fortune into a string of complicated intrigues in central Europe. There he waged desperate and brave warfare on behalf of the Hungarian nobility before being taken prisoner by the Turks. Once a prisoner, he was made a slave to a young but "noble Gentlewoman" with the romantic name of Charatza Tragabigzanda. The smitten princess "tooke (as it seemed) much compassion" on Smith, but alas, he came under the control of her sadistic brother, who reviled and taunted the captain so much, Smith lost his temper one day in the granary and "beat out [his] braines with his threshing bat" and made a daring escape, reaching England in time to sign on with the Virginia Company's expedition.

In Virginia the adventures came nearly as thick and fast. While the colony's governing council quarreled at Jamestown, Captain Smith went off on an exploring and food-gathering mission. He established the first European contact with many of the Indian tribes around Chesapeake Bay, succeeded in buying needed corn from them, and was captured by a party of Indians loyal to Powhatan, the principal chief in the Cheaspeake region. With Smith facing execution, once again he managed to win the affections of a beautiful princess—this one, Powhatan's young daughter Pocahontas.

How much of this romantic adventure story do we believe? The tone of Captain Smith's narrative makes it reasonably apparent that he was not the sort of man to hide his light under a bushel. (In writing of his adventures, he compared himself implicitly with Julius Caesar, "who wrote his owne Commentaries, holding it no less honour to write, than fight.") Indeed, several nineteenth-century scholars, including Henry Adams, challenged Smith's account of his Indian rescue as mere embellishment. Adams pointed out that the Pocahontas story did not appear in Smith's earliest published descriptions of the Virginia colony. Only in 1624, when the *Generall Historie* was issued, did the public first read of the Indian maiden's timely devotion. Captain Smith, Adams argued, probably invented the story out of whole cloth in order to enhance his reputation.

We can, of course, look for independent evidence that would corroborate Smith's claims, but in the case of the Pocahontas story, no independent records survive. Yet other historians have defended Smith, Philip Barbour prime among them. Barbour has checked Smith's tales against available records in both Hungary and England and found them generally accurate as to names, places, and dates. Smith claimed, for example, that he used an ingenious system of torch signals to coordinate a nighttime attack by his Hungarian friends, "Lord Ebersbaught" and "Baron Kisell." No other records mention Smith's role, but we do know such an attack was launched—and that it was led by two Hungarians named Sigismund Eibiswald and Jakob Khissl. Similarly, although the records show no princess named Charatza Tragabigzanda, that may have been Smith's fractured pronunciation of the Greek *koritsi* [girl] *Trapedzoûndos* [from Trebizond]. Possibly, when he tried to discover the identity of his new mistress, someone merely replied that she was *"koritsi Trapedzoûndos"*—a "girl from Trebizond."

Yet even if we grant Smith the virtue of honesty, significant problems remain when using his account; problems common to all historical evidence. To say that Smith is truthful is only to say that he reported events *as he saw them.* The qualification is not small. Like every observer, Smith viewed events from his own perspective. When he set out to describe the customs of the Chesapeake Indians, for instance, he did so as a seventeenth-century

Englishman. Behind each observation he made stood a whole constellation of presuppositions, attitudes, and opinions that he took for granted without ever mentioning them. His descriptions were necessarily limited by the experience and education—or lack of it—that he brought with him.

The seriousness of these limitations becomes clearer if we take a hypothetical example of what might happen if Captain Smith were to set down a history, not of Indian tribal customs, but of a baseball game between the Boston Red Sox and the New York Yankees:

> Not long after, they tooke me to one of their great Counsells, where many of the generalitie were gathered in greater number than ever I had seen before. And they being assembled about a great field of open grass, a score of their greatest men ran out upon the field, adorned each in brightly hued jackets and breeches, with letters cunningly woven upon their Chestes, and wearinge uppon their heades caps of a deep navy blue, with billes, of a sort I know not what. One of their chiefs stood in the midst and would at his pleasure hurl a white ball at another chief, whose attire was of a different colour, and whether by chance or artyfice I know not the ball flew exceeding close to the man yet never injured him, but sometimes he would strike att it with a wooden club and so giveing it a hard blow would throw down his club and run away. Such actions proceeded in like manner at length too tedious to mention, but the generalitie waxed wroth, with great groaning and shoutinge, and seemed withall much pleased.

Before concluding any more than that Smith would make a terrible writer for the *New York Post* (we don't even know if the Yankees won!), compare the description of the baseball game with the account by the real Smith of what happened to him after his capture. (Smith writes in the third person, referring to himself as "he" and "Captain Smith.")

> At last they brought him to Meronocomoco, where was Powhatan their Emperor. . . . Before a fire upon a seat like a bedsted, [Powhatan] sat covered with a great robe, made of Rarowcun skinnes, and all the tayles hanging by. On either hand did sit a young wench of 16 or 18 yeares, and along on each side the house, two rowes of men, and behind them as many women, with all their heads and shoulders painted red; many of their heads bedecked with the white down of Birds; but every one with something: and a great chayne of white beads about their necks. At his entrance before the King, all the people gave a great shout. The Queene of Appamatuck was appointed to bring him water to wash his hands, and another brought him a bunch of feathers, in stead of a Towell to dry them. Having feasted him after their best barbarous manner they could, a long consultation was held, but the conclusion was, two great stones were brought before Powhatan. Then as many as could layd hands on him, dragged him to them, and thereon laid his head, and being ready with their clubs, to beat out his braines, Pocahontas the Kings dearest daughter, when no intreaty could prevaile, got his head in her armes, and laid her owne upon his to save him from death: whereat the Emperour was contented he should live to make him hatchets, and her bells, beads, and copper.

The Country wee now call Virginia beginneth at Cape Henry distant from Roanoack 60 miles, where was Sr Walter Raleigh's plantation: and because the people differ very little from them of Powhatan in any thing, I have inserted those figures in this place because of the conveniency.

King Powhatan comands C: Smith to be slaine, his daughter Pokahontas begges his life his thankfullnes and how he subiected 39 of their kings. reade: histor

"**Then as many as could layd hands on him,** dragged him to them, and thereon laid his head, and being ready with their clubs, to beat out his braines, Pocahontas the Kings dearest daughter, when no intreaty could prevaile, got his head in her armes, and laid her owne upon his to save him from death. . . ." The tale has been passed down as a romantic rescue, but from Powhatan's point of view, was this event an adoption ceremony designed to cement a political alliance? (Library of Congress)

If we had not first read the account of the baseball game, it would not be nearly as obvious just how little Smith has told us about what is going on here. Indeed, anyone who reads the *Generall Historie* or any of the captain's writings will be impressed by their freshness and the wealth of detail. But that is because we, like Smith, are unfamiliar with the rituals of the seventeenth-century Chesapeake Indians. Quite naturally—almost instinctively—we adopt Smith's point of view as our own. And that point of view diverts us from asking questions to which Smith does not have the answer. What, after all, is the reason the Indians painted their heads and shoulders red and wore white down on their heads? We know no more than we did when baseball players were described as wearing bright outfits with letters woven upon their chests.

Even more to the point, consider the *form* of Smith's narrative as it has been passed down to us over the years. The good captain is about to die until he is suddenly rescued at the last moment by "the Kings dearest daughter." Does the story have a familiar ring? Indeed—there is at least half an echo of Smith's being pitied by Princess Tragabigzanda. And—equally important—the story has become prominent in our folklore because the romantic traditions of the nineteenth century delighted in such stories: a pure and noble-born woman saves the life of a brave commoner. Smith tells a story that fits a narrative pattern we love to hear.

But what if we lay aside the narrative perspective of Smith's story and consider the same facts from the point of view of Powhatan? Powhatan was the leader of a confederacy of Algonquian Indians living around Chesapeake Bay. He was, in short, the most powerful person in the region. But his control over the lesser chiefs in the area varied. Some tribal groups resisted paying tribute to him; others at a greater distance showed no allegiance and were indeed rivals.

Into this situation stepped Smith, along with the strange new tribe of white people who had just arrived from across the salt water. In hindsight, we see the arrival of Europeans as a momentous event that changed North America radically. But from Powhatan's point of view, here was simply another new group of people—strange indeed, but human beings nonetheless—whom he would have to set into the balance of his own political equation. Should he treat the newcomers as allies or enemies? Some historians and anthropologists have suggested that Powhatan's behavior toward Smith was in fact a kind of ritualized adoption ceremony and that Smith's supposed execution was a kind of initiation rite in which the captain was being ritually humiliated and subordinated. Once Smith passed the test of bravery in the face of apparent death, Powhatan was willing to adopt him as a vassal. As Smith himself puts it, Powhatan decides his prisoner can make hatchets for him and bells and beads for Pocahontas.

Powhatan's subsequent actions also suggest that he now considered Smith a chief, or *werowance*, over this new tribe of English allies. At the end of another ceremony two days later, the chief told Smith "now they were friends" and that Smith should go to Jamestown and send back "two great gunnes, and a gryndstone"—just as other Indian allies supplied Powhatan with tribute. In return, Powhatan would give Smith land and treat him "as his sonne."

This interpretation of Smith's capture and adoption must remain speculative, but it is responsible speculation, informed by study of the ways of Algonquian Indians by historians and anthropologists. And we would have been blind to the interpretation without having separated Smith's information from the narrative perspective in which it came to us.

It is easy enough to see how a point of view is embedded in the facts of an eloquent narration. But consider for a moment evidence recorded by one of the pedestrian clerks whose jottings constitute the great bulk of history's raw material. The following excerpts are taken from the records of Virginia's general assembly and the proclamations of the Governor:

> We will and require you, Mr. Abraham Persey, Cape Marchant, from this daye forwarde to take notice, that . . . you are bounde to accepte of the Tobacco of the Colony, either for commodities or upon billes, at three shillings the beste and the second sorte at 18d the punde, and this shalbe your sufficient dischardge.

> Every man to sett two acres corn (Except Tradesmen following their trades) penalty forfeiture of corn & Tobacco & be a Slave a year to the Colony. No man to take hay to sweat Tobacco because it robs the poor beasts of their fodder and sweating Tobacco does it little good as found by Experience.

With these excerpts we face the opposite of Smith's description: small bits of information dependent on a great deal of assumed knowledge. Whereas Smith attempted to describe the Indian ceremony in some detail because it was new to him, Virginia's general assembly knows all too much about tobacco prices and the planting of corn. Policy is stated without any explanation, just as the box score in the paper lists the single line, "Yankees 10, Red Sox 3." In each case the notations are so terse, the "narratives" so brief, that the novice historian is likely to assume they contain no point of view at all, only the bare facts. But the truth is, each statement has a definite point of view that can be summed up as simple questions: (1) Did the Yankees win and if so by how much? (2) Should the price of tobacco be three shillings or eighteen pence or how much? (3) What should colonists use hay for? And so on. These viewpoints are so obvious, they would not bear mentioning—except that, unconsciously, we are led to accept them as the only way to think about the facts. Because the obvious perspective often appears irrelevant, we tend to reject the information as not worth our attention.

But suppose a fact is stripped of its point of view—suppose we ask, in effect, a completely different question of it? Historians looking back on twentieth-century America would undoubtedly learn little from baseball box scores, but at least by comparing the standings of the 1950s with those of the 1970s, they would soon discover that the Giants of New York had become the Giants of San Francisco and that the Brooklyn Dodgers had moved to Los Angeles. If they knew a bit more about the economic implications of major league baseball franchises, they could infer a relative improvement in the economic and cultural status of the West Coast. Similarly, by refusing to accept the evidence of tobacco prices or corn planting at its face value, historians might make inferences about economic and cultural conditions in seventeenth-century Virginia.

In adopting a perspective different from any held by the historical participants, we are employing one of the most basic tactics of sociology. Sociologists have long recognized that every society functions, in part, through structures and devices that remain unperceived by its members. "To live in society means to exist under the domination of society's logic," notes sociologist Peter Berger. "Very often men act by this logic without knowing it. To discover this inner dynamic of society, therefore, the sociologist must frequently disregard the answers that the social actors themselves would give to his questions and look for explanations that are hidden from their own awareness."

Using that approach, historians have taken documents from colonial Virginia, stripped them of their original perspectives, and reconstructed a striking picture of Virginia society. Their research reveals that life in the young colony was more volatile, acquisitive, rowdy, raw—and deadly—than most traditional accounts have assumed. Between the high ideals of the colony's London investors and the disembarkation points along the Chesapeake, something went wrong. The society that was designed to be a productive and diversified settlement in the wilderness soon developed into a world in which the singleminded pursuit of one crop, tobacco, made life nasty, brutish, and short. And the colony that had hoped to pattern itself on the free and enlightened customs of England instead found itself establishing something that the government of England had never thought to introduce at home: the institution of human slavery.

A COLONY ON THE EDGE OF RUIN

None of the English colonial ventures found it easy to establish successful and independent settlements along the Atlantic coast, but for the Virginia colony, the going was particularly rough. In the first ten years of the colony's existence, £75,000 had been invested to send around 2,000 settlers across the ocean to what Captain Smith described as a "fruitfull and delightsome land" where "heaven and earth never agreed better to frame a place for mans habitation." Yet at the end of that time, the attempt to colonize Virginia could be judged nothing less than unmitigated disaster.

Certainly most members of the Virginia Company viewed it that way. In 1606 King James had granted a charter to a group of London merchants who became formally known as "The Treasurer and Company of Adventurers and Planters of the City of London for the First Colony in Virginia." The Virginia Company, as it was more commonly called, allowed merchants and gentlemen of quality to "adventure" money in a joint stock arrangement, pooling their resources to support an expedition to Virginia. The expedition would plant a colony and extract the riches of the new country, such as gold or iron, and also begin cultivating crops that would yield a high return, such as grapes for the production of wine or mulberry trees for the production of silk. King James, a silkworm buff, even donated some of his own specially bred worms. The proceeds would repay the company's expenses, the investors (or "adventurers") would reap handsome profits, the colonists themselves would prosper, and England would gain a strategic foothold in the Americas. So the theory went.

The reality ran rather differently. After four difficult months at sea, only 105 of the original 144 settlers reached Chesapeake Bay in April of 1607.

The site chosen at Jamestown for a fort was swampy, its water unhealthy, and the Indians less than friendly. By the end of the first hot and humid summer, 46 more settlers had perished. When the first supply ship delivered 120 new recruits the following January, it found only 38 men still alive.

The company correctly blamed part of the failure on the colony's original system of government. A president led a council of thirteen men, but in name only. Council members refused to take direction and continually bickered among themselves. In 1609 the company obtained a new charter providing for centralized control in a governor, but when it sent another 600 settlers across, the results were even worse. Because a hurricane scattered the fleet on its way over, only 400 settlers arrived, leaderless, in September of 1609. Captain Smith, the one old hand who had acted decisively to pull the colony together, was sent packing on the first ship home, and as winter approached, the bickering began anew.

Nobody, it seemed, had planted enough corn to last through the winter. Settlers preferred to barter, bully, or steal supplies from the Indians. And the Indians knew that the English depended on them—knew that they could starve out the newcomers simply by moving away. When several soldiers took French leave to seek food from the natives, the other settlers discovered their comrades not long after, "slayne with their mowthes stopped full of Breade, being donn as it seemeth in Contempte and skorne thatt others might expect the Lyke when they shold come to seek for breade and reliefe amongst them."

As the winter wore on, the store of hogs, hens, goats, sheep, and horses were quickly consumed; the colonists then turned to "doggs Catts Ratts and myce." Those settlers who were healthy enough searched the woods for roots, nuts, and berries, while others resorted to boiling boot leather. Conditions became so desperate that one man "did kill his wife, powdered [i.e., salted] her, and had eaten part of her" before leaders discovered his villainy and had him executed. By May 1610, when Deputy Governor Thomas Gates and the rest of the original fleet limped in from Bermuda, only 60 settlers out of 500 had survived the winter, and these were "so Leane thatt they looked Lyke Anotamies Cryeing owtt we are starved We are starved."

Grim as such tales are, we have almost come to expect them in the first years of a new colony. The Virginia experiment broke new ground in a new land. Mistakes were inevitable. But as the years passed, the colonists seemed to have learned little. Ten years after the first landing, yet another governor, Samuel Argall, arrived to find Jamestown hardly more than a slum in the wildnerness: "but five or six houses [remaining standing], the Church downe, the Palizado's [stockade fence] broken, the Bridge in pieces, the Well of fresh water spoiled; the Storehouse they used for the Church; the marketplace and streets, and all other spare places planted with Tobacco." Of the 2,000 or so settlers sent since 1607, only 400 remained alive and only 200 of them, Argall complained, were either trained or fit enough to farm. Even John Rolfe, a prominent settler who was usually willing to put as good a face on affairs as possible, could not help taking away with the left hand the praises he bestowed with the right. "Wee found the Colony (God be thanked) in good estate," he wrote home hopefully, "however in buildings, fortyfications, and of boats, much ruyned and greate want." All in all, it was not much of a progress report after ten years.

In England, Sir Edwin Sandys was one of the adventurers who watched with distress as the company's efforts came to naught. Sandys lacked the financial means of bigger investors like Thomas Smith, who had often presided as the company's treasurer. But Sandy's limited resources was precisely the point. Smith and the other big investors considered the Virginia enterprise just one venture among many: the East India Company, trading in the Levant, the Muscovy Company. If Virginia did not pay immediate dividends, they could afford to wait. Sandys and his followers, with less capital and less margin for error, pressed for immediate reform. By 1618 Smith had agreed to introduce significant changes into the colony's organization; the following year Sandys was elected treasurer of the company. With real power in his hands for the first time, he set out to reconstruct the failing colony from the bottom up.

BLUEPRINT FOR A VIRGINIA UTOPIA

Sandys knew that if his schemes for reform were to succeed, he would have to attract both new investors to the company and new settlers to the colony. Yet the Virginia Company was deeply in debt and the colony was literally falling apart. In order to entice both settlers and investors, Sandys offered the only commodity the company possessed in abundance—land.

In the first years of the colony, Virginia land had remained company land. Settlers who worked it might own shares in the company, but even so, they did not profit directly from their labor, because all proceeds went into the treasury to be divided only if there were any profits. There never were. In 1617 the company formally changed its policy. Old Planters, those settlers who had arrived in Virginia before the spring of 1616, were each granted 100 acres of land. Freemen received their allotment immediately, while those settlers who were still company servants received their land when their terms of service expired.

Sandys lured new investors with the promise of property too. For every share they purchased, the company granted them 100 acres. More important, Sandys encouraged immigration to the colony by giving investors additional land if they would pay the ship passage of tenant laborers. For every new tenant imported to Virginia, the investor received 50 additional acres. Such land grants were known as *headrights*, because the land was apportioned per each "head" imported. Of course, if Old Planters wished to invest in the company, they too would receive 100 acres plus additional 50-acre headrights for every tenant whose passage they paid. Such incentives, Sandys believed, would attract needed funds to the company while also promoting immigration.

And so private property came to Virginia. This tactic was the much-heralded event that every schoolchild is called upon to recite as the salvation of the colony. "When our people were fed out of the common store and labored jointly together, glad was he could slip away from his labour, or slumber over his taske," noted one settler. But "now for themselves they will doe in a day" what before they "would hardly take so much true paines in a weeke." It is important to understand, however, that the company still had its own common land and stock from which it hoped to profit. Thus a company shareholder had the prospect of making money in two ways: from any goods marketed by company servants working company lands, or directly from his newly granted private lands, also known as "Particular Plantations."

Sandys's administration provided still other openings for private investment. By 1616 the company had already granted certain merchants a four-year monopoly on providing supplies for the colony. The "Magazine," as it was called, sent supply ships to Virginia where its agent, a man known as the Cape Merchant, sold the goods in return for produce. In 1620 the company removed the Magazine's monopoly and allowed other investors to send over supply ships.

Sandys and his friends also worked to make the colony a more pleasant place to live. Instead of being governed by martial law, as the colony had since 1609, the company instructed the new governor, George Yeardly, to create an assembly with the power to make laws. The laws would be binding so long as the company subsequently approved them. Inhabitants of the various company settlements as well as of the particular plantations were to choose two members each as their burgesses, or representatives. When the assembly convened in 1619 it became the first representative body in the English colonies.

Historians have emphasized the significance of this first step in the evolution of American democracy, and significant it was. But the colony's settlers may have considered it equally important that the company had figured out a way to avoid saddling them with high taxes to pay for their government. Once again, the answer was land, which the company used to pay officials' salaries. Thus the governor received a parcel of 3,000 acres plus 100 tenants to work it, the treasurer of the colony received 1,500 acres and 50 tenants, and so on. Everybody won, or so it seemed. The officers got their salaries without having to "prey upon the people"; the settlers were relieved "of all taxes and public burthens as much as may be"; and the sharecropping tenants, after splitting the profits with company officials for seven years, got to keep the land they worked. If the company carried out its policy, John Rolfe observed enthusiastically, "then we may truly say in Virginia, we are the most happy people in the world."

In 1619, with the reforms in place and Sandys in the treasurer's seat, the company moved into high gear. New investors sent scores of tenants over to work the particular plantations; the company sent servants to tend officers' lands; and lotteries throughout England provided income to recruit ironmongers, vine-tenders, and glassblowers for the New World. The records of the Virginia Company tell a story of immigration on a larger scale than ever before: more than a thousand settlers in 1619, Sandys's first year, and equal numbers in the following three years. Historians who do a little searching and counting in company records will find that some 3,570 settlers were sent to join a population that stood, at the beginning of Sandys's program, around 700.

It would have been an impressive record, except that in 1622, three years later, the colony's population still totaled only about 700 people.

The figures are in the records; you can check the addition yourself. What it amounts to is that in 1622, there are 3,500 Virginians missing. No significant number returned to England; most, after all, could hardly afford passage over, let alone back. No significant number migrated to other colonies. We can account for the deaths of 347 colonists, slain in an Indian attack of 1622. But that leaves more than 3,000 settlers. There seems to be only one way to do the accounting: those immigrants died.

Who—or what—was responsible for the deaths of 3,000 Virginians? Something had gone terribly wrong with Sandys's plans. The magnitude of the failure was so great that the leaders of the company did not care to announce it openly. When the king got word of it, only after the company had virtually bankrupted itself in 1624, he revoked its charter. The historian who confronts the statistical outlines of this horror is forced to ask a few questions. Just what conditions would produce a society in which the death rate was in the neighborhood of 75 to 80 percent? A figure that high is simply staggering; for comparison, the death rate during the first (and worst) year at the Pilgrims' Plymouth colony stayed a little below 50 percent. During the severe plague epidemics that swept Britain in the fourteenth century, the death rate probably ranged from 20 to 45 or 50 percent.

Obvious answers suggest themselves. The colony could not sustain such an influx of new settlers, especially since Sandys, in his eagerness to increase the population, sent so many people unprepared. Immigrants often arrived with little or no food to tide them over until they could begin raising their own crops. Housing was inadequate; indeed, the records are full of letters from the company in London begging the colony's governors to build temporary "guest houses" for the newcomers, while the governors' letters in return begged the company to send more adequate provisions with their recruits.

Disease took its toll. Colonists had discovered early on that Virginia was an unhealthy place to live. For newcomers, the first summer proved particularly deadly, so much so that it was called the "seasoning time." Those who survived the first summer significantly raised their chances of prospering. But dangers remained year round, especially for those weakened by the voyage or living on a poor diet. Contaminated wells most likely contributed to outbreaks of typhoid fever, and malaria claimed victims.

The obvious answers do much to explain the devastating death rates, but anomalies remain. Even granting the seriousness of typhoid and other diseases, why a death rate higher than the worst plague years? Virginia's population was made up of younger men primarily and lacked the older men and women who would have been most weakened by these conditions. Even healthy settlers, of course, may be affected by malnutrition and semistarvation, but that brings the problem right back to the question of why, after more than ten years, the Jamestown colony was not yet self-sufficient.

To be self-sufficient required that colonists raise their own food. And the principal food raised in the area was corn. So the historian asks a simple question. How much work did it take to grow corn? A quick look at the records confirms what might be suspected—that no Virginian in those first years bothered to leave behind a treatise on agriculture. But a closer search of letters and company records provides bits of data here and there. The Indians, Virginians discovered, spent only a few days out of the year tending corn, and they often produced surpluses that they traded to the Virginians. A minister in the colony reported that "in the idle hours of one week," he and three other men had planted enough corn to last for four months. Other estimates suggested that forty-eight hours' work would suffice to plant enough corn to last a whole year. Even allowing for exaggeration, it seems clear that comparatively little effort was needed to grow corn.

Yet if corn can be grown easily, and if it is needed to keep the colonists alive, what possible sense is the historian to make of a document we encountered earlier—Governor Argall's proclamation of 1618, requiring "Every man to sett 2 acres corn (Except Tradesmen following their trades)." That year is not the last time the law appears on the books. It was reentered in the 1620s and periodically up through the 1650s.

The situation is a puzzle: a law *requiring* Virginians to plant corn? The colony is continually running out of corn, people are starving, and planting and reaping take only a few weeks out of the year. Under these circumstances, the government has to *order* settlers to plant corn?

Yet the conclusion is backed up by other company records. Virginians had to be forced to grow corn. The reason becomes clearer if we reexamine

Virginia's early planters marketed their tobacco to the Dutch as well as the English. This painting on an early-seventeenth-century ceramic tile shows a Dutch smoker attempting the novel accomplishment of blowing smoke through his nose. The new habit of smoking, at once popular and fairly disreputable, led to a demand for Virginia tobacco in Europe that drove up prices and sent enterprising colonists scrambling for laborers to help raise the profitable crop. (Niemeyer Tabaksmuseum, Holland)

Governor Argall's gloomy description of Jamestown when he stepped off the boat in 1617. The church is down, the palisades pulled apart, the bridge in pieces, the fresh water spoiled. Everything in the description indicates the colony is decrepit, falling apart, except for one paradoxical feature—the weeds in the street. The stockades and buildings may have languished from neglect, but it was not neglect that caused "the market-place and streets, and all other spare places" to be "planted with Tobacco." Unlike corn, tobacco required a great deal of attention to cultivate. It did not spring up in the streets by accident. Thus Governor Argall's description indicates that at the same time that settlers were willing to let the colony fall apart, they were energetically planting tobacco in all the "spare places" they could find.

Settlers had discovered as early as 1613 that tobacco was marketable, and they sent small quantities to England the following year. Soon shipments increased dramatically, from 2,500 pounds in 1616 to 18,839 pounds in 1617 and 49,518 pounds in 1618. Some English buyers thought that tobacco could be used as a medicine, but most purchased it simply for the pleasure of smoking it. Sandys and many other gentlemen looked upon the "noxious weed" as a vice and did everything to discourage its planting. There had been "often letters from the Counsell" in London, he complained, "sent lately to the Governour for restraint of that immoderate following of Tobacco and to cause the people to apply themselves to other and better commodities." But his entreaties, as well as the corn laws, met with little success. Tobacco was in Virginia to stay.

VIRGINIA BOOM COUNTRY

The Virginia records are full of statistics like the tobacco export figures given in the previous paragraph. Number of pounds shipped, price of the "better sort" of tobacco for the year 1619, number of settlers arriving on the *Bona Nova*. These statistics are the sort of box score evidence, recorded by pedestrian clerks for pedestrian reasons, that we noted earlier. Yet once the historian strips the facts of their pedestrian perspective and uses them for his or her own purposes, they begin to flesh out an astonishing picture of Virginia. Historian Edmund Morgan, in his own reconstruction of the situation, aptly labeled Virginia "the first American boom country."

For Virginia had indeed become a boom country. The commodity in demand—tobacco—was not as glamorous as gold or silver, but the social dynamics operated in similar fashion. The lure of making a fortune created a volatile society where wealth changed hands quickly, where an unbalanced economy centered on one get-rich-quick commodity, and where the values of stability and human dignity counted for little.

The implications of this boom-country society become clearer if we ask the same basic questions about tobacco that we asked about corn. Given the fact that Virginians seemed to be growing tobacco, just how much could one person grow in a year? If tobacco was being grown for profit, could Virginians expect to get rich doing it?

Spanish tobacco grown in the West Indies fetched 18 shillings a pound on the English market. Even the highest quality Virginia product was markedly inferior and sold for only 3 shillings. And that price fluctuated throughout the 1620s, dropping as low as 1 shilling. What that price range meant in terms of profits depended, naturally, on how much tobacco a planter could grow in a year. As with corn, the few available estimates are widely scattered. John Rolfe suggested 1,000 plants in one year. William Capps, another seasoned settler, estimated 2,000 and also noted that three of his boys, whose labor he equated with one and a half men, produced 3,000 plants. Fortunately Capps also noted that 2,000 plants made up about 500 "weight" (or pounds) of tobacco, which allows us to convert numbers of plants into number of pounds.

By comparing these figures with other estimates, we can calculate roughly how much money a planter might receive for the crop. The chart below summarizes how many plants or pounds of tobacco one or more workers might harvest in a year. The extrapolated numbers in parentheses show the number of pounds harvested per worker and the income such a harvest would yield if tobacco were selling at either 1 or 3 shillings a pound.

Tobacco Production and Income Estimates

	One-Year Production			*Income*	
Number of Workers	Number of Plants	Number of Lbs.	One Man Lbs./yr	1s	3s
1 (Rolfe)	1,000		(250)	£12	£37.5
1 (Capps)	2,000	500	(500)	25	75
3 boys (1½ men)	3,000		(500)	25	75
4 men		2,800	(930)	46.5	139.5
6–7 men	3,000–4,000		(540)	27	81

Source: Based on data presented in Edmund Morgan, *American Slavery, American Freedom* (New York, 1975).

These estimates indicate that the amount of tobacco one man could produce ranged from 250 to 930 pounds a year, an understandable variation given that some planters undoubtedly worked harder than others, that some years provided better growing weather, and that, as time passed, Virginians developed ways to turn out bigger crops. Even by John Rolfe's estimate, made fairly early and therefore somewhat low, a man selling 250 pounds at 1 shilling a pound would receive £12 sterling for the year. On the high side, the estimates show a gross of £140 sterling, given good prices. Indeed, one letter tells of a settler who made £200 sterling after the good harvest of 1619. Such windfalls were rare, but considering that an average agricultural worker in England made from 30 to 50 shillings a year (less than £3), even the lower estimates look good.

The estimates look particularly good for another reason—namely, because they indicate what a planter might do working *alone*. In a society where servants, tenants, and apprentices were commonplace, Virginians quickly discovered that if they could get other people to work for them, handsome profits could be made.

Back to the basic questions. How did an Englishman get others to work for him? In effect, he simply hired them and made an agreement, a bond indicating what he gave in return for their service and for how long the agreement was to run. The terms varied from servant to servant but fell into several general classes. Most favorable, from the worker's point of view, was the position of tenant. A landowner had fields that needed working; the tenant agreed to work them for a certain period of time, usually from four to seven years. In return, the tenant kept half of what he produced. From the landowner's point of view, a servant served the purpose better, since he was paid only room and board, plus his passage from England. In return he gave his master everything he produced. Another class of workers was the apprentices, usually called "Duty boys" in Virginia because the ship *Duty* brought many of them over. Apprentices served for seven years, then another seven as tenants. Again the master's cost was only transportation over and maintenance once in Virginia.

Little in the way of higher mathematics is required to discover that if it cost a master about £10 to £12 sterling to bring over a servant—as it did—and that if that master obtained the labor of several such servants for seven years, or even for two or three, he stood fair to make a tidy fortune. In the good harvest of 1619 one master with six servants managed a profit of £1,000 sterling. That was unusual perhaps, but by no means impossible. And Sandys's headright policies unwittingly played into the hands of the fortune-makers: every servant imported meant another fifty acres of land that could be used for tobacco.

The opportunities were too much to resist. Virginians began bending every resource in the colony toward growing tobacco. The historian can now appreciate the significance of Governor Argall's proclamation (page 6) that no hay should be used to "sweat," or cure, tobacco: obviously, colonists were diverting hay from livestock that desperately needed it ("it robs the poor beasts of their fodder"), thus upsetting Virginia's economy. The scramble for profits extended even to the artisans whom Sandys sent over to diversify the colony's exports. The ironmongers deserted in short order, having "turned good honest Tobaccoemongers"; and of similar well-intentioned projects, the report came back to London that "nothinge is done in anie of them but all is vanished into smoke (that is to say into Tobaccoe)." The boom in Virginia was on.

Planters were not the only people trying to make a fortune. The settler who raised tobacco had to get it to market in Europe somehow, had to buy corn if he neglected to raise any himself, and looked to supply himself with as many of the comforts of life as could be had. Other men stood ready to deal with such planters, and they had a sharp eye to their own profit.

The company, of course, sought to provide supplies through the magazine run by the Cape Merchant, Abraham Peirsey. And if we now return to the

Virginia assembly's order, quoted earlier, requiring Peirsey to accept 3 shillings per pound for the "better sort" of tobacco, we can begin to understand why the assembly was upset enough to pass the regulation. Peirsey was charging exorbitant prices for his supplies. He collected his fees in tobacco because there was virtually no currency in Virginia. Tobacco had become the economic medium of exchange. If Peirsey counted a pound of the better sort of tobacco as worth only 2 shillings instead of 3, that was as good as raising his prices by 50 percent. As it happened, Peirsey charged two or three times the prices set by the investors in London. Further, he compounded injury with insult by failing to reimburse the company for their supplies that he sold. Sandys and the other investors never saw a cent of the magazine's profits.

Another hunt through the records indicates what Peirsey was doing with his ill-gotten gain: he ploughed it back into the most attractive investment of all, servants. We learn this not because Peirsey comes out and says so, but because the census of 1625 lists him as keeping thirty-nine servants, more than anyone else in the colony. At his death in 1628 he left behind "the best Estate that was ever yett knowen in Virginia." When the company finally broke the magazine's monopoly in 1620, other investors moved in. They soon discovered that they could make more money selling alcohol than the necessities of life. So the Virginia boom enriched the merchants of "rotten Wynes" as well as the planters of tobacco, and settlers went hungry, in part, because liquor fetched a better return than food.

Given these conditions in Virginia—given the basic social and economic structures deduced from the historical record—put yourself in the place of most tenants or servants. What would life be like for them under these conditions? What were their chances for success?

For servants, the prospect is bad indeed. First, they face the fierce mortality rate. Chances are they will not survive the first seasoning summer. Even if they do, their master is out to make a fortune by their labor. Being poor to begin with, they are in no position to protect themselves from abuse. In England the situation was different. Agricultural workers usually offered their services once a year at hiring fairs. Since their contracts lasted only a year, servants could switch to other employers if they became dissatisfied. But going to Virginia required the expense of a long voyage; masters would hire people only if they signed on for four to seven years. Once in Virginia, what could servants do if they became disillusioned? Go home? They had little enough money for the voyage over, and likely even less to get back.

Duty boys, the children, were least in a position to improve their lot. The orphans Sandys hoped to favor by taking them off the London streets faced a hard life in Virginia. They were additionally threatened by a law the Virginia labor barons put through the assembly declaring that an apprentice who committed a crime during his service had to begin his term all over again. What constituted a crime, of course, was left up to the governor's council. One Duty boy, Richard Hatch, appeared before the council because he had commented, in a private house, on the recent execution of a settler, one Richard Cornish, for sodomy. Hatch had remarked "that in his consyence he thought that the said Cornishe was put to death wrongfully." For this offense he was to be "whipt from the forte to the gallows and from thence be whipt back againe, and be sett uppon the Pillory and there to loose one of his eares." Although Hatch had nearly completed his term of service—to Governor George Yeardly, who also sat on the council—he was ordered to begin his term anew.

Tenants would seem to have been better off, but they too were subject to the demand for labor. If immigrants could pay their passage over but were unable to feed themselves upon arrival, they had little choice but to hire themselves out as servants. And if their masters died before their terms were up, there was virtually always another master ready to jump in and claim them, legally or not, either as personal servants, or as company tenants due in payment of a salary. When George Sandys, Sir Edwin's brother, finished his term as colony treasurer, he dragged his tenants with him even though they had become freemen. "He maketh us serve him whether wee will or noe," complained one, "and how to helpe it we doe not knowe for hee beareth all the sway."

Even independent small planters faced the threat of servitude if their crops failed or if Indian attacks made owning a small, isolated plantation too dangerous. William Capps, the small planter who recorded one of the tobacco production estimates, described his own precarious situation vividly. His plantation threatened by Indians, Capps proposed that the governor's council outfit him with an expedition against the neighboring tribes. The council refused, and the indignant Capps angrily suggested what was going through the wealthy planters' minds. "Take away one of my men to join the expedition," he imagines them saying,

> there's 2000 Plantes gone, thates 500 waight of Tobacco, yea and what shall this man doe, runne after the Indians? soft, I have perhaps 10, perhaps 15, perhaps 20 men and am able to secure my owne Plantacion; how will they doe that are fewer? let them first be crusht alitle, and then perhaps they will themselves make up the Nomber for their owne safetie. Theis I doubt are the Cogitacions of some of our worthier men.

AND SLAVERY?

This reconstruction of Virginia society, from the Duty boy at the bottom to the richer planters at the top, indicates that all along the line labor had become a valuable and desperately sought commodity. Settlers who were not in a position to protect themselves found that the economy put constant pressure on them. Their status as freemen was always in danger of debasement: planters bought, sold, and traded servants without their consent, and on occasion, even used them as stakes in gambling games. There had been "many complaints," acknowledged John Rolfe, "against the Governors, Captaines, and Officers in Virginia: for buying and selling men and boies," something that "was held in England a thing most intolerable." One

"About the last of August came in a dutch man of warre that sold us twenty Negars." So wrote John Smith in 1619. The illustration is by Howard Pyle, a nineteenth-century artist who prided himself on his research into costume and setting. Yet even here, Pyle's depiction of the first African Americans probably reflects illustrations he saw of the very different slave traffic of the eighteenth and nineteenth centuries. These early arrivals may have been sold as servants, not slaves. Court records indicate that in the 1640s at least some black slaves had been freed and were purchasing their own land. (Library of Congress)

Englishman put the indignity quite succinctly: "My Master Atkins hath sold me for £150 sterling like a damnd slave."

Indeed, quite a few of the ingredients of slavery are found in Virginia: the feverish economic boom that sparked a fierce demand for human labor; the mortality rate that encouraged survivors to become callous about human life; the servants who were being bought and sold, treated as property—treated, almost, as slaves. If we were looking in the abstract to construct a society in which social and economic pressures combined to encourage the development of human slavery, boom-town Virginia would seem to fit the model neatly. Yet the actual records do not quite confirm the hypothesis.

The earliest known record of Africans in Virginia is a muster roll of March 1619 (discovered only in the 1990s), which shows 32 Africans (15 men and 17 women) "in the service of sev[er]all planters." But are these Africans working as servants or as slaves? The muster roll doesn't say. Historians have combed the sparse records of early Virginia, looking at court records, inventories, letters, wills, church records—anything that might shed light on the way blacks were treated. Precious little information is available—but what little there is has been studied intensively. What we find is that very few Africans come to Virginia in the colony's first half century. People of African descent made up no more than 5 percent of the population at any time during those years.

Furthermore, the status of Africans who did come to Virginia varied widely. Before 1660, some were held as slaves for life, but others worked as servants. Still others either were given their freedom or were able to purchase it. Even the names in the record supply a clue to the mixed status of these early African newcomers. In the eighteenth century, once slavery was well established, planters tried to control the naming process, giving their slaves diminuitive names such as Jack or Sukey, or perhaps a classical Caesar or Hercules, bestowed in jest. But during Virginia's early years Africans tended to keep their full names—names that often reflected the complex cultural landscape of the African coast, where Europeans and Africans of many backgrounds mixed: Bashaw Farnando, John Graweere, Emanuel Driggus. Other Africans tried to assimilate into English life. The man who first appeared in the colony's records as only "Antonio a Negro" changed his name to Anthony Johnson. "Francisco a Negroe" eventually became the freeman Frank Payne.

Only during the 1660s did the Virginia assembly begin to pass legislation that separated blacks from whites, that defined slavery, legally, as an institution. Black Virginians, in other words, lived with white Virginians for more than forty years before their status became fully and legally debased. The facts in the records force us to turn the initial question around. If the 1620s with its boom economy was such an appropriate time for slavery to have developed, why *didn't* it?

Here, the talents of historians are stretched to their limits. They can expect no obvious explanations from contemporaries like John Rolfe, Captain Smith, or William Capps. The development of slavery was something that snuck up on Virginians. It was part of the society's "inner dynamic," as sociologists would say—hidden from the awareness of the social actors in the situation. Even the records left by the clerks are scant help. The best that can be done is intelligent conjecture, based on the kind of society that has been reconstructed.

Was it a matter of the simple availability of slaves? Perhaps. During the time that Virginia was experiencing its boom of the 1620s, West Indian islands like Barbados and St. Kitts were being settled. There, where the cultivation of sugar demanded even more intensive labor than tobacco did, the demand for slaves was extremely high, and slavery developed more rapidly. If traders sailing from Africa could carry only so many slaves, and if the market for them was better in the Barbados than in Virginia, why sail all the way up to Chesapeake Bay? Slave traders may not have found the effort worth it. That is the conjecture of one historian, Richard Dunn. Other historians and economists have argued that Chesapeake planters preferred white servants, but that during the 1670s the supply of servants from England began to decrease, sending prices higher. At the same time, an economic depression in the West Indies sent the price of slaves falling and sent slave dealers looking to sell more slaves along the Cheaspeake.

Edmund Morgan has suggested another possibility, based on the continuing mortality rate in Virginia. Put yourself in the place of the planter searching for labor. You can buy either servants or slaves. Servants come cheaper than slaves, of course, but you get to work them for only seven years before they receive their freedom. Slaves are more expensive, but you get their labor for the rest of their lives, as well as the labor of any offspring. In the long run, the more expensive slave would have been the better buy. But in Virginia everyone is dying anyway. What are the chances that either servants or slaves are going to live for more than seven, five, even three years? The chances are not particularly good. Wouldn't it make more sense to pay less and buy servants on the assumption that whoever is bought may die shortly anyway?

It is an ingenious conjecture, but it must remain that. No plantation records or letters have been found indicating that planters actually thought that way. Available evidence does suggest that the high death rate in Virginia began to drop only in the 1650s. It makes sense that only then, when slaves became a profitable commodity, would laws come to be passed formally establishing their chattel status. Whatever the reasons may have been, Virginia remained until the 1680s and 1690s what historian Ira Berlin has termed a "society with slaves" rather than a full-fledged "slave society" whose economy and culture revolved around the institution of slavery based on race. During the boom of the 1620s slavery did not flourish markedly.

Sometime between 1629 and 1630, the economic bubble popped. The price of tobacco plummeted from 3 shillings to a penny a pound. Virginians tried desperately to prop it up again, either by limiting production or by simple edict, but they did not succeed. Planters still could make money, but the chance for a quick fortune had vanished—"into smoke," as Sandys or one of his disillusioned investors would no doubt have remarked. It is much to the credit of historians that the feverish world of the Chesapeake has not, like its cash crop, entirely vanished into smoke.

❧ ❧ ❧ ADDITIONAL READING ❧ ❧ ❧

The works of Captain John Smith make a delightful introduction to Virginia. Smith is one of those Elizabethans whose prose struts, bounces, jars, and jounces from one page to the next. Although caution is necessary in reading Smith, he has provided historians with excellent source material for early encounters between Europeans and native Americans. His writings are gathered in Philip L. Barbour, ed., *The Complete Works of Captain John Smith*, 3 vols. (Chapel Hill, 1986). A briefer sampling can be found in Karen Ordahl Kupperman, ed., *Captain John Smith: A Select Edition of His Writings* (Chapel Hill, 1988). Kupperman provides a good introduction to historians' treatments of Smith, as does J. A. Leo Lemay, *The American Dream of Captain John Smith* (Charlottesville, Va., 1991). Lemay is a strong defender of Smith, sometimes unneccessarily contentious, but worth reading. Henry Adams's attack on the Pocahontas story can be found in Charles Francis Adams, *Chapters of Erie and Other Essays* (Boston, 1871), while another modern defense of the captain's veracity is still Philip L. Barbour, *The Three Worlds of Captain John Smith* (London, 1964). The most interesting recent discussions of white–Native American relations in early Virginia are by Frederick Fausz, including an essay in William W. Fitzhugh, ed., *Cultures in Contact: The Impact of European Contacts on Native American Cultural Institutions, A.D. 1000–1800* (Washington, D.C., 1985), pp. 225–268, and "An 'Abundance of Blood Shed on Both Sides': England's First Indian War, 1609–1614," *Virginia Magazine of History and Biography* 98 (1990): 3–56.

The reconstruction of boom-country Virginia described in this chapter depends heavily on the research presented in Edmund S. Morgan's *American Slavery, American Freedom* (New York, 1975). Morgan's account combines a lucid and engaging prose style with the imaginative and thorough research that is a model for the discipline. His book makes an excellent starting place for those readers who wish to learn more about seventeenth-century Virginia. Morgan's book is only the high point, however, in a resurgence of interest by historians in the whole Chesapeake Bay region. Useful starting points for sorting out these materials are Thad W. Tate and David L. Ammerman, eds., *The Chesapeake in the Seventeenth Century: Essays on Anglo-American Society* (Chapel Hill, 1979) and Lois Green Carr et al., eds., *Colonial Chesapeake Society* (Chapel Hill, 1988). Darrett B. and Anita Rutman, *A Place in Time: Middlesex County, Virginia, 1650–1750* (New York, 1984) continues Virginia's social history, using the microcosmic techniques that we examine, for New England, in the next chapter.

Readers wishing to explore primary source material on early Virginia will probably find that contemporary narratives like Smith's provide the best introduction. Many are available in Philip L. Barbour, ed., *The Jamestown Voyages under the First Charter,* 1606–1609, 2 vols. (Cambridge, 1969) and in the older but more complete Alexander Brown, *The Genesis of the United States* (Boston, 1890). Additional details about the starving time of 1609–1610 can be found in George Percy, "A Trewe Relacyon of the Procedinges and Occurentes of Moment . . ." in *Tyler's Quarterly Historical and Genealogical Magazine* 11 (1922), 260–282. Although the official records of the Virginia Company and the colony are dense and difficult to read, they provide vital evidence. Interested readers will most profit if they bring to their reading a definite idea of the sorts of facts and the specific questions they wish to answer. For the early years, see Alexander Brown's collection; the period from 1619–1624 is covered in Susan Kingsbury, ed., *The Records of the Virginia Company of London,* 4 vols. (Washington, D.C., 1906–1935). For the later period, surviving records can be found in H. R. McIlwaine, ed., *Minutes of the Council and General Court of Colonial Virginia* (Richmond, Va., 1924) and William W. Hening, *The Statutes at Large: Being a Collection of All the Laws of Virginia* (Richmond, Va., 1809–1823).

The earliest Africans in Virginia have been studied intensively, though also inconclusively. The most recent assessment is Engel Sluiter, "New Light on the '20 and Odd Negroes' Arriving in Virginia, August 1619," *William and Mary Quarterly* 54 (1997): 395–398. The question of why slavery did not develop during the first tobacco boom is discussed in Morgan's *American Slavery, American Freedom* as well as in David W. Galenson, *White Servitude in the Colonial Labor Market: An Economic Analysis* (Cambridge, 1981). Much of the new scholarship on the development of slavery in Virginia (and elsewhere in North America) can be found in the masterful synthesis of Ira Berlin, *Many Thousands Gone: The First Two Centuries of Slavery in North America* (Cambridge, Mass., 1998). Yoked to the question of how and why slavery developed is the question of the role of racial prejudice. Winthrop Jordan explored the issue in *White over Black: American Attitudes toward the Negro, 1550–1812* (Chapel Hill, 1968). For a more recent evaluation of the debate, see Alden T. Vaughan, "The Origins Debate: Slavery and Racism in Seventeenth Century Virginia," *Virginia Magazine of History and Biography* 97 (1989): 311–354. A broad synthesis of the rise of slavery along the Chesapeake is by Allan Kulikoff, *Tobacco and Slaves: The Development of Southern Cultures in the Chesapeake, 1680–1800* (Chapel Hill, 1986). See also J. Douglas Deal, *Race and Class in Colonial Virginia: Indians, Englishmen, and Africans on the Eastern Shore of Virginia during the Seventeenth Century* (New York, 1993); T. H. Breen and Stephen Innes, *'Myne Own Ground:" Race and Freedom on Virginia's Eastern Shore, 1640–1676* (New York, 1980); and Richard S. Dunn, "Masters, Servants, and Slaves in the Colonial Chesapeake and the Caribbean," in David B. Quinn, ed., *Early Maryland in a Wider World* (Detroit, 1982).

TWO

The Visible and Invisible Worlds of Salem

Historians, we have seen, are in the business of reconstruction. Seventeenth-century Virginia, with its world of slaves, indentured servants, and tobacco barons, had to be built anew, not just lifted intact from the record. It follows, then, that if historians are builders, they must decide at the outset the scale of their projects. How much ground should be covered? A year? Fifty years? Several centuries? How will the subject matter be defined or limited? The story of slavery's arrival in Virginia might be ranked as a moderately large topic. It spans some sixty years, involves thousands of immigrants and an entire colony. Furthermore, the topic is large as much because of its content as its reach over time and space. The genesis of slavery surely ranks as a central strand of the American experience. To understand it adequately requires more breadth of vision than, for instance, understanding the history of American hats during the same period. The lure of topics both broad and significant is undeniable, and there have always been historians willing to pull on their seven-league boots, following in the honorable tradition of Edward Gibbon's *Decline and Fall of the Roman Empire*.

The great equalizer of such grand plans is the twenty-four-hour day. Historians have only a limited amount of time, and the hours, they sadly discover, are not expandable. Obviously, the more years covered, the less time available to research the events in each. Conversely, the narrower the area of research, the more the historian can become immersed in a period's details. A keen mind working on an apparently small topic may uncover relationships and connections whose significance goes beyond the subject matter's original boundaries.

Salem Village in 1692 is such a microcosm—one familiar to most students of American history. That was the place and the time witchcraft came to New England with a vengeance, dominating the life of the village for ten months. Because the witchcraft episode exhibited well-defined boundaries in both time and space, it shows well how an oft-told story may be transformed by the intensive research techniques of small-scale history. Traditionally, the outbreak at Salem has been viewed as an incident divorced from the cause-and-effect sequences of everyday village life. Even to label the events as an "outbreak" suggests that they are best viewed as an epidemic, alien to the community's normal functions. The "germs" of bewitchment break out suddenly and inexplicably—agents, presumably, of some invading disease.

Over the past decades, however, historians have studied the traumatic experiences of 1692 in great detail. In so doing they have created a more sophisticated model of the mental world behind the Salem outbreaks. They have also suggested ways in which the witchcraft episode was tied to the more mundane events of village life. The techniques of small-scale history, in other words, have provided a compelling psychological and social context for the events of 1692.

BEWITCHMENT AT SALEM VILLAGE

Most accounts of the trouble at Salem begin during the winter of 1691–92 in the kitchen of the village's minister, Samuel Parris. There, a group of girls met to discover what sort of men their future husbands might be, a subject of natural enough interest. Lacking a crystal ball, they used the next available substitute, the white of a raw egg suspended in a glass of water. At some point during these sessions, things went sour. One of the girls thought she detected "a specter in the likeness of a coffin" in the glass—hardly an auspicious omen. Soon nine-year-old Betty Parris, daughter of the minister and the youngest of the girls, began complaining of pinching, prickling sensations, knifelike pains, and the feeling that she was being choked. In the weeks that followed, three more girls exhibited similar symptoms.

The Reverend Parris was at a loss to understand the afflictions, as were several doctors and ministers he brought in to observe the strange behaviors. When one doctor hinted at the possibility of witchcraft, a neighbor, Mary Sibley, suggested putting to use a bit of New England folklore, to reveal whether indeed there had been any sorcery. Sibley persuaded two slaves living in the Parris household, John Indian and his wife, Tituba, to bake a "witch cake" made of rye meal and urine given them by the girls. The cake was fed to a dog—the theory of bewitchment confirmed, presumably, if the dog suffered torments similar to those of the afflicted women.

This experiment seems to have frightened the girls even more, for their symptoms worsened. Now they complained of being bitten and pinched by invisible specters: "their arms, necks, and backs turned this way and that way, and returned back again," according to one minister, "so [violently] as it was impossible for them to do of themselves, and beyond the power of any Epileptick Fits, or natural Disease to effect." Thoroughly alarmed by these convulsions, Parris and several other adults pressed the girls for the identity of the specters they believed were tormenting them. When the girls named three women, a formal complaint was issued, and on February 29 the suspects were arrested. For indeed, seventeenth-century New Englanders conceived of witchcraft as a crime. If the girls were being tormented, it was necessary to punish whoever was responsible.

Two of the women arrested, Sarah Good and Sarah Osbourne, were already unpopular in the village. The third accused was Parris's Indian slave, Tituba. Tituba may have been purchased by Parris during a visit to the

Caribbean and was perhaps originally from South America, though we have little firm information about her. Under examination by village magistrates, Sarah Good angrily denied the accusations against her, suggesting instead that Sarah Osbourne was guilty. Osbourne denied the charges, but the dynamics of the hearings changed abruptly when Tituba confessed to being a witch. One account of the trials, published eight years later, reported that her admission came after an angry Reverend Parris had beaten Tituba. For whatever reason, she testified that four women and a man were causing the afflictions of the young women. Good and Osbourne were among them. "They hurt the children," Tituba reported. "And they lay all upon me and they tell me if I will not hurt the children, they will hurt me." The tale continued, complete with apparitions of black and red rats, a yellow dog with a head like a woman, "a thing all over hairy, all the face hairy," and midnight rides to witches' meetings where plans were being laid to attack Salem.

During New England's first seventy years, few witchcraft cases had come before the courts. Those that had were dispatched quickly, and calm soon returned. Salem proved different. In the first place, Tituba had described several other witches and a wizard, though she said she was unable to identify them. The villagers felt they could not rest so long as these agents remained at large. Furthermore, the young women continued to name names—and now not just community outcasts but a wide variety of villagers, some respectable church members. The new suspects joined Tituba, Sarah Good, and Sarah Osbourne in jail. By the end of April the hunt had led to no less a personage than the Reverend George Burroughs, a former minister of the village living in Maine. Constables marched to Maine, fetched him back, and threw him in jail.

If someone confessed to witchcraft, the matter of identification seemed simple enough. But if the accused refused to admit guilt, then the magistrates looked for corroborating proof. Physical evidence, such as voodoo dolls and pins found among the suspect's possessions, were considered incriminating. Furthermore, if the devil made a pact with someone, he supposedly required a physical mark of allegiance and thus created a "witch's tit" where either he or his familiar, a likeness in animal form, might suck. Prisoners in the Salem trials were often examined for any abnormal marks on their bodies.

Aside from physical signs, the magistrates sought evidence that a witch's malice might have led to suffering on the part of the victim. This kind of black magic—harm by occult means—was known as *maleficium*. Villager Sarah Gadge, for example, testified that two years earlier she had refused Sarah Good lodging for the night. According to Gadge, Good "fell to muttering and scolding extreamly and so told said Gadge if she would not let her in she should give her something . . . and the next morning after, to said Deponents best remembrance, one of the said Gadges Cowes Died in a Sudden terrible and Strange unusuall maner."

The magistrates also considered what they called "spectral evidence," at once the most damning and dangerous kind of proof. Spectral evidence involved the visions of specters—likenesses of the witches—that victims reported seeing during their torments. In an attempt to confirm the connection between malice and injury, the magistrates kept the afflicted women in the courtroom to observe their behavior while the accused were being examined. "Why doe you hurt these children?" asked John Hathorne, one of the magistrates, in a typical examination. "I doe not hurt them," replied Sarah Osbourne. The record continues: "The children abovenamed being all personally present accused her face to face which being don, they ware all hurt, afflicted and tortured very much: which being over and thay out of theire fitts thay sayd that said Sarah Osburne did then Come to them and hurt them."

The problem with spectral evidence was that it could not be corroborated by others. Only the victim saw the shape of the tormentor. Such testimony was usually controversial, for theologians in Europe as well as in New England believed that spectral evidence should be treated with caution. After all, what better way for the devil to spread confusion than by assuming the shape of an innocent person? In Salem, however, the magistrates considered spectral testimony as paramount. When they handed down indictments, almost all the charges referred only to the spectral torments exhibited by accusers during the pretrial hearings.

Throughout the spring of 1692, no trials of the accused had been held, for the simple reason that Massachusetts was without legal government. In 1684 the Crown had revoked the colony's original charter and set up a new and unpopular government known as the Dominion of New England. But in 1689, William of Orange forced King James to flee England, and New Englanders took that opportunity to overthrow the Dominion. In the ensuing confusion, court cases had been brought largely to a standstill. The new governor of Massachusetts, Sir William Phips, at last arrived in May 1692 with a royal charter and quickly established a special court of Oyer and Terminer to deal with the witchcraft cases.

On June 2 the court heard its first case, that of a woman named Bridget Bishop. Even before the Salem outbreak Bishop had been suspected of witchcraft by a number of villagers. She was quickly convicted and, eight days later, hanged from a scaffold on a hill just outside Salem Town. The site came to be known as Witch's Hill—with good reason, since on June 29 the court again met and convicted five more women. One of them, Rebecca Nurse, had been found innocent, but the court's chief justice disapproved the verdict and convinced the jurors to change their minds. On July 19 Nurse joined the other four women on the scaffold, staunch churchwoman that she was, praying for the judges' souls as well as her own. Sarah Good remained defiant to the end. "I am no more a witch than you are a wizard," she told the attending minister, "and if you take away my life, God will give you blood to drink."

Still the accusations continued; still the court sat. As the net was cast wider, more and more accused were forced to work out their response to the crisis. A few, most of them wealthy, went into hiding until the furor subsided.

Giles Cory, a farmer whose wife, Martha, was executed as a witch, refused to "put himself on the country"—that is, submit to a trial by jury. The traditional penalty for such a refusal was the *peine fort et dure*, in which the victim was placed between two boards and heavy stones placed on him until he agreed to plead. Although that punishment had been outlawed in Massachusetts, the court nonetheless carried it out. Cory was slowly crushed to death, stubborn to the end. His last words were said to be, "More weight."

Some of the accused admitted guilt, the most satisfactory solution for the magistrates. Puritans could be a remarkably forgiving people. They were not interested in punishment for its own sake. If a lawbreaker gave evidence of sincere regret for his or her misdeeds, Puritan courts would often reduce or suspend the sentence. So it was in the witchcraft trials at Salem (unlike most trials in Europe, where confessing witches were executed). But the policy of forgiveness had unforeseen consequences. Those who were wrongly accused quickly realized that if they did *not* confess, they were likely to be hanged. If they did confess, they could escape death but would have to demonstrate their sincerity by providing details of their misdeeds and names of other participants. The temptation must have been great to confess and, in so doing, to implicate other innocent people.

Given such pressures, the web of accusations continued to grow. August produced six more trials and five hangings. Elizabeth Proctor, the wife of a tavern keeper, received a reprieve because she was pregnant, the court being unwilling to sacrifice the life of an innocent child. Her husband, John, was not spared. September saw another eight victims hanged. More than a hundred suspected witches remained in jail.

Pressure to stop the trials had been building, however. One member of the court, Nathaniel Saltonstall, resigned in protest after the first execution. More important, the ministers of the province were becoming uneasy. In public they had supported the trials, but privately they wrote letters cautioning the magistrates. Finally in early October Increase Mather, one of the most respected divines in the colony, published a sermon signed by fourteen other pastors that strongly condemned the use of spectral evidence. Mather argued that to convict on the basis of a specter, which everyone agreed was the devil's creation, in effect took Satan at his own word. That, in Mather's view, risked disaster. "It were better that ten suspected witches should escape, than that one innocent person should be condemned," he concluded.

Mather's sermon convinced Governor Phips that the trials had gone too far. He forbade any more arrests and dismissed the court of Oyer and Terminer. The following January a new court met to dispose of the remaining cases, but this time almost all the defendants were acquitted. Phips immediately granted a reprieve to the three women who were convicted and in April released the remaining prisoners. Satan's controversy with Salem was finished.

That, in outline, is the witchcraft story as it has come down to us for so many years. Rightly or wrongly, the story has become an indelible part of American history. The startling fits of possession, the drama of the court examinations, the eloquent pleas of the innocent condemned—all these make for a superb drama that casts into shadow the rest of Salem's more pedestrian history.

Indeed, the episode is unrepresentative. Witchcraft epidemics were not a serious problem in New England and were even less of a problem in other American colonies. Such persecutions were much more common in old England and Europe, where they had reached frightening proportions. The death of 20 people at Salem is sobering, but the magnitude of the event diminishes considerably alongside the estimate of 40,000-60,000 people executed for witchcraft in early modern Europe. Furthermore, it can be safely said that the witchcraft affair had no lasting effect on the political or religious history of America or even of Massachusetts.

Now, a curious thing has resulted from this illumination of a single, isolated episode. Again and again the story of Salem Village has been told, quite naturally, as a drama complete unto itself. The workaday history that preceded and followed the trials—the petty town bickerings, the arguments over land and ministers—all these elements were for many years largely passed over. Yet the disturbances at Salem did not occur in a vacuum. They may indeed have constituted an epidemic, but not the sort caused by some mysterious germ pool brought into the village over the rutted roads from Boston. So the historian's first task is to take the major strands of the witchcraft affair and see how they are woven into the larger fabric of New England society. Salem Village is small enough that virtually every one of its residents can be identified. We can find out who owned what land, the amount of taxes each resident paid, what sermons people listened to on Sundays. In so doing, a richer, far more intriguing picture of New England life begins to emerge.

THE INVISIBLE SALEM

Paradoxically, the most obvious facet of Salem life that the historian must re-create is also the most insubstantial: what ministers of the period would have called the "invisible world." Demons, familiars, witchcraft, and magic all shaped seventeenth-century New England. For most Salem Villagers, Satan was a living, supernatural being who might appear to people, bargain with them, even enter into agreements. The men and women who submitted to such devilish compacts were said to exchange their souls in return for special powers or favors: money and good fortune, perhaps, or the ability to revenge themselves on others.

Most often, ordinary folk viewed witchcraft as a simple matter of *maleficium:* Sarah Good, for example, being thought to have caused one of Sarah Gadge's cows to die after a hostile encounter. The process by which certain people in a community gained a reputation for wielding occult power was described well in 1587 by George Gifford, an English minister who was himself quite skeptical of the reality of witchcraft:

Some woman doth fall out bitterly with her neighbour: there followeth some great hurt . . . There is a suspicion conceived. Within few years after, [the same woman] is in some jar [argument] with another. He is also plagued. This is noted of all. Great fame is spread of the matter. Mother W is a witch. She had bewitched Goodman B. Two hogs died strangely: or else he is taken lame.

Well, Mother W doth begin to be very odious and terrible unto many. Her neighbours dare say nothing but yet in their hearts they wish she were hanged. Shortly after, another [person] falleth sick and doth pine; he can have no stomach unto his meat, nor he cannot sleep. The neighbours come to visit him. 'Well neighbour,' sayeth one, 'do ye not suspect some naughty dealing: did ye never anger Mother W?' 'Truly neighbour (sayeth he) I have not liked the woman a long time.'

Such suspicions of witchcraft were widespread in the early modern world. Indeed, the belief in *maleficium* was only one part of a worldview filled with magic and wonders—magic that could be manipulated and pursued by someone with the proper knowledge. Fortune-tellers provided a window into the future; objects like horseshoes brought good luck; earthquakes and comets warned of God's judgments. People who possessed more than the usual store of supernatural knowledge were known as "cunning folk," who might be called upon in times of trouble to heal the illness of a sick villager, cast horoscopes for a merchant worried about a ship's upcoming voyage, or discover what sort of children a woman might bear.

The outlines of such beliefs are easily enough sketched, but they convey the emotions of witchcraft about as successfully as a recital of the Apostle's Creed conveys the fire of the Christian faith. Historians who do not believe in a personal, witch-covenanting devil are entering a psychological world in which they are outsiders. It may seem a simple matter to predict how a Salem Villager who believed in such wonders might behave, but people who hold beliefs foreign to our own do not always act the way that we think they should. Over the years, historians of the witchcraft controversy have faced the challenge of re-creating Salem's mental world.

One of the first people to review Salem's troubles was Thomas Hutchinson, who in 1750 published a history of New England's early days. Hutchinson did not believe in witchcraft; fewer and fewer educated people did as the eighteenth century progressed. Therefore he faced an obvious question, which centered on the motivations of the accusers. If the devil never actually covenanted with anyone, how were the accusers' actions to be explained? Some of Hutchinson's contemporaries argued that the bewitched were suffering from "bodily disorders which affected their imaginations." He disagreed. "A little attention must force conviction that the whole was a scene of fraud and imposture, begun by young girls, who at first perhaps thought of nothing more than being pitied and indulged, and continued by adult persons who were afraid of being accused themselves." Charles Upham, a minister who published a two-volume study of the episode in 1867, was equally hard on the young women. "There has seldom been better acting in a theatre than displayed in the presence of the astonished and horror-stricken rulers," he concluded tartly.

Indeed, the historical record does supply some evidence to substantiate the view that the possessed were shamming. When Elizabeth Proctor was accused of being a witch, a friend of hers testified that he had seen one of the afflicted women cry out, "There's Goody Procter!"[1] But when people in the room challenged the woman's claim as evidently false, she backed off, saying only that "she did it for sport; they must have some sport."

A month and a half after the hearings had begun, one of the tormented young women, Mary Warren, stopped having her fits. She began to claim "that the afflicted persons did but dissemble"—that is, that they were shamming. Suddenly the other accusers began to declare that Mary's specter was afflicting them. Placed on the witness stand, Mary again fell into a fit "that she did neither see nor hear nor speak." The examination record continued:

> Afterwards she started up, and said I will speak and cryed out, Oh! I am sorry for it, I am sorry for it, and wringed her hands, and fell a little while into a fit again and then came to speak, but immediately her teeth were set, and then she fell into a violent fit and cryed out, oh Lord help me! Oh Good Lord Save me!
>
> And then afterward cryed again, I will tell I will tell and then fell into a dead fit againe.
>
> And afterwards cryed I will tell, they did, they did they did and then fell into a violent fit again.
>
> After a little recovery she cryed I will tell they brought me to it and then fell into a fit again which fits continueing she was ordered to be had out.

The scene is tantalizing. It appears as if Mary Warren is about to confess when pressure from the other girls forces her back to her former role as one of the afflicted. In the following weeks the magistrates questioned Mary repeatedly, with the result that her fits returned and she again joined in the accusations. Such evidence suggests that the girls may well have been acting.

Yet such a theory leaves certain points unexplained. If the girls were only acting, what are we to make of the many other witnesses who testified to deviltry? One villager, Richard Comans, reported seeing Bridget Bishop's specter in his bedroom. Bishop lay upon his breast, he reported, and "so oppressed" him that "he could not speak nor stur, noe not so much as to awake his wife" sleeping next to him. Comans and others who testified were not close friends of the girls; there appears no reason why they might be conspiring with each other. How does the historian explain their actions?

Even some of the afflicted women's behavior is difficult to explain as conscious fraud. It is easy enough to imagine counterfeiting certain fits: whirling

---

1. Goody was short for *Goodwife*, a term used for most married women. Husbands were addressed as Goodman. The terms *Mr.* and *Mrs.* were reserved for those of higher social standing.

through the room crying "whish, whish"; being struck dumb. Yet other behavior was truly sobering. Being pinched, pummeled, nearly choked to death; contortions so violent several grown men were required to restrain the victims. Even innocent victims of the accusations were astounded by such behavior. Rebecca Nurse on the witness stand could only look in astonishment at the "lamentable fits" she was accused of causing. "Do you think these [afflicted] suffer voluntary or involuntary?" asked John Hathorne. "I cannot tell what to think of it," replied Goody Nurse hesitantly. Hathorne pressed others with similar results. What ails the girls, if not your torments? "I do not know." Do you think they are bewitched? "I cannot tell." What do you think does ail them? "There is more than ordinary."

More than ordinary. Historians may accept that possibility without necessarily supposing, with Hathorne, the presence of the preternatural. Psychiatric research has long established what we now take almost for granted: that people may act for reasons they themselves do not fully understand, from motives buried deep within the unconscious. Even more: that emotional problems may be the unconscious cause of apparently physical disorders. The rationalistic psychologies of Thomas Hutchinson and Charles Upham led them to reject any middle-ground explanations of motivation. The Salem women had not really been tormented by witches, Hutchinson and Upham reasoned; therefore they must have been acting voluntarily, consciously. But given the mental attitudes that accompanied a belief in devils and witches, it is possible to understand the Salem episode, not as a game of fraud gone out of control, but as a study in abnormal psychology on a community-wide scale.

Scholars of the twentieth century have been more inclined to adopt this medical model as an explanation of Salem's troubles. Indeed, one of the first to make the suggestion was a pediatrician, Ernest Caulfield. The accused "were not impostors or pests or frauds," he wrote in 1943; "they were not cold-blooded malignant brats. They were sick children in the worst sort of mental distress—living in fear for their very lives and the welfare of their immortal souls." Certainly, the fear that gripped susceptible subjects must have been extraordinary. They imagined themselves pursued by agents of the devil, intent on torment or even murder, and locked doors provided no protection. Anthropologists who have examined witchcraft in other cultures note that bewitchment can be traumatic enough to lead to death. An Australian aborigine who discovers himself bewitched will

> stand aghast. . . . His cheeks blanch and his eyes become glassy. . . . He attempts to shriek but usually the sound chokes in his throat, and all that one might see is froth at his mouth. His body begins to tremble and the muscles twist involuntarily. He sways backwards and falls to the ground, and after a short time appears to be in a swoon; but soon after he writhes as if in mortal agony.

Afterward the victim refuses to eat, loses all interest in life, and dies. Although there were no documented cases of bewitchment death in Salem, the anthropological studies indicate the remarkable depth of reaction possible in a community that believes in its own magic.[2]

Historian Chadwick Hansen has compared the behavior of the bewitched with the neurotic syndrome that psychiatrists refer to as conversion hysteria. A neurosis is a disorder of behavior that functions to avoid or deflect intolerable anxiety. Normally, an anxious person deals with an emotion through conscious action or thought. If the ordinary means of coping fail, however, the unconscious takes over. Hysterical patients will convert their mental worries into physical symptoms such as blindness, paralysis of various parts of the body, choking, fainting, or attacks of pain. These symptoms, it should be stressed, cannot be traced to organic causes. There is nothing wrong with the nervous system during an attack of paralysis, or with the optic nerve in a case of blindness. Physical disabilities are mentally induced. Such hysterical attacks often occur in patterns that bear striking resemblance to some of the Salem afflictions.

Pierre Janet, the French physician who wrote the classic *Major Symptoms of Hysteria* (1907), reported that a characteristic hysterical fit begins with a pain or strange sensation in some part of the body, often the lower abdomen. From there, he explained, it

> seems to ascend and to spread to other organs. For instance, it often spreads to the epigastrium [the region lying over the stomach], to the breasts, then to the throat. There it assumes rather an interesting form, which was for a very long time considered as quite characteristic of hysteria. The patient has the sensation of too big an object as it were, a ball rising in her throat and choking her.

Most of us have probably experienced a mild form of the last symptom—a proverbial "lump in the throat" that comes in times of stress. The hysteric's lump, or *globus hystericus,* is more extreme, as are the accompanying convulsions: "the head is agitated in one direction or another, the eyes closed, or open with an expression of terror, the mouth distorted."

Compare those symptoms with the ones manifested by Richard Comans, who (we have already seen) was struck down in bed by the weight of Bridget Bishop's specter and so frightened, "he could not speak nor stur." Or the fits of another tormented accuser, Elizabeth Brown, described during the Salem hearings:

> When [the witch's specter] did come it was as birds pecking her legs or pricking her with the motion of thayr wings and then it would rize up into her stamak with pricking pain as nayls and pins of which she did bitterly complayn and cry out like a women in travail and after that it would rise to her throat in

---

2. The records hint that at least one bewitchment death may have occurred, however. Daniel Wilkins apparently believed that John Willard was a witch and meant him no good. Wilkins sickened, and some of the afflicted girls were summoned to his bedside where they claimed that they saw Willard's specter afflicting him. The doctor would not touch the case, claiming it "preternatural." Shortly after, Wilkins died.

A hysterical convulsive attack of one of the patients in Salpêtrière Hospital during the nineteenth century. J. M. Charcot, the physician in charge of the clinic, spent much of his time studying the disorder. Note the crossed legs, similar to some of the Salem girls' fits. (Sterling Memorial Library, Yale University)

a bunch like a pullets egg and then she would tern back her head and say witch you shant choak me.

The diagnosis of hysteria, or at least of unconscious psychological pressures of one sort or another, has gained ground over the past decades. Yet the issue of fraud cannot be put so easily to rest. Studies of witchcraft in Europe have discovered a wide variety of behaviors, ranging from bewitchment deaths through hysteria to the more routine claims of *maleficium*, to cases of confessed outright fraud. Bernard Rosenthal, a scholar who has recently reexamined the Salem court records, argues that a close reading of the depositions suggests that fraud and hysteria were intermingled.

Admit, Rosenthal proposes, that some behaviors fit the pattern of hysterical behavior. Even so, the records reveal other conduct that is difficult to explain through mere psychological distress. What are we to make, for example, of the testimony given against Sarah Good and another accused, Lydia Dustin, regarding their "torments" of one Susannah Sheldon?

> Susannah Sheldon being at the house of William Shaw she was tied her hands a cross in such a manner we were forced to cut the string before we could git her hand loose and when shee was out of her fit she told us it [was] Goody Dustin that did tye her hands after that manner, and 4 times shee hath been tyed in this manner in towe weeks time[.] The 2 first times shee sayth it was Goode Dustin and the 2 last times it was Sarah Goode that did tye her. We furder testifie that when ever shee doth but touch this string shee is presently bit.

It is one matter to have "fits" through terror; another to have wrists tied four times by a specter who is then said to bite Sheldon if she tries to untie them. Unless we believe in invisible specters, the only reasonable answer would seem to be that Susannah Sheldon had a confederate who tied her hands. Similarly Deodat Lawson, a minister who devoutly believed in witchcraft, reported in March 1692 that

> Some of the afflicted, as they were striving in their fits in open court, have (by invisible means) had their wrists bound fast together with a real cord, so as it could hardly be taken off without cutting. Some afflicted have been found with their arms tied, and hanged upon an hook, from whence others have been forced to take them down, that they might not expire in that posture.

The conclusion, argued Rosenthal, must be similar: "Whether the 'afflicted' worked these shows out among themselves or had help from others cannot be determined; but there is little doubt that such calculated action was deliberately conceived to perpetuate the fraud in which the afflicted were involved, and that theories of hysteria or hallucination cannot account for people being bound, whether on the courtroom floor or on hooks." Similarly, on more than one occasion, some of the accused produced pins that they claimed had been stuck in them by specters.

Such evidence suggests a complex set of behaviors in which both hysteria and fraud played a part. "Differences between malingerers and hysterics are not absolute," notes one modern psychiatry text, "and we often find many hysterical traits in malingerers and some near-conscious play acting in the hysterical patient."

What seems clear, however, is the frightening dynamic unleashed by the decision of the magistrates to regard confession and cooperation as tokens of repentance while viewing denials of witchcraft as a sign of guilt. Indeed, the magistrates appeared not to want to take no for an answer. John Proctor complained that when his son was examined, "because he would not confess that he was Guilty, when he was Innocent, they tyed him Neck and Heels till the Blood gushed out at his Nose, and would have kept him so 24 Hours, if one more Merciful than the rest, had not taken pity on him." Once Bridget Bishop was executed in June, the lesson was chilling and direct. Those who confessed to witchcraft—like Tituba—avoided being hanged. Those who maintained their innocence were headed for the gallows.

Sarah Churchill, a young woman of about seventeen, experienced these pressures. She apparently succumbed to her fears and testified that she was a witch. Soon, however, she had second thoughts, for she came crying and wringing her hands to an older friend, Sarah Ingersoll. "I asked her what she ailed?" reported Ingersoll.

> She answered she had undone herself. I asked her in what. She said in belying herself and others in saying she had set her hand to the devil's Book whereas she said she never did. I told her I believed she had set her hand to the book. She answered crying and said no no no, I naver, I naver did. I asked then what had made her say she did. She answered because they threatened her and told her they would put her into the dungeon and put her along with Mr. Burroughs, and thus several times she followed [me] on up and down telling me that she had undone herself in belying herself and others. I asked her why she didn't tell the truth now. She told me because she had stood out so long in it that now she darst not. She said also that if she told Mr. Noyes [an investigating minister] but once that she had set her hand to the Book he would believe her, but if she told the truth and said she had not set her hand to the book a hundred times he would not believe her.

Thus psychological terrors sprang from more than one source. The frights of the invisible world, to be sure, led many villagers to fear for their lives and souls. But the determination of the magistrates not to accept the denials of the innocent led to equally terrifying pressures to belie oneself in order to escape execution. In a cataclysm involving hundreds of people in the community, either as accused witches, horrified onlookers, or active accusers, it is perhaps not surprising that individuals behaved in a wide variety of ways.

THE VISIBLE SALEM

It would be tempting, after we have explored the psychological dynamics of Salem, to suppose that the causes of the outbreak have been fairly well explained. There is the natural satisfaction of placing the symptoms of the modern hysteric side by side with those of the seventeenth-century bewitched and seeing them match, or of carefully reading the trial records to distinguish likely cases of fraud from those of hysteria. Yet by narrowing our inquiry to the motivations of the possessed, we have left other important facets of the Salem episode unexplored.

In the first place, the investigation thus far has dealt with the controversy on an individual rather than a social level. But step back for a moment. For whatever reasons, approximately 150 people in Salem and other towns found themselves accused. Why were those particular people singled out? Does any common bond explain why they, and not others, were accused? Only after we have examined their social identities can we answer that question.

Another indication that the social context of Salem Village needs to be examined is the nature of hysteria itself. Hysterics are notably suggestible, that is, sensitive to the influence of their environment. Nineteenth-century patients who were kept in insane asylums along with epileptics, for example, began having seizures that mimicked those suffered by the epileptics. If hysterics, then, are influenced by the behavior of those around them, what were the expectations of the general community? Scattered testimony in the records suggests that sometimes when the young women saw specters whom they could not identify, adults suggested names. "Was it Goody Cloyse? Was it Rebecca Nurse?" If true, such conditions confirm the need to move beyond strictly personal motivations to the social setting of the community.

In doing so, a logical first step would be to look for correlations, or characteristics common to groups that might explain their behavior. Are the accusers all church members and the accused nonchurch members? Are the accusers wealthy and respectable while the accused are poor and disreputable? The historian assembles the data, patiently shuffles them around, and looks for matchups.

Take the two social characteristics already mentioned, church membership and wealth. Historians can compile lists from the trial records of both the accusers and the accused. With those lists in hand, they can begin checking the church records to discover which people on each list were church members. Or they can search tax records to see whose tax rates were highest and thus which villagers were wealthiest. Records of land transactions are recorded, indicating which villagers owned the most land. Inventories of personal property are made when a member of the community dies, so at least historians have some record of an individual's assets at death, if not in 1692. Other records may mention a trade or occupation, which will give a clue to relative wealth or social status.

If you make such calculations for the Salem region, you will quickly find yourself at a dead end, a spot altogether too familiar to practicing historians. True, the first few accused witches were not church members, but soon enough the faithful found themselves in jail along with nonchurch members. A similar case holds for wealth: although Tituba, Sarah Good, and Sarah Osbourne were relatively poor, merchants and wealthy farmers were accused as the epidemic spread. The correlations fail to check.

This dead end was roughly the point that had been reached when two historians, Paul Boyer and Stephen Nissenbaum, were inspired to take literally the advice about going back to the drawing board. More than a hundred years earlier Charles Upham had made a detailed map of Salem for his own study of the witchcraft episode. Upham examined the old town records, paced the actual sites of old houses, and established to the best of his knowledge the residences of a large majority of Salem Villagers. Boyer and Nissenbaum took their list of accusers and accused and noted the location of each village resident. The results were striking, as can be seen from the map on page 37.

Of the fourteen accused witches in the village, twelve lived in the eastern section. Of the thirty-two adult villagers who testified against the accused, thirty lived in the western section. "In other words," concluded Boyer and Nissenbaum, "the alleged witches and those who accused them resided on

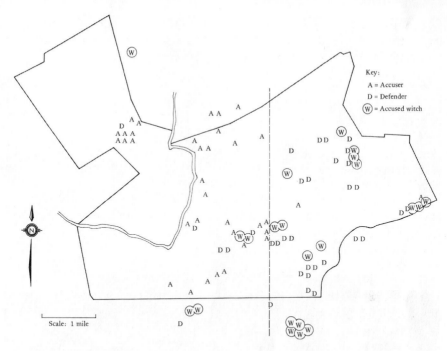

"The Geography of Witchcraft" (after Boyer and Nissenbaum, *Salem Possessed,* Harvard University Press, 1974).

opposite sides of the Village." Furthermore, of twenty-nine residents who publicly defended the accused in some way (marked by a "D" on the map), twenty-four lived in the eastern half of the village. Often they were close neighbors of the accused. It is moments like these that make the historian want to behave, were it not for the staid air of research libraries, like Archimedes leaping from his fabled bathtub and shouting "Eureka!"

The discovery is only the beginning of the task. The geographic chart suggests a division, but it does not at all indicate what that division is, other than a general east-west split. So Boyer and Nissenbaum began to explore the history of the village itself, expanding their microcosm of 1692 backward in time. They investigated a social situation that historians had long recognized but had never associated with the Salem witch trials: Salem Village's uneasy relation to its social parent, Salem Town.

Salem Town's settlement followed the pattern of most coastal New England towns. Original settlers set up houses around a central location and carved their farmlands out of the surrounding countryside. As a settlement prospered, the land in its immediate vicinity came to be completely taken up. As houses were erected farther and farther away from the central meeting house, outlying residents found it inconvenient to come to church or attend to other civic duties. In such cases, they sought recognition as a separate village, with their own church, their own taxes, and their own elected officials.

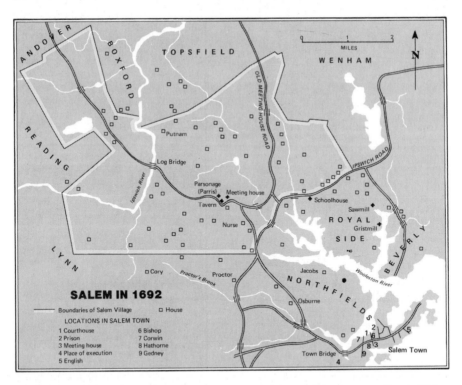

"Salem in 1692" (From *The Pursuit of Liberty: A History of the American People*, Vol. I, by R. Jackson Wilson, et al. Copyright 1966 by HarperCollins College Publishers. Reprinted by permission of Addison-Wesley Educational Publishers Inc.)

Here the trouble started. The settlers who lived toward the center of town were reluctant to let their outlying neighbors break away. Everyone paid taxes to support a minister for the town church, to maintain the roads, and to care for the poor. If a chunk of the village split off, revenue would be lost. Furthermore, outlying settlers would no longer share the common burdens, such as guarding the town at night. So the centrally located settlers usually resisted any movement for autonomy by their more distant neighbors. Such disputes were a regular feature of New England life.

Salem Town had followed this pattern. Its first settlers located on a peninsula extending into Massachusetts Bay, where they pursued a prosperous colonial trade. By 1668 four outlying areas (Wenham, Manchester, Marblehead, and Beverly) had already become separate towns. Now the "Salem Farmers," living directly to the west, were petitioning for a similar settlement, and the "Townsmen" were resisting. In 1672 Massachusetts's legislature allowed Salem Village to build its own meeting house, but in other matters, the village remained dependent. Salem Town still collected village taxes, chose village constables, and arranged for village roads. The colony's records include petition after petition from villagers complaining about tax rates, patrol duties, boundary rulings.

Here, then, is one east-west split—between the village and the town. But the line so graphically drawn on Boyer and Nissenbaum's map is *within* the village. What cause would the village have for division?

Many causes, the records indicate—chief among them the choice of a minister. When the village built its own meeting house, it chose James Bayley to be its pastor in 1673. Soon enough, however, some churchgoers began complaining. Bayley didn't attend regularly to his private prayers. Church members had not been fully consulted before his selection. After a flurry of petitions and counterpetitions, Bayley left in 1680, and George Burroughs was hired. Three years later Burroughs left in another dispute. He was succeeded by Deodat Lawson, who lasted through four more years of quarrels. Finally Samuel Parris occupied the pulpit after 1688. His term was equally stormy, and in 1696 his opponents finally succeeded in starving him out of the job by refusing to collect taxes to pay his salary.

The maneuverings that went on during the years of bickering seem bewilderingly complex. But Boyer and Nissenbaum recognized that the church records, the petitions and counterpetitions, and the minutes of the village committee provided an invaluable key to local divisions. At bottom, it was not the piety of the ministers alone that was in dispute. Equally crucial was who held power—over piety or anything else. When the lists from the different quarrels were compared, Boyer and Nissenbaum found that the same names were being grouped together. The people who supported James Bayley usually supported George Burroughs and then opposed the second two ministers. Conversely, the supporters of Deodat Lawson and Samuel Parris had been the people who complained about Bayley and Burroughs. And— here is the link—the two lists from those disputes coincide closely with the divisions in 1692 between accusers and accused.

Suddenly the Salem witch trials take on an entirely new appearance. Instead of being a dramatic disruption that appears out of nowhere in a village kitchen and then disappears equally suddenly at the end of ten months, it becomes an elaboration of a quarrel that has gone on for nearly twenty years!

What lay behind the divisions? One reading of the evidence suggests that the larger split between Salem Town and Salem Village was reflected in the village itself, with the villagers on the east retaining enough in common with the town to continue their affiliation and the westerners favoring complete separation. Boyer and Nissenbaum argue that the division also went beyond the simple geographical one to a difference in outlook and lifestyle. Salem Town was entering into its own as one of the major commercial centers of New England. It boasted a growing merchant class whose wealth would soon support the building of fine mansions. By contrast the farmers in the western portion of Salem Village were tied more closely to traditional agrarian life: subsistence farming, spartan daily lives, a suspicion of the commercial habits of offering credit and making speculative investments. Worse, the Salem farmers found themselves increasingly hard-pressed. The land

.e in the village was dwindling. What land there was proved less fer-
an the broad plains on the eastern side of the village and along the
noruiern flats of Salem Town.

Look, too, at the occupations of the accused witches and their defenders.
Many lived along the Ipswich Road, a route that passed by the village rather
than through it, a main thoroughfare for travelers and for commerce. The
tradespeople who had set up shop there included a carpenter, sawmill operator, shoemaker, miller. And of course there were the taverns, mainstays of
travelers, yet always slightly suspect to Puritans. The people along the
Ipswich Road were not rich, most of them, but their commercial links were
with Salem Town and with outsiders. They were small-scale entrepreneurs
rather than farmers. Out of twenty-one villagers who lived along or near the
road, only two signed petitions linking them with the western faction; thirteen signed petitions linking them with the eastern faction. Tavern keeper
John Proctor was hanged as a witch; his wife Elizabeth barely escaped with
her life; and Joshua Rea, another tavern keeper on the road, signed a petition defending Goody Nurse.[3]

Boyer and Nissenbaum's reconstruction of village factions thus suggests
an alternate way of looking at the Salem trials. Traditional accounts place
Samuel Parris and his supporters as leaders of the village, terrorizing innocent villagers and controlling the trials. Certainly Parris's supporters had
their day in 1692, but from the longer perspective they appear to have been
fighting a losing battle. If Boyer and Nissenbaum are correct, the Salem trials were an indirect yet anguished protest of a group of villagers whose
agrarian way of life was being threatened by the rising commercialism of
Salem Town.

In large part, the brilliance of Boyer and Nissenbaum's research was to
place the individual dramas of Salem into a larger social context. But their
maps are not the only maps that can be drawn, nor their connections the
only connections to be made. Boyer and Nissenbaum focused their attention
on Salem Village. But as the witchcraft trials gained momentum, the fever
spread to a few neighboring villages. In the summer of 1692, several of the
possessed women of Salem were invited to Andover by concerned residents.
The resulting round of accusations led to the arrest of nearly forty Andover
villagers. A month later, a smaller outbreak centered in the fishing port of
Gloucester, where six people were arrested. Several more of the accused
from Salem had Gloucester ties. All these people were tried by the same
court that dealt with the Salem cases.

Taking these additional episodes into account makes it more difficult to
generalize about embattled farmers arrayed against a rising commercialism.
Gloucester was a fishing port, while Andover, though it was just as agrarian

---

3. Many historians, including Boyer and Nissenbaum (and ourselves, in earlier editions of this book),
counted Bridget Bishop as a tavern keeper. But new research indicates that the "Goody Bishop" who
was accused of "drinking and playing shovelboard" at late hours of the night was a Salem Villager
named Sarah Bishop. Bridget Bishop lived in Salem Town and had no connection with a tavern.

as Salem Village, had no commercial "parent" the likes of Salem Town. Several historians have pointed out that during the time of the witch trials, King William's War had been in progress for several years. Both Andover and Gloucester in the past had suffered raids by the French and their Indian allies. Indeed in January 1692, just as the controversy was getting started, word came from York, Maine, that Indians had massacred residents there. Historian James Kences has drawn his own maps, similar to those of Boyer and Nissenbaum, suggesting connections between Salem accusers and Indian threats. A number of the accusers were orphans of the Indian wars. Mercy Lewis, for example—one of the principal accusers—only two years earlier saw her mother, father, sister, and brother murdered in an Indian attack. With so much anxiety present over the threats from external enemies, did Lewis and others project their worries onto an imaginary attack from Satan's invisible world?

If not the fear of Indian "devils," did the accusers perhaps fear religious demons? For years the colony's ruling Congregationalists had worried about the heresies spread by Quakers, members of the Society of Friends. In the 1650s and 1660s, Massachusetts Bay hanged four Quaker missionaries on the Boston Common. Other members of this Protestant sect had been whipped, thrown into prison, or driven from the colony. The Quaker belief that every person possessed his or her own divine inner light seemed to Congregationalists to suggest the blasphemous notion that God could speak directly to and through individuals. Even more upsetting to Puritans, Friends caught up in their enthusiasm would "quake" when the holy spirit possessed them, behavior that seemed all too much like the fits of the Salem afflicted. "Diabolical Possession was the thing which did dispose and encline men unto Quakerism," warned Boston minister Cotton Mather in 1689.

By 1692, Congregationalists no longer had the power to persecute Quakers, for Massachusett's new charter guaranteed toleration to all Protestants. Yet many ordinary folk continued to harbor suspicions, and within Essex County, the largest concentration of Quakers lived in Salem. Aside from Salem, the next largest group lived in Gloucester. In Andover too, Quaker connections seemed to figure in the arrests. In most cases, hostility was directed not so much at the Quakers themselves as at Congregationalists who established social ties with them. Rebecca Nurse, who was pious and well respected in other ways, had taken an orphaned Quaker boy into her family. John and Elizabeth Proctor, the tavern keepers, counted a large number of Quakers among Elizabeth's family.

If you plot the location of Quaker residences on the same map used by Boyer and Nissenbaum, you will find that the largest concentration is located in the area to the east of the village, along the border between Salem Village and Salem Town. Christine Heyrman, the historian who researched these connections, concluded that the western farmers of Salem may have worried less about how near they lived to commercial Salem than about "the even shorter physical distance separating the residences of the accused from Salem's Quaker enclave."

"WOMEN ALONE"

Whereas Boyer, Nissenbaum, and other historians have pursued correlations based on the social geography of witchcraft, another striking connection can be made. That connection is the link between witchcraft and gender.

By a large majority, the accused witches of Salem were women. Out of 178 accused who can be identified by name, more than three out of four were female. And it turns out that nearly half the accused men were husbands, sons, or other relatives of accused women. The gender gap widens further when witchcraft outside Salem is examined. Of 147 additional accused witches in seventeenth-century New England, 82 percent were women. In those cases that actually came to trial (forty-one), thirty-four involved women and only seven involved men. Of the women tried, 53 percent were convicted. Of the men, only two were convicted, or 29 percent. And of those people who were not only convicted but executed, women outnumbered men 15 to 2.

When historian Carol Karlsen examined the trial records in more detail, she found that the authorities tended to treat accused women differently from men. Magistrates and ministers often put pressure on women to confess their guilt. In New England cases (excluding Salem), when that pressure led a woman to confess a "familiarity with Satan," she was invariably executed, in accordance with the Biblical command, "Thou shalt not suffer a witch to live." But when men were accused, pressure was seldom applied to make them confess. In fact, confessions from men were not always accepted. In 1652, one John Broadstreet of Rowley admitted having familiarity with Satan. The court ordered him whipped and fined twenty shillings "for telling a lie." In 1674, Christopher Brown confessed to "discoursing with . . . the devil," but the court rejected his statement as being "inconsistent with truth." Hugh Crotia admitted that he had "signed the Devills book and then seald it with his blud." A Hartford grand jury refused to indict him.

Such evidence suggests that, by and large, most seventeenth-century New Englanders expected women to be witches, whereas men who confessed were seldom believed. But why should women be singled out for such attention?

Part of the answer, Karlsen argues, lay in the cultural position of women. Like Martin Luther and other Reformation theologians, the Puritans exalted the role of motherhood over the chaste life of the convent; they saw women as partners and helpmates in marriage. Even so, Puritans retained a distinctly hierarchical conception of marriage. They viewed families as miniature commonwealths, with the husband as the ruler and his family as willing subjects. "A true wife accounts her subjection [as] her honor and freedom," noted Governor John Winthrop of Massachusetts.

A wife's unequal status was reflected legally as well: she was known in law as a *feme covert*—one whose identity was "covered" by that of her husband. As such, she had no right to buy or sell property, sue or be sued, or make contracts. Similarly, the patterns of inheritance in New England were male dominated. A husband might leave his widow property—indeed, the law required him to leave her at least a third of his estate. But she was to "have and enjoy" that property only "during term of her natural life." She could not waste or squander it, for it was passed on to the family's heirs at her death. Similarly, daughters might inherit property, but if they were already married, it belonged to the husband. If a young woman had not yet married, property usually seems to have been held for her, "for improvement," until she married.

Thus the only sort of woman who held any substantial economic power was a widow who had not remarried. Such a woman was known as a *feme sole*, or "woman alone." She did have the right to sue, to make contracts, and to buy or sell property. Even when remarrying, a widow could sometimes protect her holdings by having her new husband sign a prenuptial contract, guaranteeing before marriage that the wife would keep certain property as her own. In male-dominated New England, these protections made the *feme sole* stand out as an anomaly—a woman alone who did not fit comfortably into the ordinary scheme of things.

Given that women in Puritan society were generally placed in subordinate roles, how does that fact help explain the preponderance of female witches? As it turns out, a significant number of accused witches were women who were *not* subordinate in some way. In refusing to conform to accepted stereotypes, they threatened the traditional order of society and were more likely to be accused of subverting it as witches.

Older women—especially those who were reputed to have medical knowledge of herbs and potions—often came under suspicion of witchcraft both in England and in America. This English drawing of 1622 portrays the stereotypical image of a willful older woman: a supposed witch by the name of Jennet Dibble. She was said to have been attended for forty years by a spirit in the shape of a great black cat called Gibb.

A woman might stand out, for example, through a contentious, argumentative nature. If a woman's duty was to submit quietly to the rule of men and to glory in "subjection," then quite a few witches refused to conform to the accepted role. We have already seen how Sarah Good's "muttering and scolding extreamly" were perceived by Salem Villagers to have caused the death of cattle. Trial records are filled with similar accusations.

Often, more than short tempers were at stake. A remarkably high percentage of accused women were women alone in an economic sense. Of the 124 witches whose inheritance patterns can be reconstructed from surviving records, as many as seventy-one (57 percent) lived or had lived in families with no male heirs. Another fourteen accused witches were the daughters or granddaughters of witches who did not have brothers or sons to inherit their property. This figure is at least twice the number that would be expected, given the usual percentage of women alone in the New England population. Furthermore, of the women executed at Salem, more than half had inherited or stood to inherit their own property. Such statistics suggest why witchcraft controversies so often centered on women.

TANGLED WEBS

The early modern world, including that of colonial New England, was uncertain, unpredictable, full of chance. Livestock upon which farm families depended might die suddenly. The primitive knowledge of physicians proved all but useless in curing the ills of the poor and wealthy alike. Amidst so many unpredictable tragedies, witchcraft offered a simple, clear explanation for misfortunes that otherwise might have seemed inexplicable. Witchcraft made the unpredictable predictable and the obscure sometimes all too terrifyingly clear.

Unlike diviners or witch doctors, historians have followed the example of the natural sciences in seeking testable, rational links between cause and effect. Yet the longing for a simple, coherent story remains strong in all of us. We all wish to see the confusing welter of events lock together with a clarity that leads us, like Archimedes, to cry Eureka—conversion hysteria! Or Eureka—the pressures of the new commercial economy! Or Eureka—women alone!

Instead, the discipline of small-scale, local history forces humility. As historians sift the web of relationships surrounding the Salem outbreak, most have come to believe that its causes are multiple rather than singular. "Irreducible to any single source of social strain," concludes Christine Heyrman. No single "governing explanation," argues Bernard Rosenthal. The very fact that witchcraft outbreaks did not recur elsewhere in New England suggests that the magnitude of Salem's calamity depended on an unusual combination of psychological and social factors.

Certainly an agrarian faction in the village did not consciously devise the trials to punish their commercial rivals or Quaker-loving neighbors. Nor was the male Puritan patriarchy launching a deliberate war against women. But the invisible world of witchcraft did provide a framework that amplified village anxieties and focused them. As the accusations of a small circle of young women widened and as controversy engulfed the town, it was only natural that long-standing quarrels and prejudices were drawn into the debate. The interconnections between a people's religious beliefs, their habits of commerce, even their dream and fantasy lives, are intricate and fine, entwined with one another like the delicate root system of a growing plant. Historians who limit their examination to a small area of time and space are able, through persistent probing, to untangle the strands of emotions, motivations, and social structures that provided the context for those slow processions to the gallows on Witch's Hill.

⇒ ⇒ ⇒ ADDITIONAL READING ⇐ ⇐ ⇐

David Hall's *Worlds of Wonder, Days of Judgment* (New York, 1988) provides an excellent introduction to the way witchcraft fits into the larger belief systems of popular religion and magic. Hall also lays out historians' contrasting approaches to Salem in "Witchcraft and the Limits of Interpretation," *New England Quarterly* 58 (1985): 253–281. Since that article, however, significant new material has appeared.

Some changes seem merely a matter of detail, such as the exact manner in which the outbreak began in Samuel Parris's kitchen. But details matter. Many accounts (including ours, in earlier editions) assumed that Tituba's knowledge of African magic sparked the baking of the witch cake and possibly even the original fortune-telling episode. Other historians have even assumed Tituba was African. In fact, that notion is a nineteenth-century addition, amplified over the years, as Chadwick Hansen shows in "The Metamorphosis of Tituba, or Why American Intellectuals Can't Tell an Indian Witch from a Negro," *New England Quarterly* 47 (1974): 3–12. Bernard Rosenthal, in *Salem Story: Reading the Witch Trials of 1692* (New York, 1993), makes it clear that a white New England neighbor, not Tituba, had the idea of baking a witch cake. See also Elaine G. Breslaw, *Tituba, Reluctant Witch of Salem: Devilish Indians and Puritan Fantasies* (New York, 1996) and Bernard Rosenthal, "Tituba's Story," *New England Quarterly* 71 (1998): 190–203. David C. Brown debunks other venerable myths in "The Case of Giles Corey," *Essex Institute Historical Collections* 121 (1985): 282–299.

Chadwick Hansen's *Witchcraft at Salem* (New York, 1969) presents the most detailed case for conversion hysteria among the accusers. But Rosenthal's *Salem Story* argues convincingly that conscious deception played some role, especially among the core accusers. Another theory has suggested that the accusers' fits can be explained by ergot, a fungus that sometimes grows on bread grains such as rye. See Mary A. K. Matossian, *Poisons of the Past* (New Haven, 1989), as well as Linnda R. Caporael, "Ergotism: The Satan Loosed in Salem?" in *Science* 192 (1976): 21–26. To our mind, ergot is another of those monocausal explanations (Eureka!) that simply do not hold up. For a rebuttal, see Nicholas P. Spanos and Jack Gottlieb,

"Ergotism and the Salem Village Witch Trials," *Science* 194 (1976): 1390–1394.

Paul Boyer and Stephen Nissenbaum apply the techniques of social history with unusual lucidity and grace in *Salem Possessed: The Social Origins of Witchcraft* (Cambridge, Mass., 1974). Other historians, however, have been skeptical about leaning too hard on rising commercialism as the outbreak's chief catalyst. For the contribution of anxiety over war and Indian raids, see James Kences, "Some Unexplored Relationships of Essex City Witchcraft to the Indian Wars of 1675 and 1689," *Essex Institute Historical Collections* 120 (1984): 179–212; for Quaker connections, Christine Leigh Heyrman, "Specters of Subversion, Societies of Friends" in David D. Hall et. al., eds. *Saints and Revolutionaries: Essays on Early American History* (New York, 1984). Our discussion of gender and witchcraft relies on Carol Karlsen, *The Devil in the Shape of a Woman: Witchcraft in Colonial New England* (New York, 1987). Other approaches to the gender question can be found in John Putnam Demos, *Entertaining Satan: Witchcraft and the Culture of Early New England* (New York, 1982) and Elizabeth Reis, *Damned Women: Sinners and Witches in Puritan New England* (Ithaca, N.Y., 1997).

Other studies of witchcraft include Richard Godbeer, *The Devil's Dominion: Magic and Religion in Early New England* (New York, 1992) and Richard Weisman, *Witchcraft, Magic, and Religion in Seventeenth-Century Massachusetts* (Amherst, Mass., 1984). Peter Charles Hoffer, *The Devil's Disciples: Makers of the Salem Witchcraft Trials* (Baltimore, 1996) provides useful legal background, though the author is often speculative. (He vividly describes Tituba's *African* years, for example, and her supposed Middle Passage voyage to the Caribbean.)

Comparison of the Salem trials with witchcraft in early modern Europe is useful. The place to begin is with Robin Briggs, *Witches and Neighbors* (New York, 1996). Briggs notes that although a belief in *maleficium* was widespread among the peasantry, it less often embodied grandiose satanic conspiracies. (Godbeer's *Devil's Dominion* also makes this point about Salem, contrasting the elaborate plots and witches' meetings described by the primary accusers with the testimony of simple *maleficium* elicited from other villagers.) Older studies of English witchcraft worth consulting include Brian P. Levack, *The Witch-Hunt in Early Modern Europe* (2d ed., New York, 1995); Alan Macfarlane, *Witchcraft in Tudor and Stuart England* (New York, 1970); and Keith Thomas, *Religion and the Decline of Magic* (London, 1971).

The most fascinating primary sources are the records of pretrial examinations made by the Salem magistrates. These records can be found in *The Salem Witchcraft Papers: Verbatim Transcripts of the Legal Documents of the Salem Witchcraft Outbreak of 1692*, 3 vols. (New York, 1977). The collection sorts documents alphabetically, by the names of the accused witches. This arrangement is quite inconvenient in some ways, because many documents, obviously, refer to more than one of the accused. Bernard Rosenthal is preparing a new edition of the work that will be arranged chronologically, which when it appears should be definitive. George Lincoln Burr, ed., *Nar-*

ratives of the Witchcraft Cases, 1648–1706 (New York, 1914; reissued 1968) is a convenient compendium of some contemporary accounts. Boyer and Nissenbaum have collected their own anthology of primary documents in *Witchcraft at Salem Village* (Belmont, Calif., 1972), oriented more toward the social background of Salem.

Finally, parallels between the outbreak at Salem and modern controversies are worth pursuing. The question of whether repressed incidents of child abuse can be deduced through "recovered memory" are explored in a volume that makes explicit comparisons with the Salem witch trials. See Mark Pendergrast, *Victims of Memory: Sex Abuse Accusations and Shattered Lives* (2d ed., Hinesburg, Vt., 1996) as well as Michael Shermer, *Why People Believe Weird Things: Pseudoscience, Superstition, and Other Confusions of Our Time* (New York, 1997). Also useful is Frederick Crews, "The Revenge of the Repressed," *The New York Review of Books*, 17 November 1994 and 1 December 1994. (Crews has collected these essays along with responses by his critics in *The Memory Wars: Freud's Legacy in Dispute* (New York, 1995). Elaine Showalter puts some of these controversies in the broader context of hysteria as it has been expressed over the years in *Hysteries* (New York, 1997).

❊ ❊ THREE ❊ ❊

Declaring Independence

Good historians share with magicians a talent for elegant sleight of hand. In both professions, the manner of execution conceals much of the work that makes the performance possible. Like the magician's trapdoors, mirrors, and other hidden props, historians' primary sources are essential to their task. But the better that historians are at their craft, the more likely they will focus their readers' attention on the historical scene itself and not on the supporting documents.

Contrary to prevailing etiquette, we have gone out of our way to call attention to the problems of evidence to be solved before a historical narrative is presented in its polished form. As yet, however, we have not examined in detail the many operations to be performed on a single document. What at first seems a relatively simple job of collecting, examining, and cataloging may become remarkably complex, especially when the document in question is of major importance.

So let us narrow our focus even more than in the previous two chapters, by concentrating not on a region (Virginia) or a village (Salem), but on one document. The document in question admittedly carries more import than most, yet it remains brief enough to be read in several minutes. It also has the merit of being one of the few primary sources that virtually every reader of this book already will have encountered: the Declaration of Independence.

The Declaration, of course, is one of the most celebrated documents in the nation's history. Drafted by Thomas Jefferson, adopted by the Second Continental Congress, published for the benefit of the world, memorialized in countless patriotic speeches, it is today displayed within the rotunda of the National Archives, carefully encased in a glass container filled with helium to prevent any long-term deterioration from oxygen. Every schoolchild knows that Congress declared the colonies' independence by issuing the document on July 4, 1776. Nearly everyone has seen the painting by John Trumbull that depicts members of Congress receiving the parchment for signing on that day.

So the starting place is familiar enough. Yet there is a good deal to establish when unpacking the facts about such a seminal document. Under what circumstances did Jefferson write the Declaration? What people, events, or

Along with the Constitution and the Bill of Rights, the Declaration of Independence (center) is displayed within the rotunda of the National Archives. Since 1952, when the nuclear arms race was in full swing, these documents have been lowered every night into a 55-ton vault of reinforced concrete and steel, whose massive doors swing shut to protect them from the threat of atomic attack. (Jon Wallen)

other documents influenced him? Only when such questions are answered in more detail does it become clear that quite a few of the "facts" enumerated in the previous paragraph are either misleading or incorrect. And the confusion begins in trying to answer the most elementary questions about the Declaration.

THE CREATION OF A TEXT

In May 1776 Thomas Jefferson traveled to Philadelphia, as befit a proper gentleman, in a coach and four with two attending slaves. He promptly took his place on the Virginia delegation to the Second Continental

Congress. Even a year after fighting had broken out at Lexington and Concord, Congress was still debating whether the quarrel with England could be patched up. Sentiment for independence ran high in many areas but by no means everywhere. The greatest reluctance lay in the middle colonies, particularly in Pennsylvania, where moderates like John Dickinson still hoped for reconciliation.

Such cautious sentiments infuriated the more radical delegates, especially John and Samuel Adams of Massachusetts. The two Adamses had worked for independence from the opening days of Congress, but found the going slow. America, complained John, was "a great, unwieldy body. It is like a large fleet sailing under convoy. The fleetest sailers must wait for the dullest and the slowest." Jefferson also favored independence, but he lacked the Adamses' taste for political infighting. While the men from Massachusetts pulled their strings in Congress, Jefferson only listened attentively and took notes. Thirty-three years old, he was the youngest delegate, and no doubt his age contributed to his diffidence. Privately, he conversed more easily with friends, sprawling casually in a chair with one shoulder cocked high, the other low, and his long legs extended. He got along well with the other delegates and performed his committee assignments dutifully.

The debate over independence seemed to sputter on fitfully until late May, when Jefferson's colleague Richard Henry Lee arrived from Williamsburg. Lee was under instructions from the Virginia convention to force Congress to act. On Friday, June 7, he rose in Congress and offered the following resolutions:

> That these United Colonies are, and of right ought to be, free and independent States, that they are absolved from all allegiance to the British crown, and that all political connection between them and the state of Great Britain is, and ought to be, totally dissolved.
>
> That it is expedient forthwith to take the most effectual measures for forming foreign alliances.
>
> That a plan of confederation be prepared and transmitted to the respective colonies for their consideration and approbation.

On Saturday and again on Monday, moderates and radicals earnestly debated the propositions. They knew that a declaration of independence would make the breach with England final. The Secretary of the Congress, Charles Thomson, cautiously recorded in his minutes only that "certain resolutions" were "moved and discussed"—the certain resolutions, of course, being treasonous in the extreme.

Still, sentiment was running with the radicals. When delegate James Wilson of Pennsylvania announced that he felt ready to vote for independence, Congress set the wheels in motion by appointing a five-member committee "to prepare a Declaration to the effect of the said first resolution." The events that followed can be traced, in bare outline at least, in a modern edition of Secretary Thomson's minutes (*Journals of the Continental Congress: 1774–1789*). From it we learn that on June 11, 1776, Congress constituted

Jefferson, John Adams, Benjamin Franklin, Roger Sherman, and Robert Livingston as a Committee of Five responsible for drafting the declaration. Then for more than two weeks, Thomson's Journal remains silent on the subject. Only on Friday, June 28, does it note that the committee "brought in a draught" of an independence declaration.

On Monday, July 1, Congress resolved itself into a "Committee of the Whole," in which it could freely debate the sensitive question without leaving any official record of debate or disagreement. (Thomson's minutes did not record the activities of committees.) On July 2, the Committee of the Whole went through the motions of "reporting back" to Congress (that is, to itself). The minutes note only that Richard Lee's resolution, then "being read" in formal session, "was agreed to."

Thus the official journal makes it clear that Congress voted for independence on July second, not the fourth, adopting Richard Henry Lee's original proposal of June 7. When John Adams wrote home on July 3 to his wife, Abigail, he enthusiastically predicted that July second would be remembered as "the most memorable Epoca in the History of America. I am apt to believe that it will be celebrated, by succeeding Generations, as the great anniversary Festival. . . . It ought to be solemnized with Pomp and Parade, with Shews, Games, Sports, Guns, Bells, Bonfires and Illuminations from one End of this Continent to the other from this Time forward forever more."

As it turned out, Adams picked the wrong date for the fireworks. Although Congress had officially broken the tie with England, the declaration *explaining* the action had not yet been approved. On July 3 and 4 Congress again met as a Committee of the Whole. Only then was the formal declaration reported back, accepted, and sent to the printer. Thomson's *Journal* notes, "The foregoing declaration was, by order of Congress, engrossed, and signed by the following members. . . ." Here is the enactment familiar to everyone: the "engrossed" parchment (one written in large, neat letters) beginning with its bold "IN CONGRESS, JULY 4, 1776" and concluding with the president of the Continental Congress's signature, so flourishing that we still speak of putting our John Hancock to paper. Below that, the signatures of fifty-five other delegates appear more modestly inscribed.

If mention of the Declaration in Thomson's minutes concluded with the entry on July 4, schoolchildren might emerge with their memories reasonably intact. But later entries of the journal suggest that in all likelihood, the Declaration was not signed on July 4 after all, but on August 2. To muddy the waters further, not all the signers were in Philadelphia even on August 2. Some could not have signed the document until October or November.

So the upshot of the historian's preliminary investigation is that (1) Congress declared independence on the second of July, not the fourth; (2) most members officially signed the engrossed parchment only on the second of August; and (3) all the signers of the Declaration never met together in the same room at once, despite the appearances in John Trumbull's painting. In the matter of establishing the basic facts surrounding a document, historians are all too ready to agree with John Adams's bewildered search of his

The committee of five—Adams, Sherman, Livingston, Jefferson, and Franklin—present their work to John Hancock, president of the Continental Congress, in a detail from *The Declaration of Independence* by John Trumbull. When Hancock finally put his elaborate signature to the engrossed copy, he is reported to have said, "There! John Bull can read my name without spectacles, and may now double his reward of £500 for my head." (National Archives)

recollections: "What are we to think of history? When in less than 40 years, such diversities appear in the memories of living men who were witnesses."

Yet even with the basic facts in place, many important points remain to be answered about the Declaration's creation. Although Jefferson drafted it, what did the Committee of Five contribute? If the delegates made changes during the congressional debate on July 3 and 4, for what purpose? A historian will want to know which parts of the completed document were most controversial; surviving copies of earlier drafts could shed valuable light on these questions.

The search for accurate information about the Declaration's drafting began even while the protagonists were still living. Some forty years after the signing, both Jefferson and John Adams tried to set down the sequence of events. Adams recalled the affable and diplomatic Jefferson suggesting that Adams write the first draft. "I will not," replied Adams.

"You shall do it," persisted Jefferson.

"Oh no!"

"Why will you not do it? You ought to do it."

"I will not."

"Reasons enough." And Adams ticked them off. "Reason 1st. You are a Virginian and a Virginian ought to be at the head of this business. Reason 2nd. I am obnoxious, suspected and unpopular; you are very much otherwise. Reason 3rd. You can write ten times better than I can."

"Well," said Jefferson, "if you are decided, I will do as well as I can."

Jefferson, for his part, did not remember this bit of diplomatic shuttle-cock. In a letter to James Madison in 1823 he asserted that

> The Committee of 5 met . . . [and] they unanimously pressed on myself alone to undertake the draught. I consented; I drew it; but before I reported it to the committee I communicated it separately to Dr. Franklin and Mr. Adams requesting their corrections; . . . and you have seen the original paper now in my hands, with the corrections of Dr. Franklin and Mr. Adams interlined in their own handwriting. Their alterations were two or three only, and merely verbal [that is, changes of phrasing, not substance].

So far, so good. Jefferson's "original paper"—which he endorsed on the document itself as the "original Rough draught"—is preserved in the Library of Congress. Indeed, the draft is even rougher than Jefferson suggested. As historian Carl Becker pointed out,

> the inquiring student, coming to it for the first time, would be astonished, perhaps disappointed, if he expected to find in it nothing more than the 'original paper . . . with the corrections of Dr. Franklin and Mr. Adams interlined in their own handwriting.' He would find, for example, on the first page alone nineteen corrections, additions or erasures besides those in the handwriting of Adams and Franklin. It would probably seem to him at first sight a bewildering document, with many phrases crossed out, numerous interlineations, and whole paragraphs enclosed in brackets.

These corrections make the rough draft more difficult to read, but in the end also more rewarding. For the fact is, Jefferson continued to record on this copy successive alterations of the Declaration, not only by Adams and Franklin, but by Congress in its debates of July 3 and 4.

Thus by careful comparison and reconstruction, we can accurately establish the sequence of changes made in one crucial document, from the time it was first drafted, through corrections in committee, to debate and further amendment in Congress, and finally on to the engrossed parchment familiar to history. The changes were not slight. In the end, Congress removed about a quarter of Jefferson's original language. Eighty-six alterations were made by one person or another, including Jefferson, over those fateful three weeks of 1776.

THE TACTICS OF INTERPRETATION

Having sketched the circumstances of the Declaration's composition, the historian must attempt the more complicated task of interpretation. And here, historians' paths are most likely to diverge—understandably so. To determine a document's historical significance requires placing it within the larger, more complex context of events. There is no single method for doing this, of course. If there were, historians would all agree upon their reconstructions of the past, and history would be a good deal duller. On the other hand, historians do at least share certain analytical tactics that have consistently yielded profitable results. All historians do not employ all these tactics each time they confront a document, but they will usually employ more than one in order to approach their subject from several perspectives. Each new approach requires the historian to read the document afresh, subjecting it to different questions, searching it for previously unnoticed relationships.

What follows, then, is one set of tactical approaches to the Declaration. These approaches are by no means the only ways of making sense of the document. But they do suggest some range of the options historians normally call upon.

The document is read, first, to understand its surface content. This step may appear too obvious to bear mentioning, but not so. The fact is, most historians examine a document from a particular and potentially limiting viewpoint. A diplomatic historian, for instance, may approach the Declaration with an eye to the role it played in cementing a formal alliance with France. A historian of political theory might prefer to focus on the theoretical justifications of independence. Both perspectives are legitimate, but by beginning with such specific interests, historians risk prejudging the document. They are likely to notice only the kinds of evidence they are seeking.

So it makes sense to begin by temporarily putting aside any specific questions and approaching the Declaration as a willing, even uncritical reader. Ask only the most basic questions. How is the document organized? What are its major points, briefly summarized?

The Unanimous Declaration of the Thirteen United States of America.

When in the Course of human events, it becomes necessary for one people to dissolve the political bands, which have connected them with another, and to assume among the powers of the earth, the separate and equal station to which the Laws of Nature and of Nature's God entitle them, a decent respect to the opinions of mankind requires that they should declare the causes which impel them to the separation.—We hold these truths to be self-evident, that all men are created equal, that they are endowed by their Creator with certain unalienable Rights, that among these are Life, Liberty and the pursuit of Happiness.—That to secure these rights, Governments are instituted among Men, deriving their just powers from the consent of the governed,—That whenever any Form of Government becomes destructive of these ends, it is the Right of the People to alter or to abolish it, and to institute new Government, laying its foundation on such principles and organizing its powers in such form, as to them shall seem most likely to effect their Safety and Happiness. Prudence, indeed, will dictate that Governments long established should not be changed for light and transient causes; and accordingly all experience hath shewn, that mankind are more disposed to suffer, while evils are sufferable, than to right themselves by abolishing the forms to which they are accustomed. But when a long train of abuses and usurpations, pursuing invariably the same Object evinces a design to reduce them under absolute Despotism, it is their right, it is their duty, to throw off such Government, and to provide new Guards for their future security. Such has been the patient sufferance of these Colonies; and such is now the necessity which constrains them to alter their former Systems of Government. The history of the present King of Great Britain is a history of repeated injuries and usurpations, all having in direct object the establishment of an absolute Tyranny over these States. To prove this, let Facts be submitted to a candid world.—He has refused his Assent to Laws, the most wholesome and necessary for the public good.—He has forbidden his Governors to pass Laws of immediate and pressing importance, unless suspended in their operation till his Assent should be obtained; and when so suspended, he has utterly neglected to attend to them.—He has refused to pass other Laws for the accommodation of large districts of people, unless those people would relinquish the right of Representation in the Legislature, a right inestimable to them and formidable to tyrants only.—He has called together legislative bodies at places unusual, uncomfortable, and distant from the depository of their public Records, for the sole purpose of fatiguing them into compliance with his measures.—He has dissolved Representative Houses repeatedly, for opposing with manly firmness his invasions on the rights of the people.—He has refused for a long time, after such dissolutions, to cause others to be elected; whereby the Legislative powers, incapable of Annihilation, have returned to the People at large for their exercise; the State remaining in the meantime exposed to all the dangers of invasion from without, and convulsions within.—He has endeavoured to prevent the population of these States; for that purpose obstructing the Laws for Naturalization of Foreigners; refusing to pass others to encourage their migrations hither, and raising the conditions of new Appropriations of Lands.—He has obstructed the Administration of Justice, by refusing his Assent to Laws for establishing judiciary powers.—He has made judges dependent on his Will alone, for the tenure of their offices, and the amount and payment of their salaries.—He has erected a multitude of New Offices, and sent hither swarms of Officers to harass our people, and eat out their substance.—He has kept among us, in times of peace, Standing Armies without the Consent of our legislatures.—He has affected to render the Military independent of and superior to the Civil power.—He has combined with others to subject us to a jurisdiction foreign to our constitution, and unacknowledged by our laws; giving his Assent to their Acts of pretended Legislation:—For quartering large bodies of armed troops among us:—For protecting them, by a mock Trial, from punishment for any Murders which they should commit on the inhabitants of these States:—For cutting off our Trade with all parts of the world:—For imposing Taxes on us without our Consent:—For depriving us in many cases, of the benefits of Trial by Jury:—

For transporting us beyond Seas to be tried for pretended offenses:—For abolishing the free System of English Laws in a neighboring Province, establishing therein an Arbitrary government, and enlarging its Boundaries so as to render it at once an example and fit instrument for introducing the same absolute rule into these Colonies:—For taking away our Charters, abolishing our most valuable Laws, and altering fundamentally the Forms of our Governments:—For suspending our own Legislatures, and declaring themselves invested with power to legislate for us in all cases whatsoever.—He has abdicated Government here, by declaring us out of his Protection and waging War against us.—He has plundered our seas, ravaged our Coasts, burnt our towns, and destroyed the lives of our people.—He is at this time transporting large Armies of foreign Mercenaries to compleat the works of death, desolation and tyranny, already begun with circumstances of Cruelty & perfidy scarcely paralleled in the most barbarous ages, and totally unworthy the Head of a civilized nation.—He has constrained our fellow Citizens taken Captive on the high Seas to bear Arms against their Country, to become the executioners of their friends and Brethren, or to fall themselves by their Hands.—He has excited domestic insurrections amongst us, and has endeavoured to bring on the inhabitants of our frontiers, the merciless Indian Savages, whose known rule of warfare, is an undistinguished destruction of all ages, sexes and conditions. In every state of these Oppressions We have Petitioned for Redress in the most humble terms: our repeated Petitions have been answered only by repeated injury. A Prince whose character is thus marked by every act which may define a Tyrant, is unfit to be the ruler of a free people. Nor have We been wanting in attentions to our Brittish brethren. We have warned them from time to time of attempts by their legislature to extend an unwarrantable jurisdiction over us. We have reminded them of the circumstances of our emigration and settlement here. We have appealed to their native justice and magnanimity, and we have conjured them by the ties of our common kindred to disavow these usurpations, which would inevitably interrupt our connections and correspondence. They too have been deaf to the voice of justice and of consanguinity. We must, therefore, acquiesce in the necessity, which denounces our Separation, and hold them, as we hold the rest of mankind, Enemies in War, in Peace Friends.

We, therefore, the Representatives of the United States of America, in General Congress, Assembled, appealing to the Supreme Judge of the world for the rectitude of our intentions do, in the Name, and by Authority of the good People of these Colonies, solemnly publish and declare, That these United Colonies are, and of Right ought to be Free and independent States; that they are Absolved from all Allegiance to the British Crown, and that all political connection between them and the State of Great Britain, is and ought to be totally dissolved: and that as Free and independent States, they have full Power to levy War, conclude Peace, contract Alliances, establish Commerce, and to do all other Acts and Things which independent States may of right do.—And for the support of this Declaration, with a firm reliance on the protection of divine Providence, we mutually pledge to each other our Lives, our Fortunes and our sacred Honor.

As befits a reasoned public document, the Declaration can be separated fairly easily into its component parts. The first sentence begins by informing the reader of the document's purpose. The colonies, having declared their independence from England, intend to announce "the causes which impel them to the separation."

The causes that follow, however, are not all of a piece. They break naturally into two sections: the first, a theoretical justification of revolution, and the second, a list of the specific grievances that justify this revolution. Because the first section deals in general, "self-evident" truths, it is the one most often remembered and quoted. "All men are created equal," "unalienable Rights," "Life, Liberty and the pursuit of Happiness," "consent of the governed"—these principles have relevance far beyond the circumstances of the colonies in the summer of 1776.

But the Declaration devotes far greater space to a list of British actions that Congress labeled "a long train of abuses and usurpations" designed to "reduce [Americans] under absolute despotism." Because the Declaration concedes that revolution should never be undertaken lightly, the document proceeds to demonstrate that English rule has been not merely unwieldy and inconvenient, but so full of "repeated injuries," that "absolute tyranny" is the result. What threatens Americans most, the Declaration proclaims, is not the individual measures, but the existence of a deliberate plot by the king to deprive a "free people" of their liberties.

The final section of the Declaration turns to the colonial response. Here the Declaration incorporates Richard Lee's resolution passed on July 2 and ends with the signers solemnly pledging their lives, fortunes, and sacred honor to support the new government.

Having begun with this straightforward reading, the historian is less likely to wrench out of context a particular passage, magnifying it at the expense of the rest of the document. Yet taken by itself, the reading of "surface content" may distort a document's import. Significance, after all, depends upon the circumstances under which a document was created. Thus historians must always seek to place their evidence in context.

The context of a document may be established, in part, by asking what the document might have said but did not. When Jefferson retired to his second-floor lodgings on the outskirts of Philadelphia, placed a portable writing desk on his lap, and put pen to paper, he had many options open to him. Yet the modern reader, seeing only the final product, is tempted to view the document as the logical, even inevitable result of Jefferson's deliberations. Perhaps it was, but the historian needs to ask how it might have been otherwise. What might Jefferson and the Congress have declared but did not?

We can get a better sense of what Congress and Jefferson rejected by looking at a declaration made some ten years earlier by another intercolonial gathering, the Stamp Act Congress. Like Jefferson's, this declaration began by outlining general principles. In reading the first three resolves, note the difference between their premises and those of the Declaration.

I. That his Majesty's Subjects in these Colonies, owe the same Allegiance to the Crown of *Great-Britain*, that is owing from his Subjects born within the Realm, and all due Subordination to that August Body the Parliament of *Great-Britain*.

II. That his Majesty's Liege Subjects in these Colonies, are entitled to all the inherent Rights and Liberties of his Natural born Subjects, within the Kingdom of *Great-Britain*.

III. That it is inseparably essential to the Freedom of a People, and the undoubted Right of *Englishmen*, that no Taxes be imposed on them, but with their own Consent, given personally, or by their Representatives.

The rights emphasized by the Stamp Act Congress in 1765 differ significantly from those emphasized in 1776. The Stamp Act resolutions claim that colonials are entitled to "all the inherent Rights and Liberties" of "Subjects, within the Kingdom of *Great-Britain*." They possess "the undoubted Right of *Englishmen*." Nowhere in Jefferson's Declaration are the rights of Englishmen mentioned as justification for protesting the king's conduct. Instead, the Declaration magnifies what the Stamp Act only mentions in passing—natural rights inherent in the "Freedom of a People," whether they be English subjects or not.

The shift from English rights to natural rights resulted from the changed political situation. In 1765, Americans were seeking relief within the British imperial system. Logically, they cited rights they felt due them as British subjects. But in 1776, the Declaration was renouncing all ties with its parent nation. If the colonies were no longer a part of Great Britain, what good would it do to cite the rights of Englishmen? Thus the natural rights "endowed" all persons "by their Creator" took on paramount importance.

The Declaration makes another striking omission. Nowhere in the long list of grievances does it use another word that appears in the first resolve of the Stamp Act Congress—"Parliament." The omission is all the more surprising because the Revolutionary quarrel had its roots in the dispute over Parliament's right to tax and regulate the colonies. The Sugar Act, the Stamp Act, the Townshend duties, the Tea Act, the Coercive Acts, the Quebec Act—Parliament is at the center of the dispute. The Declaration alludes to those legislative measures but always in the context of the king's actions, not Parliament's. Doing so admittedly required a bit of evasion: in laying out Parliamentary abuses, Jefferson complained, rather indirectly, that the king had combined with "others"—namely Parliament—"to subject us to a jurisdiction foreign to our constitution and unacknowledged by our laws, giving his Assent to their acts of pretended Legislation."

Obviously, the omission came about for much the same reason that Jefferson excluded all mention of the "rights of Englishmen." At the Stamp Act

Congress of 1765, virtually all Americans were willing to grant Parliament some jurisdiction over the colonies. Not the right to lay taxes without American representation, certainly, but at least the right to regulate colonial trade. Thus Congress noted (in Resolution I) that Parliament deserved "all due Subordination."

By 1775 more radical colonials would not grant Parliament any authority over the colonies. They had come to recognize what an early pamphleteer had noted, that Americans could be "as effectually ruined by the powers of legislation as by those of taxation." The Boston Port Bill, which closed Boston harbor, was not a tax. Nor did it violate any traditional right. Yet the radicals argued, quite correctly, that Parliament could take away Americans' freedoms by such legislation.

Although many colonials had totally rejected all Parliamentary authority in 1775, most had not yet advocated independence. How, then, were the colonies related to England if not through Parliament? The only link, radicals argued, was through the king. The colonies possessed their own sovereign legislatures, but they shared with all British subjects one monarch. Thus, when the final break with England came, the Declaration carefully laid all blame at the king's feet. Even to recognize Parliament would be to tacitly admit that it had some legitimate connection with the colonies.

What the Declaration does *not* say, then, proves to be as important as what it did say. Historians can recognize the importance of such unstated premises by remembering that the actors in any drama possess more alternatives than the ones they finally choose.

A document may be understood by seeking to reconstruct the intellectual worlds behind its words. We have already seen, in the cases of Virginia and Salem, the extent to which history involves the task of reconstructing whole societies from fragmentary records. The same process applies to the intellectual worlds that lie behind a document.

The need to perform this reconstruction is often hidden, however, because the context of the English language has changed over the past two hundred years—and not simply in obvious ways. For example, what would Jefferson have made of the following excerpt out of a recent issue of a computer magazine?

> *Macworld*'s Holiday Gift Guide. It's holiday shopping season again. *Macworld* advises you on the best ways to part with your paycheck. . . . It could be an audio CD, but it could also be a CD-ROM containing anything from an encyclopedia to a virtual planetarium to an art studio for the kids.

To begin with, terms like *audio CD* and *CD-ROM* would mystify Jefferson simply because they come from a totally unfamiliar world. Beyond the obvious, however, the excerpt contains words that might seem familiar but would be deceptively so, because their meaning has changed over time. Jefferson probably would have recognized *planetarium*, though he might have preferred the more common eighteenth-century term *orrery*. He would recognize *virtual* as well. But a *virtual planetarium?* Today's notion of virtual reality would be lost to him unless he read a good deal more about the computer revolution.

Even more to the point, look at the innocuous phrase, "It's holiday shopping season again." The words would be completely familiar to Jefferson, but the world that surrounds them certainly would not. To understand the phrase, he would have to appreciate how much the holiday of Christmas has evolved into a major commercial event, bearing scant resemblance to any eighteenth-century observance. (In John Adams's puritan New England, of course, even to celebrate Chrismas would have been frowned upon as a popish superstition.) Or to make an even subtler linguistic point: unlike a magazine article from the 1950s, this one from the 1990s never uses the word *Christmas*. The social reasons for this deliberate omission would undoubtedly have interested Jefferson, for it reflects a multicultural nation sensitive to the questions of equality and the separation of church and state. But unless he were aware of the ways in which American society had evolved, Jefferson would miss the implications hidden within language that seems at first glance quite straightforward.

By the same token, eighteenth-century documents may appear deceptively lucid to twentieth-century readers. When Jefferson wrote that all men were "endowed by their Creator with certain unalienable Rights," including "Life, Liberty and the pursuit of Happiness," the meaning seems reasonably clear. But as essayist and historian Garry Wills has insisted, "To understand any text remote from us in time, we must reassemble a world around that text. The preconceptions of the original audience, its tastes, its range of reference, must be recovered, so far as that is possible."

In terms of reassembling Jefferson's world, historians have most often followed Carl Becker in arguing that its center lay in the political philosophy of John Locke. Locke's *Second Treatise on Government* (1690) asserted that all governments were essentially a compact between individuals based on the principles of human nature. Locke speculated that if all the laws and customs that had grown up in human society over the years were stripped away, human beings would find themselves in "a state of perfect freedom to order their possessions and persons, as they think fit, within the bounds of the law of nature." But because some individuals inevitably violate the laws of nature—robbing or murdering or committing other crimes—people have always banded together to make a compact, agreeing to create governments that will order human society. And just as people come together to allow themselves to be governed, likewise they can overturn those governments wherein the ruler has become a tyrant who "may do to all his subjects whatever he pleases."

Jefferson's colleague Richard Henry Lee in later years commented that Jefferson, in writing the Declaration, had merely "copied from Locke's treatise on government." Yet as important as Locke was, his writings were only one facet of the Enlightenment tradition flourishing in the eighteenth century. Jefferson shared with many European philosophes the belief that the study of human affairs should be conducted as precisely as the study of the natural world had come to be. Just as Sir Isaac Newton in the 1680s had used mathematical equations to derive the laws of gravity, optics, and planetary motion, so the philosophes of Jefferson's day looked to quantify the study of the human psyche.

The results of such endeavors seem quaint today, but the philosophes took their work seriously. Garry Wills has argued that even more important to Jefferson than Locke were the writings of Scottish Enlightenment thinkers, chief among them Francis Hutcheson. In 1725 Hutcheson attempted to quantify such elusive concepts as morality. The result was a string of equations where qualities were abbreviated by letters (B = benevolence, A = ability, S = self-love, I = interest) and placed in their proper relations:

$$M = (B + S) \times A = BA + SA; \text{ and therefore } BA = M - SA = M - I, \text{ and } B = \frac{M - I}{A}.$$

Jefferson possessed a similar passion for quantification. He repeatedly praised the American astronomer David Rittenhouse and his orrery, a mechanical model of the solar system whose gears replicated the relative motions of the earth, moon, and planets. Jefferson also applied classification and observation as a gentleman planter. If it were possible to discover the many relationships within the natural order, he reasoned, farmers might better plant and harvest to those rhythms. Even in the White House, Jefferson kept his eye on the Washington markets and recorded the seasons' first arrivals of thirty-seven different vegetables.

Wills argues that Jefferson conceived the "pursuit of Happiness" in equally precise terms. Francis Hutcheson had suggested that a person's actions be judged by how much happiness that person brought to other people. "That action is best," he argued, "which accomplishes the greatest happiness for the greatest number." According to Enlightenment science, because happiness could be quantified, a government's actions could be weighed in the balance scales to discover whether they hindered a citizen's right to pursue happiness as he or she saw fit. Thus for Jefferson, the pursuit of happiness was not a phrase expressing the vague hope that all Americans should have the chance to live happily ever after. His language reflected the conviction that the science of government, like the science of agriculture or celestial mechanics, would gradually take its place in the advancing progress of humankind.

Historians' reconstructions of Jefferson's intellectual world, imaginative as they are, must remain speculative. We do not have Jefferson's direct testimony of what he was thinking, aside from a few recollections made decades after the event. When Garry Wills made his case for the importance of Scottish moral philosophy, he was forced to rely on circumstantial evidence, such as the presence of Francis Hutcheson's works in Jefferson's library or the topics Jefferson's professors lectured on during his college years—or even more generally, what ideas and opinions were "in the air." Whether or not Wills's specific case stands up to examination, his method of research is one that historians commonly employ. By understanding the intellectual world from which a document arose—by tracing, in effect, its genealogy or intellectual ancestors—we come to understand the document itself.

ACTIONS SPEAK LOUDER?

More than a few historians, however, become uneasy about depending too heavily on a genealogy of ideas. To be sure, a historian can speak of theories as being "in the air" and of Jefferson, as it were, inhaling. But that approach may neglect the noisy and insistent world outside his Philadelphia lodgings. By June 1776, Congress was in the midst of waging a war as well as a revolution, and a hundred and one events demanded its daily attention. The morning that Richard Henry Lee submitted his motion for independence, delegates had to deal with troops being raised in South Carolina and complaints about the gunpowder manufactured by a certain Mr. Oswald of Eve's Mill. Over the following days, they learned that the British fleet had sailed from Halifax, on its way to attack New York City. Events both large and small kept Jefferson and the other members of Congress from sitting down quietly for long to ponder over the creation of a single document.

Thus, to understand the Declaration we must not only set it in the context of previous ideas, but also of contemporary events. "What was Jefferson thinking about on the eve of his authorship of the Declaration of Independence?" asked a recent biographer, Joseph Ellis. "The answer is indisputable. He was not thinking . . . about John Locke's theory of natural rights or Scottish commonsense philosophy. He was thinking about Virginia's new constitution." Throughout May and June, couriers brought news to Jefferson of doings in Williamsburg, the capital of his own "country," as he called it. There, on June 12, the Virginia convention adopted a preamble to its state constitution, written by George Mason. "All men are created equally free and independent and have certain inherent and natural rights," wrote Mason, ". . . among which are the enjoyment of life and liberty, with the means of acquiring and possessing property, and pursuing and obtaining happiness and safety."

These words reached Philadelphia little more than a week before Jefferson penned his immortal credo "that all men are created equal, that they are endowed by their Creator with certain unalienable Rights, that among these are Life, Liberty and the pursuit of Happiness." The point is not to expose Jefferson as a plagiarist, for he substantially improved Mason's version. Nor is it to deny that John Locke or Francis Hutcheson may have played a role in shaping Jefferson's (and Mason's) thinking. But seeing how closely Jefferson's language resembles George Mason's makes it clear how much Jefferson was affected by events around him.

Often enough, actions do speak louder than words. One way to put the Declaration in context is to compare it with the actions taken by other Americans during these same months. As historian Pauline Maier has noted, the Continental Congress was not the only body to issue a declaration of independence. She discovered at least ninety other resolutions to similar effect made between April and July of 1776. Some were issued by town meetings; others by gatherings of militia or workers; still others by grand juries or county conventions. These state and local declarations, argued Maier, "offer the best opportunity to hear the voice of the people . . . that we are likely to get."

Like Congress's Declaration, the local resolutions listed grievances that caused them to take up arms. Worrying less about theoretical consistency, these local declarations did not hesitate either to mention Parliament or to emphatically condemn it. Many pointed in particular to the Declaratory Act of 1766, in which Parliament asserted the right to make laws binding the colonies "IN ALL CASES WHATSOEVER," as one declaration stated in uppercase letters—underlining the act's insulting language. It was Parliament that had no right to legislate whatsoever, colonials now countered.

Once this flat assertion was made, most local declarations did not bother to list a "long train of abuses." Instead, they focused on the outrages of the preceding year. King George had received the Congress's Olive Branch Petition of July 1775 with "contempt," objected the Pennsylvania assembly. New York's mechanics complained that the king "is deaf to our petitions." The war itself supplied many more grievances, beginning with the dead from Lexington and Concord: "We hear their blood crying to us from the ground for vengeance," noted one Massachusetts town. Many resolutions condemned the "barbarous" act of hiring "foreign mercenaries" such as the German Hessians to prosecute the war for the king's "inhuman purposes."

In short, the local resolutions reflected the events around them even more strongly than the Declaration did. They underline the likelihood that sentiment for independence among most colonials did not really blossom until well after the fighting began. In that sense, the resolutions help us link the official Declaration more closely with the feelings of ordinary Americans.

Yet a problem remains. The proverb proclaims that actions speak louder than words, but all these declarations are still just words. The point of the aphorism is that we cannot always take words at face value—that often, actions are what reveal true feelings. We need not reject the Declaration's heartfelt sentiments in order to recognize that the Congress (or for that matter, colonials themselves) may have had reasons for declaring independence that they did not enunciate fully, either in the Declaration or in local resolutions.

For example, consider the vexed topic of slavery, especially interesting in a document proclaiming that "all men are created equal." It has become commonplace to point out the contradiction between the Declaration's noble embrace of human liberties and the reality that many delegates to Congress, including Jefferson, were slaveowners. Or similarly, the inconsistency between a declaration of equality and the refusal to let women participate in the equal rights of citizenship.

Though such contradictions have attained the status of truisms, they deserve to be pointed out again and again, as often as the Declaration is discussed. Indeed, much of American history can be seen as an effort to work out the full implications of the phrase "all men are created equal"—whether that history be the Civil War, wherein a vast and bloody carnage was required to bring an end to slavery, or the more peaceful Seneca Falls Convention, mounted in 1848 by women to proclaim their own Declaration of Sentiments supporting an equality of the sexes. The theme could be applied to the populist and progressive reform movements of the late nineteenth century, grappling as they did with the effect upon equality of the monopoly powers of big business; or to the debates of the late twentieth century over civil rights and affirmative action. The implications of the Declaration have engaged the republic for more than two centuries and no doubt will continue to do so.

Granting the ironies of these unstated contradictions, it may still be worthwhile to return to the notion of actions and to examine the intriguing way in which slavery *does* appear in the Declaration. At first glance, the Declaration seems to say very little about slavery. In its long list of grievances, Congress merely notes that the king has been "exciting domestic insurrections amongst us"—in other words, encouraging slaves to revolt. The five words slip by so quickly we hardly notice them.

Slavery did not slip by so quickly in Jefferson's rough draft. His discussion of the institution appeared not as a grace note, but as the climax of his long list of grievances against the king:

> He has waged cruel war against human nature itself, violating its most sacred rights of life and liberty in the persons of a distant people who never offended him, captivating & carrying them into slavery in another hemisphere or to incur miserable death in their transportation thither. This piratical warfare, the opprobrium of *infidel* powers, is the warfare of the *Christian* king of Great Britain. Determined to keep open a market where *Men* should be bought & sold, he has prostituted his negative [used his veto power] for suppressing every legislative attempt to prohibit or to restrain this execrable commerce. And that this assemblage of horrors might want no fact of distinguishing die, he is now exciting those very people to rise in arms among us, and to purchase that liberty of which he has deprived them, by murdering the people on whom he also obtruded them: thus paying off former crimes committed against the *Liberties of* one people, with crimes which he urges them to commit against the *lives of* another.

The passage is in many ways both revealing and astonishing. It reveals, first, that Jefferson was very much aware of the contradiction between slavery and the Declaration's high sentiments. Not once but twice he speaks out. The enslavement of black Africans violates "the most sacred rights of life and liberty," he insists; and again, enslavement amounts to "crimes committed against the *Liberties of* one people." Yet in admitting the wrong, he blames the king for it! Jefferson based his charge on the fact that several times during the eighteenth century, Virginia's legislature passed a tariff designed to restrict the importation of slaves. It did so not so much from humanitarian motives (although these were occasionally mentioned) but because the colony's slave population was expanding rapidly. Importing too many Africans would lower the price of domestic slaves whom Virginia planters wanted to sell. The British administration, however, consistently disallowed such laws—and thus the king had "prostituted his negative" to prevent the slave trade from being restrained. For their part, white Georgians and South Carolinians were generally happy to see the trade continue, as were many New England merchants who made a profitable livelihood from it.

To accuse the king of enslaving black colonials was far-fetched enough, but Jefferson then turned around and hotly accused the king of *freeing* black colonials. In November 1775, the loyal Governor Dunmore of Virginia proclaimed that any slave who deserted his master to fight for the king would be freed. Dunmore's Proclamation, as it was called, outraged many white patriots. Hence Jefferson called King George to account for the vile "crime" of freeing slaves who remained loyal.

What the delegates in Congress thought of the passage does not survive. But their actions speak loudly. In the final draft, Jefferson's long passage has vanished. All that remains is the general accusation that the king has been "exciting domestic insurrections." It seems likely Congress simply rejected Jefferson's logic as being so tortuous, it could hardly withstand public scrutiny. The less said, the better.

DECLARING FOR FREEDOM

Saying less, however, is not the same as saying nothing. By not deleting the accusation regarding "domestic insurrections," Congress revealed that this particular issue remained a sensitive one. Indeed, other local declarations featured it prominently. Marylanders complained that slaves "were proclaimed free, enticed away, trained and armed against their lawful masters." Pennsylvanians objected that the British had incited "the negroes to imbrue their hands in the blood of their masters." North Carolina echoed the sentiment nearly word for word. The frequency of this complaint raises a question. Leave aside for a moment the issue of white attitudes toward slavery and liberty. How did the actions of *African Americans* affect the drafters of the Declaration?

On the face of it, the chance of answering that question seems farfetched. The approximately 400,000 black slaves living in the colonies in 1776 could not leave a trail of resolutions or declarations behind them, for most were not allowed to. Yet the Declaration's complaint that Britain was stirring up American slaves brings to mind the similar laments of proslavery advocates in the 1850s and of segregationists during the 1950s and 1960s. Both repeatedly blamed "outside agitators" for encouraging southern blacks to assert their civil rights. In the eighteenth century, the phrase most commonly used was *instigated insurrection.* "The newspapers were full of Publications calculated to excite the fears of the People—" wrote one indignant South Carolinian in

1775, "Massacres and Instigated Insurrections, were words in the mouth of every Child." And hardly children alone: South Carolina's First Provincial Congress voiced their own "dread of instigated insurrections." North Carolinians echoed the sentiment, warning that "there is much reason to fear, in these Times of general Tumult and Confusion, that the Slaves may be instigated, encouraged by our inveterate Enemies to an Insurrection."

But were the British "instigating" rebellion? Or were they taking advantage of African Americans' own determination to strike for freedom? As historian Sylvia Frey has pointed out, the incidence of flight, rebellion, or protest among enslaved African Americans increased significantly in the decade following the Stamp Act, despite the long odds that weighed against success. In 1765, the Sons of Liberty paraded around Charleston harbor shouting "Liberty! Liberty and stamp'd paper!" Soon after, black slaves organized a demonstration of their own, chanting "Liberty!" Planter Henry Laurens believed this action to be merely a "thoughtless imitation" of white colonials, but it frightened many South Carolinians.

With good reason. Look more closely at events in Virginia preceding Lord Dunmore's Proclamation. Dunmore in November 1775 offered freedom to able-bodied slaves who would serve the king. Six months earlier, anticipating the outbreak of hostilities, the governor had confiscated some of the colony's gunpowder to prevent it from falling into rebel hands. At that point, "some Negroes . . . had offered to join him and take up arms." What was Dunmore's reaction? He ordered the slaves "to go about their business" and "threatened them with his severest resentment, should they presume to renew their application." Patriot forces, on the other hand, demanded the return of the gunpowder and accused Dunmore of seizing it with the intention of "disarming the people, to weaken the means of opposing an insurrection of the slaves." At this charge Dunmore became "exceedingly exasperated" and threatened to "declare freedom to the slaves and reduce the City of Williamsburg to ashes."

In other words, the slaves, not Dunmore, made the first move in this particular game of chess. And far from greeting the slaves' offer with delight, Dunmore shunned it—until patriot fears about black insurrections made him consider the advantages that black military support might provide. Similarly, in 1773 and again in 1774 the loyal governor of Massachusetts, General Thomas Gage, was approached with five separate petitions from "a grate Number of [enslaved] Blacks" offering to fight for him if he would provide arms and set them free. "At present it is kept pretty quiet," Abigail Adams reassured her husband, John, who was off at the First Continental Congress.

By 1775, unrest among black slaves was common in many areas of the Carolinas and Georgia. South Carolina had taken on "rather the appearance of a garrison town," reported one observer, because the militia were patrolling the streets at night as well as during the day, "to guard against any hostile attempts that may be made by our domesticks." White fears were confirmed when a black harbor pilot, Thomas Jeremiah, was arrested, tried,

R UN away from *Hampton*, on *Sunday* laſt, a luſty Mulatto Fellow named ARGYLE, well known about the Country, has a Scar on one of his Wriſts, and has loſt one or more of his fore Teeth; he is a very handy Fellow by Water, or about the Houſe, &c. loves Drink, and is very bold in his Cups, but daſtardly when ſober. Whether he will go for a Man of War's Man, or not, I cannot ſay; but I will give 40s. to have him brought to me. He can read and write.
NOVEMBER 2, 1775. JACOB WRAY.

R UN away from the Subſcriber, in *New* Kent, in the Year 1772, a ſmall new New Negro Man named GEORGE, about 40 Years of Age, with a Nick in one Ear, and ſome Marks with the Whip. He was about *Williamſburg* till laſt Winter, but either went or was ſent to Lord *Dunmore*'s Quarter in *Frederick* County, and there paſſes for his Property. Whoever conveys him to me ſhall have 5l. Reward.
1 ‖ JAMES MOSS.

Masters whose slaves ran away commonly posted notices in newspapers offering rewards for their return. The advertisements often assumed that slaves had gone to join kin. But these advertisements from an issue of *The Virginia Gazette* in November 1775 indicate that slaveowners were frequently convinced that their male slaves might have gone to offer service to Lord Dunmore or to the British navy ("a Man of War's Man"). (Virginia Historical Society)

hanged, and burned to death for plotting an insurrection that would enlist the help of the British navy. Jeremiah had told other blacks that "there was a great War coming soon" that "was come to help the poor Negroes." According to James Madison, a group of Virginia slaves "met together and chose a leader who was to conduct them when the English troops should arrive." The conspiracy was discovered and suppressed. Islands along the coast, as well as British cruisers, attracted slaves striking for freedom: Tybee and Sullivan's Island off South Carolina; Cockspur Island off Georgia. The slaves were not "inticed," reported one captain; they "came as freemen, and demanding protection." He could "have had near 500 who had offered."

The actions of these and other enslaved African Americans clearly affected the conduct of both British officials and colonial rebels. The British, who (like Dunmore) remained reluctant to encourage a full-scale rebellion, nevertheless saw that the mere possibility of insurrection might be used as an effective psychological threat. If South Carolinians did not stop opposing British policy, warned General Gage ominously, "it may happen that your Rice and Indigo will be brought to market by negroes instead of white People." For their part, southern white colonials worked energetically to suppress both the rebellions and all news of them. As two Georgia delegates to the Continental Congress informed John Adams, slave networks could carry news "several hundreds of miles in a week or fortnight." When Madison heard about the slave conspiracy in Virginia, he saw clearly the dangers of talking about the incident: "It is prudent such things should be concealed as well as suppressed," he warned a friend. Maryland's provisional government felt similarly about Governor Dunmore's proclamation in neighboring Virginia. It immediately outlawed all correspondence with Virginia, either by land or water. But word spread anyway. "The insolence of the Negroes in this county is come to such a height," reported one Eastern Shore Marylander, "that we are under a necessity of disarming them which we affected [sic] on Saturday last. We took about eighty guns, some bayonets, swords, etc."

Thus, the actions of African Americans helped push the delegates in Congress toward their final decision for independence, even though the Declaration remained largely silent on the subject. By striking for liberty, slaves encouraged the British to use them as an element in their war against the Americans. As Lord North told the king in October 1775, British troops sent to Georgia and the Carolinas should expect to meet with success, especially because "we all know the perilous situation . . . [arising] from the great number of their negro slaves, and the small proportion of white inhabitants."

The Americans were pushed toward independence by this knowledge. Georgia delegates told John Adams that slaves in their region were simply waiting a chance to arise, and if "one thousand regular [British] troops should land in Georgia, and their commander be provided with arms and clothes enough, and proclaim freedom to all the negroes who would join his campaign, twenty thousand would join it from [Georgia and South Carolina] in a fortnight." James Madison, worrying about Lord Dunmore, confided that the possibility of a slave insurrection "is the only part in which this Colony is vulnerable; & if we should be subdued, we shall fall like Achilles by the hand of one that knows the secret." George Washington too perceived the threat. Dunmore must be crushed instantly, he warned in December 1775, "otherwise, like a snowball, in rolling, his army will get size." Although southern delegates at first attempted to pass legislation forbidding black Americans from serving in the Continental Army, Washington changed his mind and supported the idea, having come to believe that the outcome of the war might depend on "which side can arm the Negroes the faster." Until recently, few historians have appreciated the role African Americans played in shaping the context of independence.

Actions do speak louder than words—often enough. Still, the echoes of the Declaration's words and the persistent hold of its ideals have outlasted the often contradictory actions of its creators. Jefferson's entire life embodied those contradictions. More than any American president save Lincoln, Jefferson contributed to the downfall of slavery. In addition to penning the Declaration's bold rhetoric, he pushed for the antislavery provision in the Northwest Ordinance of 1787, which served as a model for later efforts to stop slavery's expansion. Yet despite Jefferson's private criticisms of slavery, he continued to depend on the labor of enslaved African Americans throughout his life. Though he apparently maintained a sexual relationship with one of his slaves, Sally Hemings, upon his death he freed none, except five members of the Hemings family. Sally was not among them.

It lay with Abraham Lincoln to express most eloquently the notion that a document might transcend the contradictions of its creation. In 1857, Lincoln insisted that in proclaiming "all men are created equal," the founders of the nation

> did not mean to assert the obvious untruth that all were then actually enjoying that equality. They meant to set up a standard maxim for free society, which should be familiar to all, and revered by all, constantly looked to, constantly labored for, and even though never perfectly attained, constantly approximated, and thereby constantly spreading and deepening its influence, and augmenting the happiness and value of life to all people of all colors everywhere.

"For the support of this Declaration," Jefferson concluded, "we mutually pledge to each other our Lives, our Fortunes and our sacred Honor." This sentiment was no idle rhetoric. Many delegates took the final step toward independence only with great reluctance. If the war was lost, they faced a hangman's noose. Even in victory, more than a few signers discovered that their fortunes had been devastated by the war. Yet it does no dishonor to the principles of the Revolution to recognize the flawed nature of Jefferson's attempt to reconcile slavery with liberty. Even less does it dishonor the Revolution to appreciate the role enslaved African Americans played in forcing the debates about independence. They too risked all in the actions—the unspoken declarations—that so many of them took to avail themselves of life, liberty, and the pursuit of happiness.

❧ ❧ ❧ ADDITIONAL READING ❧ ❧ ❧

The Declaration of Independence, surely one of the most scrutinized documents in American history, stands at the center of the American Revolution, surely one of the most scrutinized events in that history. Consequently, the interested reader has plenty of material upon which to draw.

For background on the Revolution, Edmund S. Morgan's *Birth of the Republic*, rev. ed. (Chicago, 1977) remains brief and lucid. More recent studies include Edward Countryman, *The American Revolution* (London, 1985), good on the social and economic background; and Robert Middlekauff, *The Glorious Cause* (New York, 1982), which treats military aspects more fully. For the Declaration itself, see Carl Becker's venerable yet still engaging *The Declaration of Independence: A Study in the History of Political Ideas* (New York, 1942). Garry Wills's wide-ranging contextual analysis of the Declaration can be found in *Inventing America: Jefferson's Declaration of Independence* (New York, 1978). Wills has been called to task for overstating his case by Ronald

Hamowy in a classic cut-and-thrust maneuver entitled "Jefferson and the Scottish Enlightenment: A Critique of Garry Wills's *Inventing America*," *William and Mary Quarterly*, 3d ser., 36 (1979): 503–23. For a discussion of the local declarations of independence, see Pauline Maier, *American Scripture: Making the Declaration of Independence* (New York, 1997). Maier also examines how the Declaration outgrew its position of relative obscurity during the half century following the Revolution to become one of the "scriptural" texts of American history. In this light, Garry Wills's brilliant explication of another seminal document in American history is worth consulting. See Wills's *Lincoln at Gettysburg: The Words that Remade America* (New York, 1992).

Readers wishing to do their own textual analysis will find Julian P. Boyd's *The Declaration of Independence: The Evolution of the Text* (Princeton, N.J., 1945) a good starting place. Worthington C. Ford, ed., *Journals of the Continental Congress: 1774–1789* (Washington, D.C., 1904–1937) provides Charles Thomson's tantalizingly brief minutes. For a better sense of the delegates' concerns, see Edmund C. Burnett, ed., *Letters of Members of the Continental Congress* (Washington, D.C., 1921–1936); and the much more inclusive edition of letters, Paul H. Smith, ed., *Letters of Delegates to Congress, 1774–1789* (Washington, D.C., 1976–). A brilliant though somewhat eccentric analysis of the Declaration's text can be found in Jay Fliegelman, *Declaring Independence: Jefferson, Natural Language, and the Culture of Performance* (Stanford, Calif., 1993). Fliegelman even finds meaning in the pauses and punctuation of the document.

As for Jefferson himself, the best brief starting place is Joseph J. Ellis, *American Sphinx: The Character of Thomas Jefferson* (New York, 1996). Ellis is perceptive about Jefferson's conflicting, often self-deceptive attitudes toward slavery and race. Although Ellis argued against the likelihood of Jefferson having had an intimate and ongoing relationship with his slave Sally Hemings, he more recently reversed himself in light of evidence, based on an analysis of the DNA of Jefferson's descendants, that Jefferson fathered at least one child by Hemings. Annette Gordon-Reed, *Thomas Jefferson and Sally Hemings: An American Controversy* (Charlottesville, 1997) lays out the debate. For the DNA findings, see the articles in *Nature 396* (5 November 1998): 13–14 and in *The New York Times*, 1 November 1998, A1.

Sylvia Frey's fine study, *Water from the Rock: Black Resistance in a Revolutionary Age* (Princeton, 1991), outlines the actions taken by African Americans during the Revolutionary years. See also Woody Holton, "Rebel against Rebel: Enslaved Virginians and the Coming of the American Revolution," *Virginia Magazine of History and Biography* 105 (1997): 157–92; and Peter H. Wood, "'Taking Care of Business' in South Carolina: Republicanism and the Slave Society," in *The Southern Experience in the American Revolution*, Jeffrey J. Crow and Larry E. Tise, eds. (Chapel Hill, 1978). For the relation of African American rebellion and the Declaration itself, see Sidney Kaplan, "The Domestic Insurrections of the Declaration of Independence," *Journal of Negro History* 61 (1976): 243–55.

⇒ ⇒ FOUR ⇐ ⇐

Jackson's Frontier— and Turner's

Ceremony, merriment, and ballyhoo came to Chicago in the summer of 1893, and predictably, the crowds swelled the fairgrounds to get a taste of it. Buffalo Bill's Wild West Show went through its usual bronco-busting, war-whooping routines. Visitors gawked at a giant map of the United States fashioned entirely from pickles. Also on display were a huge telescope, destined for Yerkes Observatory; a long-distance telephone, connected with New York City; and a four-story high cross-section of a new ocean liner. The amusement park—the "Midway Plaisance"—even boasted exotic exhibits in the living flesh. Irish peasants boiled potatoes over turf fires, Arabian veiled women and turbaned elders occupied their own village, while "Prince Pomiuk" of the Eskimos drove a dogsled through the warm summery dust.

The excuse for the fuss was Chicago's "World's Columbian Exposition," held ostensibly to salute the 400th anniversary of Columbus's arrival in the Americas. More plausibly, the fair allowed proud Chicagoans to prove that they were more than hog butchers to the world and that they could out-exposition any metropolis on the globe. Given the total attendance of more than 12 million people over six months, the city made its case.

To further the exposition's reputation, several scholarly congresses were convened, including a World's Congress of Historians and Historical Students. And so on July 12, the curious tourist had the opportunity (or misfortune) of straying away from the booming cannibal drums of the Midway Plaisance and into the Art Institute, where five eager historians waited to present the fruits of their labors. On this hot evening, the papers were read back-to-back without respite, ranging from a discussion of "English Popular Uprisings in the Middle Ages," to "Early Lead Mining in Illinois and Wisconsin." The hardy souls who had not been driven off by the first four presentations saw a young man in starched collar rise to present yet another thesis, this one titled "The Significance of the Frontier in American History."

The young man was Frederick Jackson Turner, a historian from the University of Wisconsin. Although none in the audience could have suspected it, his essay would spark four generations of scholarship and historical debate. The novelty of Turner's frontier thesis resulted not from his discovery of any previously unknown facts, but because he proposed a new theory, one that took old facts and placed them in an entirely different light.

THE SIGNIFICANCE OF THEORY

Turner's thesis is only one of many theoretical concepts that historians have used to bring order out of the chaotic past. Yet thus far, this book has avoided a direct discussion of the term *theory*. It is time to make amends, for theory is an essential part of the discipline of history, profoundly affecting the way historians go about their work. Indeed, if history is not merely "the past" itself, but instead a reconstruction of it, theory could be said to supply the blueprints needed to raise the ediface.

At one level, theory can be defined simply as hypothesis. In this sense, it is the analysis that explains a relationship between two or more facts. During the Salem witch trials, certain "afflicted" townspeople acted in violent but consistent ways. Before historians can conclude that these acts might constitute symptoms of neurotic behavior, they must have accepted the concept of conversion hysteria as a valid theoretical explanation. Note that the Salem records do not provide this interpretation; theory is what supplies it.

In a broader sense, theory can be defined as a body of theorems presenting a systematic view of an entire subject. We use the term this way when speaking of the "theory of wave mechanics" or a "germ theory of disease." Often, small-scale theoretical constructs are a part of a larger theoretical framework. Conversion hysteria is only one of many behavioral syndromes classified as neuroses. In turn, the concept of neurosis is only one part of the larger body of theory accepted by modern psychology. Physicists, chemists, and other natural scientists often use mathematical formulas to summarize their general theories, but among social scientists and humanists, theorems become less mathematic and more elastic. Even so, when historians discuss a "theory of democracy" or a "theory of economic growth," they are applying a set of coherent principles to explain specific events.

Because historians study an event or period in its entirety, historical narrative usually incorporates many theories rather than just one. The historian of early Virginia will draw on theories of economic behavior (the development of joint stock companies as a means of capital formation), sociology (the rise of slavery as an institution of color), psychology (the causes of friction between white and black laboring classes), and so on. In this broadest sense, historical theory encompasses the entire range of a historian's training, from competence in statistics to opinions on politics and philosophies of human nature. It is derived from formal education, from reading, even from informal discussions with academic colleagues and friends.

It follows that theory in this wider sense—"grand theory," as it might be called—plays a crucial role in historical reconstruction. While small-scale theory is called on to explain specific puzzles (why didn't slavery become entrenched in Virginia before 1660?), grand theory is usually part of a historian's mental baggage *before* he or she is immersed in a particular topic. Grand theory encourages historians to ask certain questions and not others. It tends to single out particular areas of investigation as worthy of testing and to dismiss other areas as either irrelevant or uninteresting. Thus, anyone who ventures into the field of history—the lay reader as well as the professional researcher—needs to be aware of how grand theory exerts its influence. Nowhere in American history is this influence better illustrated than in Frederick Jackson Turner's venerable frontier thesis.

Turner began his Chicago lecture with a simple yet startling fact he had found in the recently released census of 1890. "Up to and including 1880, the country had a frontier of settlement," the census reported, "but at present the unsettled area has been so broken into by isolated bodies of settlement that there can hardly be said to be a frontier line." Turner seized upon this "event"—the passing of the frontier—as a "great historic moment." The reason for its importance to him seemed clear: "Up to our own day, American history has been in a large degree the history of the colonization of the Great West. The existence of an area of free land, its continuous recession, and the advance of American settlement westward, explain American development."

Turner's broad assertion—a manifesto, really—challenged on several counts the prevailing historical wisdom. Scholars of Turner's day had approached their subject with an Atlantic-coast bias. They viewed the East, and especially New England, as the true bearer of American culture. Developments beyond the Appalachian range were either ignored or treated

Turner in 1893, the year he presented his thesis at the Columbian World Exposition; and the Johns Hopkins University seminar room for history students. At the head of the table is Professor Herbert Baxter Adams, who argued that American democratic institutions could be traced to British and European roots. "It is just as improbable that free local institutions should spring up without a germ along American shores as that English wheat should have grown there without planting," he wrote. Turner resented the lack of interest in the West at Hopkins. "Not a man I know here," he commented, "is either studying, or is hardly aware of the country behind the Alleghenies." (*Left:* Collection of The University of Wisconsin–Madison Archives; *Right:* Reproduced by permission of The Huntington Library, San Marino, California)

sketchily. Turner, who had grown up in the rural setting of Portage, Wisconsin, and had taken his undergraduate degree at the University of Wisconsin, resented that attitude.

In addition, the reigning scholarship focused almost exclusively on political and constitutional developments. "History is past Politics and Politics present History" ran the slogan on the wall of the Johns Hopkins seminar room in which Turner had taken his Ph.D. In contrast, young Turner strongly believed that this narrow political perspective neglected the broader contours of social, cultural, and economic history. Historians who took the trouble to examine those areas, he felt, would discover that the unique physical and cultural conditions of the frontier, and not eastern cities, had shaped American character.

The frontier's effect on American character had been recognized in a casual way by earlier observers, but Turner attempted a more systematic analysis. In doing so, he drew on the scientific grand theory most prominent in his own day, Charles Darwin's theory of evolution. Whereas Darwin had proposed an explanation for evolution in the natural world, Turner suggested that America was an ideal laboratory for the study of cultural evolution. The American frontier, he argued, returned human beings to a primitive state of nature. With the trappings of civilization stripped away, the upward process of evolution was reenacted. Dramatically, Turner recreated the sequence for his audience:

> The wilderness masters the colonist. It finds him a European in dress, industries, tools, modes of travel, and thought. It takes him from the railroad car and puts him in the birch canoe. It strips off the garments of civilization and arrays him in the hunting shirt and the moccasin. It puts him in the log cabin of the Cherokee and Iroquois and runs an Indian palisade around him. Before long he has gone to planting Indian corn and plowing with a sharp stick; he shouts the war cry and takes the scalp in orthodox Indian fashion. In short, at the frontier the environment is at first too strong for the man. He must accept the conditions which it furnishes, or perish, and so he fits himself into the Indian clearings and follows the Indian trails. Little by little he transforms the wilderness, but the outcome is not the old Europe. . . . The fact is that here is a new product that is American.

Turner suggested that the evolution from frontier primitive to civilized town-dweller occurred not just once but time and time again, as the frontier moved west. Each time, settlers shed a bit more of their European ways; each time, a more distinctively American culture emerged. That was why the perspective of eastern historians was so warped: they stubbornly traced American roots to English political institutions, or even worse, the medieval organization of the Germanic town. "The true point of view in the history of this nation is not the Atlantic coast," Turner insisted, "it is the Great West."

From this general formulation of the frontier's effects, Turner deduced several specific traits that the recurring evolutionary process produced. Chief among them were nationalism, independence, and democracy.

Nationalism, Turner argued, arose as the frontier broke down the geographic and cultural identities of the Atlantic coast: New England with its Yankees and the tidewater South with its aristocratic planters. The mixing and amalgamation of sections was most clearly demonstrated in the middle states, where both Yankees and Southerners migrated over the mountains, where Germans and other northern Europeans joined the English in seeking land. There a new culture developed, possessing "a solidarity of its own with national tendencies. . . . Interstate migration went steadily on—a process of cross-fertilization of ideas and institutions." (Once again, note the Darwinian metaphor of "cross-fertilization.")

The frontier also promoted independence, according to Turner. The first English settlements had depended on the home country for their material goods, but as settlers pressed farther west, England found it difficult to extend that supply. Frontier towns became self-sufficient, and eastern merchants increasingly provided westerners with American rather than English products. The economic system became more American, more independent.

Most important, suggested Turner, the individualism of the frontier promoted democracy and democratic institutions. "Complex society is precipitated by the wilderness into a kind of primitive organization based on the family," Turner argued. "The tendency is anti-social. It produces antipathy to control, and particularly to any direct control." Thus westerners resented being taxed without being represented, whether by England and Parliament or by Carolina coastal planters. The frontier also broke down social distinctions that were so much a part of the East and Europe. Given the fluid society of the frontier, poor farmers or traders could and did become rich almost overnight. Social distinctions disappeared when placed against the greater necessity of simple survival.

Turner even argued that the West, with its vast supply of "free land," encouraged democracy in the East. The frontier acted as a safety valve, he suggested, draining off potential sources of discontent before they disrupted society. "Whenever social conditions tended to crystallize in the East, whenever capital tended to press upon labor or political restraints to impede the freedom of the mass, there was this gate of escape to the free conditions of the frontier. . . . Men would not accept inferior wages and a permanent position of social subordination when this promised land of freedom and equality was theirs for the taking."

The upshot of this leveling process was nothing less than a new American character. Turner waxed eloquent in his description of frontier traits:

> That coarseness and strength combined with acuteness and inquisitiveness; that practical, inventive turn of mind, quick to find expedients; that masterful grasp of material things, lacking in the artistic but powerful to effect great ends; that restless, nervous energy; that dominant individualism, working for good and for evil, and withal that buoyancy and exuberance which comes with freedom—these are the traits of the frontier, or traits called out elsewhere because of the existence of the frontier.

What Turner offered his Chicago listeners was not only "the American, this new man," as Hector St. John de Crevecoeur had called him in 1778, but also a systematic explanation of how the new American had come to be.

It would be proper etiquette here to scold Turner's Chicago audience for failing to recognize a masterpiece when they were read one. But in some ways it is easier to explain his listeners' inattention than to account for the phenomenal acceptance of the frontier thesis by later historians. Undeniably, Turner's synthesis was fresh and creative. But as he himself admitted, the essay was a hypothesis in need of research and testing. Of this, Turner proved constitutionally incapable. Although he loved to burrow in the archives for days on end, he found writing to be an unbearable chore.

Consequently, Turner published only magazine articles in the influential *Atlantic Monthly* and other journals. But these articles, along with numerous lectures and a gaggle of enthusiastic students, proved sufficient to make Turner's reputation. Publishers flocked to Wisconsin seeking books by the celebrated historian. Turner, with hopelessly misplaced optimism, signed contracts with four publishers to produce eight separate manuscripts. None saw the light of day. The single book he completed (*The Rise of the West*, 1906) appeared only through the frantic efforts of editor Albert Bushnell Hart, who wheedled, cajoled, and threatened in order to obtain the desired results. "It ought to be carved on my tombstone," Hart later remarked, "that I was the only man in the world that secured what might be classed an adequate volume from Turner."

Why Turner's remarkable success? Certainly not because of his detailed research, which remained unpublished. Success was due to the attraction of his grand theory. Later critics have taken Turner to task for imprecision and vagueness, but these defects are compensated by an eloquence and magnificence of scale. "The United States lies like a huge page in the history of society," Turner would declaim, and then proceed to lay out history with a continental sweep. The lure of his hypothesis for historians was much like the lure of a unified field theory for natural scientists—a set of equations, as physicist Freeman Dyson has remarked, that would "account for everything that happens in nature . . . a unifying principle that would either explain everything or explain nothing." In similar (though less galactic) fashion, Turner's theory captured historians' imaginations. "The existence of an area of free land, its continuous recession, and the advance of American settlement westward, explain American development." That proposal is about as all-encompassing as a historian could desire!

The theory seemed encompassing, too, in its methods. The techniques of social science in historical research are so familiar today that we forget the novelty and brilliance of Turner's insistence on unifying the tools of research. Go beyond politics, he argued; relate geography, climate, economics, and social factors to the political story. Not only did he propose this unification, Turner also provided a key focus—the frontier—as the laboratory in which these variables could be studied. The fresh breeze of Turner's theory succeeded in overturning the traditional approaches of eastern historians.

By the time Turner died in 1932, a tide of reaction had set in. Some critics pointed out that the frontier thesis severely minimized the democratic and cultural contributions of the English heritage. Others attacked Turner's vague definition of the "frontier." (Was it a geographical place? a type of population, such as trappers, herders, and pioneers? or a process wherein European traits were stripped off and American ones formed?) Other critics disputed the notion of the frontier as a "safety valve" for the East. Few European immigrants actually settled on the frontier; if anything, population statistics showed more farmers moving to the cities.

For our own purposes, however, it would be misleading to focus on these battles. Whether or not Turner was right, his theory dramatically influenced the investigations of other historians. To understand how, we need to take Turner's general propositions and look at the way he and others applied them to a specific topic.

An ideal subject for this task is the man whose name Turner himself shared—Andrew Jackson.[1] Jackson is one of those figures in history who, like Captain John Smith, seems always to be strutting about the stage just a bit larger than life. Furthermore, Jackson's wanderings took him straight into the most central themes of American history. Old Hickory, as his troops nicknamed him, led land-hungry pioneers into the southeastern United States, displacing Native Americans from lands east of the Mississippi, expelling the Spanish from Florida, and repelling the British from New Orleans. As president, he launched the war against the "monster" Bank of the United States, placing himself at the center of the perennial American debate over the role of economic power in a democracy. Above all, he came to be seen as the political champion of the common people. Here is a man whose career makes it impossible to avoid the large questions that grand theory will suggest.

How, then, did Turner's frontier hypothesis shape historians' perception of Jackson? What features of his career did it encourage them to examine?

JACKSON: A FRONTIER DEMOCRAT (TARNISHED)

For Frederick Turner, Andrew Jackson was not merely "one of the favorites of the west," he was "the west itself." By that rhetorical proclamation Turner meant that Jackson's whole life followed precisely the pattern of frontier evolution wherein eastern culture was stripped bare and replaced by the "contentious, nationalistic democracy of the interior."

Jackson's Scotch-Irish parents had joined the stream of eighteenth-century immigrants who landed in Pennsylvania, pushed westward until they bumped up against the Appalachians, and then filtered southwest into the

---

1. The bond of names is more than coincidence. Frederick Jackson Turner's father, Andrew Jackson Turner, was born in 1832 and named in honor of the President reelected that year.

Carolina backcountry. This was the process of "mixing and amalgamation" that Turner outlined in his essay. Turner had also shown how the frontier stripped away higher social organizations, leaving only the family as a sustaining bond. Andrew Jackson was denied even that society. His father died before Jackson's birth; his only two brothers and his mother died during the Revolution. At the age of seventeen, Andrew left Waxhaw, his boyhood home, never to return again. In effect, he was a man without a family—but not, as Turner saw it, a man without a backcountry.

Jackson first moved to the town of Salisbury, North Carolina, reading law by day and, with the help of high-spirited young friends, raising hell by night. Brawling in barrooms, sporting with young ladies, moving outhouses in the hours well past midnight—such activities gave Jackson a reputation as "the most roaring, game-cocking, horse-racing, card-playing, mischievous fellow that ever lived in Salisbury," according to one resident.

In 1788 the footloose Jackson grabbed the opportunity to become public prosecutor for the western district of North Carolina, a region that then stretched all the way to the Mississippi. There, in the frontier lands that now constitute Tennessee, Jackson hoped to make his reputation. Once settled in Nashville, he handled between a quarter and a half of all court cases in his home county during the first few years of his arrival. And he dispensed justice with the kind of "coarseness and strength" Turner associated with the frontier personality. When one enraged defendant stepped on prosecutor Jackson's toe to indicate his displeasure, Jackson calmly coldcocked the offender with a stick of wood. On another occasion, after Jackson had been appointed superior court judge in the newly created state of Tennessee, he stalked off the bench to summon a defendant before the court when no one else dared, including the sheriff and posse. The man in question, one Russell Bean, had threatened to shoot the "first skunk that came within ten feet," but when Jackson came roaring out of the courthouse, Bean pulled in his horns. "I looked him in the eye, and I saw shoot," said Bean, "and there wasn't shoot in nary other eye in the crowd; and so I says to myself, says I, hoss, it's about time to sing small, and so I did."

All in all, Jackson seemed a perfect fit for frontier democrat. Turner described in characteristic terms Jackson's election to the House of Representatives in 1796:

> The appearance of this frontiersman on the floor of Congress was an omen full of significance. He reached Philadelphia at the close of Washington's administration, having ridden on horseback nearly eight hundred miles to his destination. Gallatin (himself a western Pennsylvanian) afterwards graphically described Jackson, as he entered the halls of Congress, as "a tall, lank, uncouth-looking personage, with long locks of hair hanging over his face, and a cue down his back tied in an eel-skin; his dress singular, his manners and deportment those of a rough backwoodsman." Jefferson afterwards testified to Webster: "His passions are terrible. When I was President of the Senate, he was a Senator, and he could never speak, on account of the rashness of his feel-

Jackson the frontiersman: Russell Bean surrenders to Justice Jackson, as depicted in an 1817 biography. Wrote Turner, "If Henry Clay was one of the favorites of the West, Andrew Jackson was the West itself . . . the very personification of the contentious, nationalistic democracy of the interior." (Library of Congress)

ings. I have seen him attempt it repeatedly, and as often choke with rage." At length the frontier, in the person of its leader, had found a place in the government. This six-foot backwoodsman, angular, lantern-jawed, and thin, with blue eyes that blazed on occasion; this choleric, impetuous, Scotch-Irish leader of men; this expert duellist and ready fighter; this embodiment of the contentious, vehement, personal west, was in politics to stay.

This was Turner at his rhetorical best, marshaling all the striking personal details that supported his theory. But he was not writing a full-length biography and so confined his discussion of Jackson mostly to a few paragraphs of detail.

One of Turner's graduate students went further. Thomas Perkins Abernethy studied at Harvard during the period when the university had lured Turner east from his home ground at the University of Wisconsin. Abernethy believed that to test the frontier thesis, it ought to be examined on a local level, in more detail. In this respect, he felt, previous historians had not been scientific enough. "Science is studied by the examination of specimens, and general truths are discovered through the investigations of typical forms," he asserted. In contrast, "history has been studied mainly by national units, and the field is too broad to allow of minute examination." But Tennessee provided a perfect "specimen" of the western state. It broke away from its parent, North Carolina, during its frontier days; it was the first area of the nation to undergo territorial status; and from its backwoods settlements came Andrew Jackson himself. Why not trace the leavening effects of the frontier within this narrower compass? Abernethy set out to do just that in his book *From Frontier to Plantation in Tennessee.*

He had learned the techniques of his mentor well. Turner encouraged students to trace the effects of geography and environment on politics. Abernethy perceived that Tennessee's geography divided it into three distinct agricultural regions, providing a "rare opportunity to study the political effects of these several types of agricultural economy." Turner emphasized the role of free land as a crucial factor in the West. Abernethy agreed that land was "the chief form of wealth in the United States in its early years" and carefully studied the political controversies over Tennessee's vast tracts of land. Always he determined to look beyond the surface of the political arena to the underlying economic and geographic considerations.

These techniques were Turner's, but the results produced anything but Turner's conclusions. *From Frontier to Plantation* is dedicated to Frederick Jackson Turner, but the book directly refutes Turner's optimistic version of western history.

As Abernethy began unraveling the tangled web of Carolina-Tennessee politics, he discovered that Americans interested in western land included more than pioneer squatters and yeoman farmers of the "interior democracy." Prosperous speculators who preferred the comforts of the civilized East saw equally well that forested, uncultivated land would skyrocket in value once settlers poured over the Appalachians in search of homesteads.

The scramble for land revealed itself in the strange and contradictory doings of the North Carolina legislature. During the Revolution, inflation had plagued the state, largely because the legislature had continuously issued its own paper money when short of funds. The value of this paper money plummeted to a fraction of its original face value. After the war, the legislature retrenched by proclaiming that all debtors would have to repay their debts in specie (that is, gold or silver coins) or its equivalent in paper money. If, for example, the going rate set $1 in silver or gold as equal to $400 in paper notes, and a person owed $10, debtors who repaid using paper money would owe $4,000. In effect, the legislature was repudiating its paper currency and saying that only gold or silver would be an acceptable medium of exchange.

This move made sense if the legislature was trying to put the state's finances on a stable footing. But Abernethy noticed that in the same session, the legislature turned around and issued a *new* run of paper money—printing up a hundred thousand dollars. Why issue more paper money when you've just done your best to get rid of the older stuff?

Abernethy also noticed that during the same legislative session, land offices were opened up to sell western lands—but only under certain conditions. The claimant had to go out into the woods and mark some preliminary boundaries, then come back and enter the claim at a designated land office. Finally, a government surveyor would survey the lot, submit a report to the Secretary of State for the governor's authentication, and enter it in the county register.

The situation hardly confirmed Turner's democratic conception of the frontier, Abernethy concluded. First, who ended up being able to buy the new land? Not the squatter or yeoman farmer, certainly—few of them could fulfill the requirements of marking out land, returning East to register it, having it officially surveyed, and entering it. Instead, land speculators in the East, including state legislators, stepped in to make a killing. The career of William Blount, one of the most successful speculators, illustrated the process at work. As a state legislator, Blount helped write the new land laws. At the same time, he hired a woodsman to go west and mark out vast tracts. Blount, for his part, registered the claim and paid for the land.

Sometimes the money that paid for the land was the old paper currency, bought up for a fraction of its original price from poorer folk who had no means of claiming their own land. But the legislature also allowed purchasers to pay for the lands using the new paper money at face value. Was it coincidence only that Blount had been the legislator proposing the new issue of paper money? Abernethy thought not.

Instead of confirming Turner's version of a hardy democracy, then, Abernethy painted a picture of "free" Tennessee lands providing fortunes for already powerful men. Blount used "the entire Southwest [as] his hunting ground and he stuffed his pockets with the profits of his speculations in land. In the maw of his incredible ambition—or greed—there originated land grabs involving thousands of choice acres." And Blount was only one of many across the country. "In those days," Abernethy concluded, "America was run largely by speculators in real estate."

It was into this free-for-all country that Andrew Jackson marched in 1788, but Abernethy's new frame of reference placed his career in a different light. Compare Turner's description of Jackson's "pioneer" ride to Philadelphia with Abernethy's version of Jackson's horseback arrival in Tennessee. "Tradition has it," reported Abernethy, that Jackson

> arrived at Jonesboro . . . riding a fine horse and leading another mount, with saddlebags, gun, pistols, and fox-hounds. This was elaborate equipment for a struggling young lawyer, and within the year he increased it by the purchase of a slave girl. . . . Jackson still found time to engage in his favorite sport of horse-racing, and he fought a bloodless duel with Waightstill Avery, then the most famous lawyer in western North Carolina. All this makes it clear that the young man had set himself up in the world as a "gentleman." Frontiersmen normally fought with their fists rather than with pistols, and prided themselves more upon physical prowess, than upon manners. Though commonly looked upon as a typical Westerner, Jackson was ever an aristocrat at heart.

Jackson cemented his ties with the upper layers of society in more substantial ways. Turner had noted Jackson's practice as a "public prosecutor—an office that called for nerve and decision, rather than legal acumen." What frontier lawyering also called for, which Turner neglected to mention, was a

Jackson the gentleman: Thomas Abernethy argued that the history of Jackson's Tennessee demonstrated how "the wealthy rose to the top of affairs even on the frontier, and combined through their influence and common interests to control economic legislation. From time to time they found it necessary to make some obvious concession to democracy, such as broadening the suffrage or lowering the qualifications for office. But, while throwing out such sops with one hand, they managed to keep well in the other the more obscure field of economic legislation." The portrait of Jackson is by Thomas Sully. (Library of Congress)

knack for collecting debts, since Jackson most often represented creditors intent on recovering loans. During his first month of legal practice, he issued some seventy writs to delinquent debtors. This energetic career soon came to the notice of William Blount, who had by this time gotten himself appointed governor of the newly created Tennessee territory. He and Jackson became close political allies.

Jackson too had an eye for speculating, and it almost ruined him. Like Blount, he had cashed in on Tennessee's lands, buying 50,000 acres on the site of the future city of Memphis. In 1795 Jackson took his first ride to Philadelphia, a year before the one Turner eloquently described, in order to sell the Memphis land at a profit. Few Philadelphians wanted to buy, but Jackson finally closed a deal with David Allison, another of Blount's cronies. Allison couldn't pay in cash, so he gave Jackson promissory notes. Jackson, in turn, used the notes to pay for goods to stock a trading post he wanted to open in Tennessee.

Scant months after Jackson returned home, he learned that David Allison had gone bankrupt. Even worse, since Jackson had signed Allison's promissory notes, Allison's creditors were now after Jackson. "We take this early opportunity to make known to you that we have little or no expectations of getting paid from him," they wrote, "and that we shall have to get our money from you." This financial nightmare left Jackson "placed in the Dam'st situation ever a man was placed in," he admitted. To get himself out, he was forced to speculate even more. Buy a parcel of land here, sell it there. Cash in his trading post, make a small profit, invest it in more land. Exchange the new land for another buyer's promissory note. And so on. Not until 1824 did he settle the final claims in the tangle. Clearly, Abernethy believed that Jackson's horseback rides on behalf of real estate deserved more emphasis than any romantic notions of a galloping frontier democrat.

Despite such a devastating attack on the frontier thesis, Abernethy's admiration for Turner was genuine, no doubt because he recognized how much the thesis had guided his research. It is easy to conclude that the value of a theory rests solely on its truth. Yet even if Turner's hypothesis erred on many points, it provided a focus that prodded Abernethy to investigate important historical questions—the implications of western land policy, the effect of environment on character, the social and geographical foundations of democracy. All these topics had been slighted by historians.

Theory, in other words, is often as important for the questions it raises as for the answers it provides. In this sense it performs the same function in the natural sciences. Thomas Kuhn, a historian of science, has demonstrated how indispensable an older scientific theory is in pointing the way to the theory that replaces it. As the old theory is tested, attention naturally turns to problem areas—places where the results are not what the old theory predicts. The new theory emerges, Kuhn pointed out, "only for the man who, knowing with precision what he should expect, is able to recognize that something has gone wrong." Abernethy was able to discern that something had "gone wrong" in Tennessee politics, but only because Turner's hypothesis showed him what questions needed to be asked and where to look for answers.

JACKSON: LABORER'S FRIEND

Theory, then, can actually sharpen a historian's vision by limiting it—aiding the process of selection by zeroing in on important issues and data. It stands to reason, however, that trade-offs are made in this game. If a theory focuses attention on certain questions, it necessarily also causes a historian to ignore other facts, trends, or themes. Theory can limit in a negative as well as a positive sense.

Abernethy's disagreement with Turner illustrates this problem. Although the two historians reached diametrically opposed conclusions about Jackson, they carried on the debate within the framework of Turner's thesis. Did Jackson embody the democratic, individualistic West? Yes, argued Turner. No, countered Abernethy. Yet both accepted the premise suggested by the thesis, that the influence of the West was crucial.

That conclusion might serve well enough for a study limited to Tennessee politics, but Jackson went on to achieve national fame by winning the Battle of New Orleans and was elected to the Presidency in 1828. He triumphed in all the southern coastal states and in Pennsylvania, and he also received a majority of New York's electoral votes. In New York too he cemented an alliance with Martin Van Buren, the sophisticated eastern leader of the Albany Regency political faction.

Such facts call attention to something that Turner's frame of reference overlooked. As a national leader, Jackson made friends in the East as well as the West, in cities as well as in the country. Historian Arthur Schlesinger Jr., believing that Abernethy as well as Turner overemphasized the importance of Jackson's western roots, determined to examine the eastern sources of Jackson's democratic coalition. "A judgment on the character of Jackson's democracy must be founded on an examination of what Jackson did as President," he argued, "and on nothing else; certainly not on an extrapolation made on the basis of his career before he became President." The result of Schlesinger's research was *The Age of Jackson* (1945), a sweeping study that highlighted the influence of eastern, urban laboring classes on Jacksonian democracy.

In part, Schlesinger's theoretical approach had been the natural consequence of his upbringing. He spent his childhood within the civilized environs of Cambridge, Massachusetts, where his father, Arthur Meier Schlesinger Sr., held a chair in history at Harvard. Like Turner, Schlesinger Sr. preferred the wider horizons of social and cultural history over traditional political history. Unlike Turner, he emphasized the role of urban society and culture in American life. His article "The City in American History" sparked a generation of scholarship on peculiarly urban problems such as industrial labor and immigration. The article, Schlesinger later suggested generously, "did not seek to destroy the frontier theory but to substitute a balanced view: an appreciation of both country and city in the rise of American civilization." Nevertheless, Schlesinger Sr.'s interest clearly lay with the cities.

The younger Schlesinger admired his father—so much so that at the age of fifteen he changed his name from Arthur Bancroft Schlesinger to Arthur Meier Schlesinger Jr. More significant, the son shared the same scholarly dispositions. After schooling at the prestigious Phillips Exeter Academy,

Arthur completed a brilliant undergraduate and graduate career at Harvard.[2] It was out of this intellectual training that Schlesinger wrote his book.

The Age of Jackson also reflected a set of attitudes and emphases popular in the 1930s that distanced Schlesinger from the Progressive outlook Turner had shared at the turn of the century. The thirties saw the country plunged into a depression so severe that it shook many Americans' faith in the traditional economic system. Theories of class struggle, of conflict between capital and labor, became popular in scholarly circles. As an avid supporter of Franklin Roosevelt, Schlesinger by no means accepted the doctrines of the communist left, but he did believe that class conflict played a greater role in American history than the sectional disputes that Turner had emphasized. Significantly, Schlesinger used a quotation from George Bancroft, a radical Jacksonian from New England, as the superscription for his book. It affirmed the importance of class struggle but still embraced the liberal's hope for a nonviolent resolution of conflict:

> The feud between the capitalist and laborer, the house of Have and the house of Want, is as old as social union, and can never be entirely quieted; but he who will act with moderation, prefer fact to theory, and remember that every thing in the world is relative and not absolute, will see that the violence of the contest may be stilled.

→ LABORERS SUPPORTED JACKSON

Given Schlesinger's background and temperament, his research focused on substantially different aspects of Jackson's career. It portrayed Old Hickory as a natural leader who, though he came from the West, championed the cause of laborers in all walks of life—city "mechanicks" as well as yeoman farmers. Jackson's chief political task, argued Schlesinger, was "to control the power of the capitalist groups, mainly Eastern, for the benefit of the non-capitalist groups, farmers and laboring men, East, West, and South." Schlesinger made his opposition to Turner abundantly clear:

> The basic Jacksonian ideas came naturally enough from the East, which best understood the nature of business power and reacted most sharply against it. The legend that Jacksonian democracy was the explosion of the frontier, lifting into the government some violent men filled with rustic prejudices against big business does not explain the facts, which were somewhat more complex. Jacksonian democracy was rather a second American phase of that enduring struggle between the business community and the rest of society which is the guarantee of freedom in a liberal capitalist state.

Consequently, much of *The Age of Jackson* is devoted to people the Turner school neglected entirely: the leaders of workingmen's parties, the broader labor movement, and the efforts of Democratic politicians to bring laborers within the orbit of Jackson's party. Abernethy's treatment of Jackson as land

---

2. In fact, Schlesinger Sr. firmly believed in the virtues of public education. But he felt compelled to send Arthur Jr. to Exeter after discovering that his tenth-grade public school teacher taught that "the inhabitants of Albania were called Albinos because of their white hair and pink eyes."

Jackson, champion of the working people: "The specific problem was to control the power of the capitalistic groups, mainly Eastern, for the benefit of the noncapitalist groups, farmers and laboring men, East, West and South," wrote Arthur Schlesinger Jr. "The legend that Jacksonian democracy was the explosion of the frontier, lifting into the government some violent men filled with rustic prejudices against big business, does not explain the facts." Here, the general public (dubbed "King Mob" by Jackson's genteel opponents) goes to work on a giant cheese at a White House celebration in 1837. The odor of the cheese lingered for months. (Library of Congress)

speculator is replaced by attention to Jackson's vigorous war on the Second Bank of the United States, where Democratic leaders are shown forging an alliance with labor. "During the Bank War," Schlesinger concluded, "laboring men began slowly to turn to Jackson as their leader, and his party as their party."

Like Turner, Schlesinger came under critical fire. Other historians have argued that much of Jackson's so-called labor support was actually middle- or even upper-class leaders who hoped to channel worker sentiments for their own purposes. At the same time, many in the real laboring classes refused to support Jackson. But again—what is important for our present purposes is to notice how Schlesinger's general concerns shaped his research. It is not coincidental that Jackson's celebrated kitchen cabinet, in Schlesinger's retelling, bears a marked resemblance to the "brain trusters" of Franklin

Roosevelt's cabinet. It is not coincidental that Jackson attacks the "monster Bank" for wreaking economic havoc much the way that FDR inveighed against the "economic royalists" of the Depression era. Nor is it coincidental that *The Age of Jackson* was followed, in 1957, by *The Age of Roosevelt*. Schlesinger may have displayed his political and economic philosophy more conspicuously than most historians, but no scholar can escape bringing some theoretical framework to his or her research. One way or another, theory inevitably limits and focuses the historian's perspective.

JACKSON AND THE NEW WESTERN HISTORY

Perhaps precisely because Schlesinger does wear his political heart on his sleeve, we are forced to consider a notion that is potentially more troubling. The term *theory* implies that a historian, like some scientist in a lab, arrives at his or her propositions in a rigorous, logical way, setting aside the controversies of the present in order to study the past on its own terms. But in Schlesinger's case—like it or not—the events of his day clearly influenced his approach to Andrew Jackson. For that matter, Turner's original frontier thesis was a product of his times. It was the Census of 1890, after all, that caught Turner's attention, with its declaration that the frontier was essentially closed. It was Turner's rural, midwestern upbringing that encouraged him to dissent from eastern-trained historians in his search for an explanation of democracy in America. Indeed, Turner would have been the first to recognize the pull of contemporary affairs. "Each age writes the history of the past anew with reference to the conditions uppermost in its own time," he commented in 1891.

The notion that historians' theories are tainted by a kind of presentism troubles many, including some historians. "The present-minded contend that in writing history no historian can free himself of his total experience," wrote one scholar, clearly unhappy with the notion that others might think he could not help being swayed by contemporary "passions, prejudices, assumptions, prepossessions, events, crises and tensions." Surely he was right in believing that those who reconstruct the past should not do violence to it by making it over in the image of the present. Yet for better or for worse—perhaps we should say, for better *and* for worse—historical theories and questions are shaped by the present in which they arise. There is no escaping current events—only, through careful self-discipline, the opportunity of using new perspectives in positive rather than negative ways: to broaden our understanding rather than lessen it. A case study of present-mindedness at work can be found among those historians who more recently have reexamined the field Turner championed. Their movement has come to be known as the new western history.

The generation of historians spearheading the new western history came of age, by and large, during the social upheavals of the 1960s and 1970s, an era during which African Americans led a revolution for civil rights and equal treatment under the law. Other minorities too sought a greater voice in American society, whether they were Indians seeking tribal lands and tribal rights or Chicano migrant laborers organizing for fair working conditions. During these same years feminists rallied to obtain equal treatment, and an environmental movement questioned the prevailing boom mentality in American life that equated all economic growth with progress. All these forces for change challenged traditional ways of thinking, and regardless of whether historians themselves became social activists, many were moved to reevaluate what constituted legitimate history. For historians of the West, the experiences of these decades were eye-opening in a host of different ways.

Return for a moment to Turner's central proposition: "The existence of an area of free land, its continuous recession, and the advance of American settlement westward, explain American development." For a new generation of historians such as Patricia Limerick, the seemingly innocuous phrase "free land" served as a big, flapping red flag. The ferment of the sixties and seventies made it much more evident that calling such land "free" loaded the dice. In framing a working hypothesis, historians glided over the inconvenient fact that the lands "were not vacant, but occupied," as Limerick pointed out, by Indians who used them either for hunting or for the cultivation of their own crops. "Redistributing those lands to the benefit of white farmers required the removal of Indian territorial claims and of the Indians themselves—a process that was never simple." The title of Limerick's book, *The Legacy of Conquest* (1987), framed the issue in blunt terms. Conquest was what made land "free," for the land had been taken either without permission or with only the most token of payments dispensed under dubious circumstances.

Consider another phrase plucked out of Turner's sentence: "the advance of American settlement westward." Turner tended to view the frontier as essentially one-dimensional. Americans—by which he meant Americans primarily of English heritage—moved westward across the "wilderness," evolving a new democratic society as they went. But the notion of wilderness was a theoretical construct that implicitly denied the existence of any significant borderland cultures other than Anglo-American. The new voices of the sixties and seventies—Indian, Latino, African American, and feminist—pushed historians to recognize that the frontiers of North America were both multicultural and multidirectional. Spanish settlers spread northward from Central America and the Caribbean into Florida, Texas, New Mexico, and California. Chinese and Japanese immigrants of the mid-nineteenth century moved from west to east as they crossed the Pacific to California. And for the various Indian tribes themselves, frontier lines were shifting in all directions during the unsettled centuries following European contact with the Americas.

Turner evidenced little interest in the cultural mixing that went on in these regions, a defect the new western history sought to correct. "The invaded and subject peoples of the West must be given a voice in the region's history," argued Donald Worster in 1989. "Until very recently many western historians acted as though the West had either been empty of people prior to the coming of the white race or was quickly, if bloodily, cleared of them, once and for all, so that historians had only to deal with the white point of view." But Worster suggested that the "younger generation appearing in the 1970s and '80s" made the "new multicultural perspective their own." They replaced Turner's unidirectional frontier with a portrait of a West that "has been on the forward edge of one of modern history's most exciting endeavors, the creation, in the wake of European expansion and imperialism, of the world's first multi-racial, cosmopolitan societies." Newcomers to western cities often found as many or more foreign languages spoken there than in such cosmopolitan centers as New York, Paris, or Moscow.

Historians' attitudes toward Andrew Jackson could hardly be expected to remain untouched by these currents of change. Indeed, even before the new western history came into vogue, historians had begun reevaluating Jackson's career. For historian Michael Rogin, who wrote about Jackson during the tumultuous seventies, Old Hickory was the "embodiment" of the West for reasons entirely different from Turner's. Jackson embodied the West simply because he was instrumental in driving the Indians from their lands. "Historians have failed to place Indians at the center of Jackson's life," Rogin argued. "They have interpreted the Age of Jackson from every perspective but Indian destruction, the one from which it actually developed historically."

Robert Remini made a similar case in his biography of Jackson, the first volume of which appeared in 1977. Time after time, Jackson led efforts to force Indians to sign treaties ceding millions of acres. While he served as major general of the Tennessee militia and later as major general in the U.S. army, Jackson consistently exceeded his instructions on such matters. At the conclusion of his war against the Creek Indians, the remnants of the Creek Red Stick faction (whom Jackson had been fighting) retreated to Florida in hopes of continuing their war. Since the general could not compel his enemies to cede land, he turned around and demanded 23 million acres from his Indian *allies*, signing the treaty instead with them! Fearing that the government might revoke such a brazen action, he called for the new boundary lines to be run immediately and land sold to settlers as quickly as possible. "The sooner this country is brought in the market the better," he advised president-elect James Monroe, on yet another occasion. Over the years, Jackson's negotiations led to the acquisition by the United States of Indian lands amounting to one-third of Tennessee, three-quarters of Alabama and Florida, one-fifth of Georgia and Mississippi, and a tenth of Kentucky and North Carolina.

Of course, Jackson's involvement in land acquisition did not end with his military career. As president, he championed the movement to force the remaining 125,000 Indians east of the Mississippi onto much less valuable lands west of the river, freeing up additional millions of prime acres in the midst of the booming cotton kingdom. At the president's urging, Congress set the policy of Indian removal into motion in 1830. "In terms of acquisition," commented Remini, "it is not too farfetched to say that the physical shape of the United States today looks pretty much like it does largely because of the intentions and efforts of Andrew Jackson."

Rogin and Remini disagreed on many aspects of Jackson's career. (To begin with, Rogin used another grand theory—Freudian psychology—to interpret Jackson's sometimes contradictory attitudes toward Indians, which were at once fierce and paternalistic.)[3] Yet for all their disagreements, both scholars could not avoid having their interpretations of Jackson shaped by the demands of Native Americans during the 1970s that their cultures and their rights be taken seriously.

Perhaps ironically, none of the new western historians has yet stepped forward to recast Jackson in light of recent scholarship. In part, the lack of attention arises because younger scholars rejected Turner's definition of the frontier as a "process," continually repeated as Anglo-Americans moved westward across the continent. The new western historians preferred to focus on the trans-Mississippi West, well beyond the territory Andrew Jackson roamed. Yet there is more at work here than a geographic narrowing of field. In many ways, the questions posed by the new western historians cannot be answered by making Jackson the center of attention. To be sure, Old Hickory played a leading role in driving the Indians from their homelands. But focusing on the actions of the Anglo victors tells us little about the often vibrant intermixture of cultures that arose *before* removal began, during an era when both whites and Indians held significant power along the frontier.

One of the new western historians, Richard White, has examined the frontier of the seventeenth and eighteenth century along the Great Lakes in a book suggestively titled *The Middle Ground*. White argued that most discussions of the frontier portrayed the contrasting cultures as essentially and always in opposition. In contrast, White preferred to highlight a process of accommodation at work. By adopting the metaphor of a "middle ground," he highlighted a situation in which "whites could neither dictate to Indians nor ignore them. Whites needed Indians as allies, as partners in exchange, as sexual partners, as friendly neighbors." Only with the passing of this frontier did the middle ground break down, accompanied by a hardening of attitudes among whites, a "re-creation of the Indians as alien, as exotic, as other."

From this perspective, Jackson and his policies of Indian removal seem only the depressing endgame of what is the more interesting and neglected territory of the middle ground. Indeed, the Old Southwest from about 1780 to 1820—the middle ground Jackson traveled—was a region extraordinarily rich in cultural accommodation. For 200 years the land had witnessed a remarkable intermingling of Indian, French, Spanish, and English cultures. From its base in Florida, Spain actively courted trade with Indians, many of whom had intermarried with whites. The trader Alexander McGillivray, for example, was

---

3. We will encounter Freud's psychoanalytic theories in Chapter 6.

This Chickasaw Indian girl's elegant hair and fashionable dress suggest the complexity of cultural relations in the middle ground of the Old Southwestern frontier in Andrew Jackson's time. The girl was among the thousands of Indians removed to territory west of the Mississippi. (Edward E. Ayer Collection, The Newberry Library, Chicago)

not the white European his name conjures up, but an influential Indian leader of the Creeks, who concluded a treaty of alliance between his people and the Spanish in 1784. His parentage reflected the mixed heritage of the middle ground: a mother of French-Creek descent, a father who was a Scots trader.

Adding to the regional mixture of the Old Southwest were African Americans. White traders who intermarried with Indians were the first among the Cherokees, Creeks, and other tribes to clear cotton plantations and use slaves to work them. Often these slaves were runaways whose skills the Indians drew upon in their attempt to emulate white plantation owners. African Americans knew how to spin and weave, shoe horses, and repair guns. Often they served as translators. Ironically, as a minority of Cherokees adopted a frame of government similar to the U.S. Constitution, they also set up slave codes similar to those in the white antebellum South.

Seminole Indians also held slaves, although they gave more autonomy to these "black Seminoles," as the slaves were known. When runaways fled Spanish or American plantations for Seminole lands, the Seminoles allowed the newcomers to live in separate villages, often far from their Indian owners. In return for being allowed to raise crops, black Seminoles paid a portion of the harvest to their masters—in effect, sharecropping. If, as Donald Worster suggested, the lure of the new western history involved tracing a process of multiracial, multicultural mixing along the frontier, topics such as the middle ground held a greater attraction than did rehashing the traditional stories of Andrew Jackson as Indian fighter.

After such a procession of grand historical theories, what may be said of the "real" Andrew Jackson? Skeptics may be tempted to conclude that there was not one but four Old Hickories roaming the landscape of Jacksonian America: Jackson the frontier democrat; Jackson the aristocratic planter and speculator; Jackson, friend of labor; and Jackson, taker of Indian lands. The use of historical theory seems to have led the reader into a kind of boggy historical relativism where there is no real Jackson, only men conjured up to fit the formulas of particular historical theories or the fashionable currents of the day.

But that viewpoint is overly pessimistic. It arises from the necessary emphasis of this chapter, where our concern has been to point out the general effects of grand theory rather than to evaluate the merits of each case. Theory, we have stressed, provides a vantage point that directs a researcher's attention to significant areas of inquiry. But the initial theorizing is only the beginning. Theories can be and are continually tested. Sometimes old theories are thrown out, replaced by new ones. In such fashion did Copernicus replace Ptolemy. On the other hand, some theories stand up to testing or are merely refined to fit the facts more closely. In yet other instances, old theories are incorporated into more encompassing frameworks. Newtonian mechanics are still as valid as ever for the everyday world, but they have been found to be only a special case of the broader theories of relativity proposed by Einstein.

Historical theory will probably never attain the precision of its counterparts among the natural sciences. In part, such precision remains beyond our reach because historical narrative seeks to account for specific, unique chains of events—events that can never be replicated in the way scientists replicate experiments in the lab. The complexity of the task will no doubt ensure that our explanations will remain subject, for better *and* for worse, to contemporary concerns. Of all people, historians should be the first to acknowledge that they are shaped by the currents of their own times.

But that does not mean historians must give up on the possibility of describing and explaining an objective reality. In the present example, we may argue that, far from having four different Jacksons roaming the historical landscape, we are seeing various aspects of Jackson's personality and career that need to be incorporated into a more comprehensive framework. It is the old tale of the blind men describing the different parts of an elephant: the elephant is real enough, but the descriptions are partial and fragmentary. Frederick Jackson Turner was writing about a nebulous Jacksonian style— indeed, one may as well come out with it—"democracy" and "individualism" were, for Turner, little more than styles. Abernethy, on the other hand, was looking at the concrete material interests and class alliances that Jackson developed during his Tennessee career and paid almost no attention to the presidential years. Schlesinger did precisely the opposite: he picked up Jackson's story only after 1824 and in the end was more concerned with the Jacksonian movement than with its nominal leader. The historians who came of age in the 1960s and 1970s have replaced Turner's imaginary frontier line with a contested cultural space whose middle grounds are populated with a Jacksonian "common people" more multiracial and diverse than Turner was ever able to conceive.

A unified field theory for Jacksonian America? Perhaps the outlines are there, but the task of deciding must be left to some future Turner of the discipline. What remains clear is that, however much particular theories continue to be revised or rejected, theory itself will accompany historians always. Without it, researchers cannot begin to select from among an infinite number of facts; they cannot separate the important from the incidental; they cannot focus on a manageable problem. Albert Einstein put the proposition succinctly. "It is the theory," he concluded, "which decides what we can observe."

➢ ➢ ➢ ADDITIONAL READING ➢ ➢ ➢

Grand theory begets grand bibliography. Edward Pessen's *Jacksonian America*, rev. ed. (Homewood, Ill., 1978), which lists only the "more important" books and articles on Jacksonian America, runs to more than 700 entries. Robert V. Remini and Robert O. Rupp devote an entire book to the writings about Jackson in *Andrew Jackson: A Bibliography* (Westport, Conn., 1991).

Old Hickory himself may be approached through a number of traditional biographies. Earliest is John Reid and John Henry Eaton, *The Life of Andrew Jackson* (Philadelphia, 1817, reissued 1974). The volume has much authentic material for Jackson's early years, but beware later "campaign" editions of 1824 and 1828, to which chunks of political puffery were added. James Parton, *The Life of Andrew Jackson*, 3 vols. (Boston, 1866), includes the recollections of Jackson's boyhood neighbors, whom Parton interviewed years later. Robert Remini's eminently readable *The Life of Andrew Jackson* (New York, 1988) is a condensation of his three-volume study: *Andrew Jackson and the Course of American Empire, 1767–1821; Andrew Jackson and the Course of American Democracy, 1822–1832;* and *Andrew Jackson and the Course of American Freedom, 1833–1845* (New York, 1977–1984). Though Remini provides valuable and unsparing detail on Jackson's aggressive treaty signing, the author's approach nonetheless reflects the perspectives of an older generation whose admiration for Jackson remains uppermost. For a balanced recent portrait of Jackson's place in in the political landscape, see Harry L. Watson, *Liberty and Power* (New York, 1990).

To understand the role of theory in both science and history, readers will profit from Thomas Kuhn, *The Structure of Scientific Revolutions* (Chicago, 1962). The revised edition (1970) contains a few remarks by Kuhn on the applicability of his theory to social science disciplines. For a recent critique of Kuhn's work as it relates to the natural sciences, see Steven Weinberg, "The Revolution That Didn't Happen," *New York Review of Books* 45:15 (8 October 1998): 48–52.

Frederick Jackson Turner's key essays are reprinted in *The Frontier in American History* (New York, 1920). He also wrote *The Rise of the New West* (New York, 1906). The best accounts of Turner's life and work are by Ray Billington, the last major Turnerian, who set to print more words on Turner than Turner himself ever sent to press on American history. *Frederick Jackson Turner: Historian, Scholar, Teacher* (New York, 1973) is an entertaining biography, while *The Genesis of the Frontier Thesis* (San Marino, Calif., 1971) describes just that. A contrasting view may be found in Richard Hofstadter, *The Progressive Historians: Turner, Beard, Parrington* (New York, 1968).

In addition to Thomas Abernethy's *From Frontier to Plantation in Tennessee* (Chapel Hill, N.C., 1932), see his views in "Andrew Jackson and the Rise of Southwestern Democracy," *American Historical Review* 33 (October, 1927): 64–77, and his biography of Jackson in the *Dictionary of American Biography*. Arthur Schlesinger Jr.'s *Age of Jackson* (Boston, 1945) has generated much discussion among historians, discussion that is summarized well in Pessen's bibliographical essay. Information on Schlesinger's career may be gained from an essay on him in *Pastmasters: Some Essays on American Historians*, ed. Marcus Cunliffe and Robin Winks (New York, 1969). Although a great many scholars would probably agree with Michael Rogin on the importance of Indian removal to Jackson's career, the Marxian and Freudian approach that Rogin employs in *Fathers and Children: Andrew Jackson and the Subjugation of the American Indian* (New York, 1975) has been hotly challenged. Remini carries on a polite but firm running war in the footnotes of his biography. From the radical end of the spectrum, Elizabeth Fox-Genovese offers a critique in *Reviews in American History* 3 (December 1975): 407–17.

The views of the new western history are expounded in Patricia Limerick, *The Legacy of Conquest: The Unbroken Past of the American West* (New York, 1987); Donald Worster, *Under Western Skies: Nature and History in the American West* (New York, 1992); and William Cronon, George Miles, and Jay Gitlin, eds., *Under an Open Sky: Rethinking America's Western Past* (New York, 1992). All discuss Turner as a jumping-off point for newer perspectives. Richard White's *The Middle Ground: Indians, Empires, and the Republics in the Great Lakes Region, 1650–1815* (New York, 1991) provides one of the best models of the new approaches.

Though no single work has done for the Old Southwest what White did for the Great Lakes region, many studies have been perceptive. For the

Spanish influence, see the relevant chapters of David J. Weber, *The Spanish Frontier in North America* (New Haven, 1992). For a recent overview of Indian removal, see Anthony F. C. Wallace, *The Long, Bigger Trail: Andrew Jackson and the Indians* (New York, 1993). On Indians and African Americans, see Theda Perdue, *Slavery and the Evolution of Cherokee Society, 1540–1866* (Knoxville, Tenn., 1979) and Daniel F. Littlefield Jr., *Africans and Creeks: From the Colonial Period to the Civil War* (Westport, Conn., 1979). Writing in the 1930s, Kenneth W. Porter provided much useful information about black Seminoles, later reprinted in *The Negro on the American Frontier* (New York, 1971). (Readers of this chapter should now be able to hypothesize why Porter's research, published originally in the *Journal of Negro History*, was not elaborated on by mainstream historians and was only reprinted in 1971.) More recently, Quintard Taylor, *In Search of the Racial Frontier: African Americans in the American West, 1528–1990* (New York, 1998) provides an excellent portrait of the roles played by African Americans in the emerging new western history.

✦ ✦ FIVE ✦ ✦

The Invisible Pioneers

Sometime in the early 1700s, somewhere along the rolling foothills of Montana, a man named Shaved Head lay in hiding, staring into the distance at a group of very big dogs.

To the west lay the peaks of the Rockies and the continental divide; to the east, the short-grass plains stretching for hundreds of miles. Shaved Head's usual haunts were some distance to the north, in what is now Saskatchewan. But together with a group of Blackfeet comrades, he had run and walked south for several days, leading a war party in search of the people who came from across the mountains to hunt buffalo—probably the Snake Indians. At last he had discovered one of their camps.

And in it stood a number of these strange big dogs.

The Blackfeet had dogs, of course. They used them to haul skin lodges, cooking pots, and utensils whenever they moved camp. But these dogs were different from any Shaved Head had ever seen. They were tall as a man and more the size of elk, except they seemed to have lost their horns. Still, they couldn't be elk, for they were obviously slaves to the Snake people, just as dogs were slaves to the Blackfeet.

Shaved Head managed to steal a few of the animals. But when his warriors tried to mount them, the creatures began walking and the men quickly jumped off. Cautiously they led the animals home, where everyone in the band gathered around and marveled. At first, people tried putting robes on the animals' backs, but that made them jump. After a time a woman said, "Let's put a travois on one of them, just like we do on our small dogs." So they made a travois and attached it to one of the gentler animals. He didn't kick or jump. Then the people led him around with the travois attached. Finally a woman mounted the animal and rode it. In years after, they called these creatures *ponokamita*, or elk dogs.

The elk dogs, so strange to the Blackfeet, were actually horses. Such creatures had been extinct in North America for 10,000 years, until the Spanish reintroduced them in the sixteenth century. From Spanish outposts horses gradually spread north and east, finally reaching the Blackfeet early in the eighteenth century. Shaved Head's account of their arrival is noteworthy because it rests on a remarkable oral tradition. Anthropologist John Ewers heard the story in the 1940s from an eighty-year-old Blackfoot named Weasel Tail who, in turn, had heard it growing up as a boy, in the 1860s and

"Let's put a travois on one of them, just like we do our small dogs." This Blackfoot oral tradition related how horses were first tamed in the early 1700s. The use of horses to draw travois, as in this photograph, meant important changes in the life of a nomadic tribe, especially for women. Larger pack animals meant larger loads; hence larger, more spacious teepees could be made and carried. (D. Barry/Denver Public Library, Western History Department, Colorado)

1870s, from an elderly member of the tribe named Two Strikes Woman. She was passing along accounts that her great-grandfather had given her father. Thus the tradition passed through at least four generations. To be sure, such oral evidence lacks the authority of written or eyewitness accounts, especially since the events in question took place more than 200 years earlier. (In Chapter 7, we examine in more detail the problems of oral evidence.) Still, other available records suggest that, however the details fell out, the Blackfeet first gained the use of horses sometime in the early 1700s, well before the region was ever visited by whites.

Weasel Tail's story is useful for another reason. It suggests some of the complexity involved in portraying "the middle ground"—historian Richard White's metaphor for the borderlands in which various cultures met, mixed, and accommodated one with another. As we saw in Chapter 4, the new western historians have insisted that the interactions between peoples and cultures in North America amounted to more than just a process of "westward advance" into "wild forests, trackless plains, [and] untrodden valleys," to quote one Overland Trail guidebook of the 1840s. Weasel Tail's story reminds us that just as Europeans were discovering and adapting to conditions in their "New" World, Native Americans were discovering and adapting to the cultures that came to them from across the oceans. And the crucial adaptations cannot be described in terms of human contact alone. Horses from European culture interacted with Blackfoot society years before whites themselves appeared. There was not only a human frontier line but also a "horse frontier," as well as myriad other plant and animal frontiers—not the least of them a critical frontier of microorganisms.

We may rephrase this insight in more basic, elemental terms: human history is not merely the history of humans. Although historians have traditionally focused on the creations of humankind—social and political institutions, wars, economic and cultural systems—all human societies are inevitably constructed within a larger natural setting: physical, geographical, biological. Historians need to be aware of the interactions of human actors and their larger environment.

The boundaries that must be drawn, then, are not simply between differing cultures but between differing ecological systems. And although such lines may at first seem unimportant, they exerted a profound impact on the settlement of North America. Europeans and Indians had developed different ways of exploiting the plants and animals of their environments. When these competing methods intermingled along the middle grounds of frontier borderlands, they were all too often disastrously incompatible. A full understanding of the expansion of the United States to the Pacific must take account of these ecological conflicts. In many ways, European flora and fauna were invisible pioneers along shifting frontiers.

To watch these larger movements in action, our approach in this chapter must be nearly the opposite of the microcosmic focus used to examine the witchcraft outbreak at Salem. Instead of looking at a small patch of ground in detail, we must pull on the proverbial seven-league boots and seek out trends at work over centuries and across an entire continent. The center of the story will remain the expansion of the United States during the nineteenth century. But it is important to look first at North America when the Atlantic Ocean remained the boundary between European and American cultures. What were some of the features of this precontact era? How did the new frontier affect not only European cultures and ecologies but also those of Native Americans?

SHAPERS OF THE ENVIRONMENT

If modern Americans were somehow able to return to the North America of 1450 and trek across it, they would most likely be struck by the sheer abundance of wildlife. Certainly, the first European colonists remarked on the profusion of birds, beasts, and fish.

Francis Higginson, an early settler of Massachusetts Bay, knew that his friends in England would be skeptical of the reports he was sending. "The aboundance of Sea-Fish are almost beyond beleeving," he noted, "and sure I should scarce have beleeved it except I had seene it with mine owne eyes."

In Virginia, settlers fording streams on horseback sometimes found that the hooves of their mounts killed fish, the rivers were so thick with them. Governor Thomas Dale, in one setting of his seine, hauled in 5,000 sturgeon.

And size! Some of the sturgeon in Governor Dale's nets were twelve feet long, while Virginia crabs ran to a foot in length. A Dutch visitor to Brooklyn reported being treated to a pail of "Gowanes oysters which are the best in the country . . . large and full, some of them not less than a foot long." As for the lobsters coming out of New York Bay, another traveler reported that "those a foot long are better for serving at table." He meant in comparison to the five- and six-footers that were being taken. Such granddaddy lobsters continued to be trapped from time to time through much of the eighteenth century.

As with fish, so with wildfowl. Governor Berkeley of Virginia spoke of massive flocks of ducks, geese, brant, and teal, whose beating wings sounded "like a great storm coming over the water." And the number of passenger pigeons—a bird that had been hunted into extinction by 1914—astounded everyone, including naturalist John James Audubon. In 1813, along the banks of the Ohio River, Audubon watched flocks pass that darkened the sun with their numbers. In "almost solid masses, they darted forward in undulating and angular lines, descended and swept close over the earth with inconceivable velocity, mounted perpendicularly so as to resemble a vast column, and, when high, were seen wheeling and twisting within their continued lines, which then resembled the coils of a gigantic serpent." At night when they arrived at their roosting place, Audubon was waiting, along with hunters who had come with poles to knock them down.

> As the birds . . . passed over me, I felt a current of air that surprised me. . . . The fires were lighted [by the hunters], and a magnificent as well as wonderful and almost terrifying sight presented itself. The pigeons, arriving by thousands, alighted everywhere, one above another, until solid masses, as large as hogsheads, were formed on the branches all round . . . it was a scene of uproar and confusion. I found it quite useless to speak or even to shout to those persons who were nearest to me.

Similar tales were told of mammals. Red and fallow deer congregated along the Virginia coasts in the hundreds. Gray and black squirrels ate so much of the colonists' grain that bounties for squirrels were offered. In Pennsylvania, more than 600,000 squirrels were killed in one year alone. When settlers crossed the Great Plains in the 1840s and 1850s, they were amazed by the villages and even entire "cities" of prairie dogs. In 1905 a scientist from the U.S. Biological Survey reported finding the remnants of a Texas prairie dog colony whose underground passages stretched for nearly 25,000 square miles, an area the size of West Virginia. The colony's estimated population had been 400 million.

Above ground, bison roamed the prairies in herds estimated to number 50 million, and not only on the prairies and plains. Herds had moved east as far as Pennsylvania, Kentucky, and a few even into Virginia along the Potomac

River. Pronghorn antelope may have even outnumbered buffalo. Beaver swelled the streams of eastern forests as well as those of the Rockies, and grizzly bears "were everywhere," reported one mountain man, "upon the plains, in the valleys, and on the mountains, so that I have often killed as many as five or six in one day, and it is not unusual to see fifty or sixty within the twenty-four hours." Another trapper, James Ohio Pattie, claimed to have sighted 220 in one day.

It is possible, then, to assemble a picture of the North American continent as a sort of natural Eden teeming with life. Yet although this picture is accurate in many details, it presents problems. The accounts from which it is drawn were written by a wide variety of people. Some, like Audubon, possessed well-deserved reputations for accuracy; a few, like the scientists from the U.S. Biological Survey, were even conducting systematic research. On the other hand, how seriously are we to take James Ohio Pattie's report of seeing 220 grizzlies in one day? (In ten hours of wandering, 220 grizzlies would mean sighting an average of twenty-two bears every hour, or about one every three minutes.) Was 220 based on an actual count, or was it merely his rough translation for "a hell of a lot more bears than I saw most days"? Even if we believe Pattie, we cannot assume that such densities applied equally throughout the Rockies or even in that particular region at all times. (Grizzlies, for example, are more likely to congregate during mating season than other times of the year.) Individual observations, in other words, must be evaluated as critically in ecology as in history.

There is a second reason for proceeding cautiously. We must be critical not only of data provided by observers but also of ecological theory itself. Ecologists, like historians, need coherent hypotheses to organize their information; and as with historians, theory shapes the way facts are analyzed. In describing the ecological systems of precontact America, it is easy to assume not only that existing plants and animals were abundant but that they lived together in a kind of mutually adjusting, harmonious balance. Indeed, ecologists of the early twentieth century encouraged this notion. The influential Frederic Clements argued that although natural systems went through certain stages of growth, eventually they reached a "climax," or mature phase. At that point, the animals and plants within the system remained in dynamic balance. Under such conditions, stability was the norm.

More recently, ecologists have suggested that this model idealizes too much the notion of stability. Few ecosystems settle into a long-term equilibrium without experiencing disruptions. Such changes ought not to be seen as aberrations but as something to be expected. Even without human intervention, instability is normal. As a case in point, the abundant beaver of the Rockies were subject to cycles of disruption. When populations built up along streams, closer contact allowed disease to spread from one colony to another. At such times epizootics (epidemics in animal populations) wiped out large numbers of beaver. A dry year, too, lowered stream levels, making the spread of disease easier.

Epizootics are only one example of dramatic change. The overabundance of a particular species often altered other parts of the ecosystem. As large herds of buffalo cropped the grasses of the plains too closely, the older vegetation was driven out by faster-growing, hardier weeds. When Lewis and Clark complained that their moccasins were constantly pierced by spikes of the prickly pear cactus along the upper Missouri, they were describing not vegetation that had grown there since time immemorial but relatively new growth that was taking advantage of the conditions of overgrazing.

It would be equally misleading to assume that Native Americans before 1492 harmonized so well with their world that they were a "natural" part of the system's ecology, unlike the white invaders of 1492. The idea that Indians were protoecologists of some sort is only a more sophisticated version of the pioneers' belief that the Indians were "children of nature" and the land still virgin wilderness. In truth, Native Americans were quite active in altering and controlling their environment.

To begin with, horticulture played a crucial role in many Native American cultures. In the Southwest, the Anasazi devised a sophisticated system of dikes and dams to flood their fields, while the Hohokam dug canals, some of them thirty miles long. The peoples east of the Mississippi, whom popular literature tends to portray primarily as hunters, in fact regularly raised "vast quantities of pease, beans, potatoes, cabbages, Indian corn, pumpions [pumpkins], melons" to supply the greater part of their food needs. Both men and women worked to clear fields, plow, sow, and weed. In the early years of the Virginia colony, it was Indian surplus corn that kept the English alive. Even in the plains region, horticulture was important to many tribes.

The most widespread way in which Native Americans altered their environment was through fire. All across the continent, Indians regularly burned large tracts of land. Cabeza de Vaca, the Spanish explorer who crossed much of the Southeast during the 1530s, noted that the Ignaces Indians of Texas went about

> with a firebrand, setting fire to the plains and timber so as to drive off the mosquitoes, and also to get lizards and similar things which they eat, to come out of the soil. In the same manner they kill deer, encircling them with fires, and they do it also to deprive the animals of pasture, compelling them to go for food where the Indians want.

Plains Indians used fires for communication—to report a herd of buffalo or warn of danger—as well as to drive off enemies in war. In California, where grass seeds were an important food, Indians burned fields annually to remove old stocks and increase the yield. In fact, in 1602 the Spanish explorer Vizcaino reported that near San Diego the Indians "made so many columns of smoke on the mainland that at night it looked like a procession and in the daytime the sky was overcast."

Along the Atlantic coast, Indians regularly set fires to keep down the scrub brush. As William Wood observed in New England, fire consumed "all the underwood and rubbish which otherwise would overgrow the country, making it unpassable, and spoil their much affected hunting." The

Fires could spread quickly through parched prairie grass, and in such cases Indians of the plains used fire defensively as well as offensively, as artist Alfred Jacob Miller recorded in this watercolor painted in 1837. The approach of a prairie fire was "insidious enough," Miller noted; "at first a slight haze is seen near the horizon, but the experienced eye of the Trapper or Indian immediately detects the nature of the visitor, and all hands in the camp are immediately busy in setting fire to the long grass about them;—not suffering it to make much headway, but beating it down with cloths & blankets. In this manner large spaces are cleared, horses, mules, and tents are secured in the burnt areas, which are enlarged as time permits, and escape from certain death is thus averted. . . . The fire sweeps round with the speed of a race horse, licking up every thing that it touches with its fiery tongue,—leaving nothing in its train but a blackened heath." (Walters Art Gallery, Baltimore, Maryland)

resulting forest was almost parklike, with large, widely spaced trees, few shrubs, and plenty of succulent grasses. Historian William Cronon has pointed out that such tended forests not merely attracted game but helped create much larger populations of it. Indian burning promoted the increase of exactly those species whose abundance so impressed English colonists: elk, deer, beaver, hare, porcupine, turkey, quail, ruffed grouse, and so on. When these populations increased, so did the carnivorous eagles, hawks, lynxes, foxes, and wolves. In short, Indians who hunted game animals were not just taking the "unplanted bounties of nature"; in an important sense, they were harvesting a foodstuff that they had consciously been instrumental in creating.

Such carefully nurtured abundance did not mean that Native Americans lived free from want in a land of milk and honey. Scarcity was an equally crucial element of their ecology. For abundance was above all seasonal, a fact many enthusiastic European explorers failed to take into account. "When I remember the high commendations some have given of the place," wrote one New Englander, "I have thought the reason thereof to be this, that they wrote surely in strawberry time." Governor Thomas Dale's 5,000 sturgeon were caught in spring or summer, when the fish were running, not during the sluggish days of February. Furthermore, animal populations fluctuated from year to year, and herds of antelope, bison, and caribou migrated along unpredictable routes. To survive, Indians had to take advantage of different seasons of abundance at different locations as well as get through the lean winter. Ecologists summarize these constraints in what is known as Liebig's law: that biological populations are limited not by the total resources available but by the minimum amount of food that can be found during the scarcest times of the year.

Often scarcity led Indians to extract every conceivable benefit from available resources. The buffalo, for example, provided not only meat but also hides for teepees and clothing, sinew for thread and bowstrings, bones for tools, and horns for eating utensils. Even the dung was burned as fuel. On the other hand, a "feast or famine" attitude also developed, encouraging practices of questionable ecological value. Before the coming of horses, Plains Indians most often caught buffalo by stampeding them over cliffs or into rude corrals. Such stampedes could kill many more buffalo than were needed. "Today we passed . . . the remains of a vast many mangled carcases of Buffalow," wrote Lewis in 1804, "which had been driven over a precipice of 120 feet by the Indians & perished; the water appeared to have washed away a part of this immence pile of slaughter and still there remained the fragments of at least a hundred carcases, they created a most horrid stench." More than 120 years earlier, Father Louis Hennepin noted that in times of plenty, Indians "sometimes kill'd forty or fifty [buffalo], but took only the Tongues, and some other of the best Pieces."

From the Indian point of view, some of these practices were quite defensible. While a successful hunt might lead to much waste, success itself was never certain. A herd might easily flee if it scented its pursuers. On other occasions, only a small number of animals might be killed while the rest broke through the ranks of Indian herders. Yet for all that, Indians ought not to be portrayed merely as the spiritual forerunners of today's environmentalists. They had developed many ways of controlling and altering their surroundings—some remarkably ingenious in terms of husbanding resources, others relatively wasteful.

THE QUESTION OF NUMBERS

The frontier, then, was not merely a buffer zone between settled white regions and untouched wilderness. Indians actively shaped the land in which they lived. But a more vexing question remains: How many Native

Americans were living in the land when white Europeans first came into it? The image of an untamed wilderness encourages the notion that the Indians of North America were relatively few, scattered in small villages and separated by miles of dense forest or empty, rolling plains.

Unfortunately, the question of population in the precontact era is immensely difficult. Hundreds of separate cultures spread across North America with no census to enumerate them. Farther south, the Aztecs were known to have kept detailed records of taxation and population, but the vast majority of these records were destroyed by the Spanish. How can historians even begin to calculate a precontact population?

One common method has been to collect, adjust, and average available estimates from early white explorers and settlers. By proceeding across the continent, region by region and tribe by tribe, numbers can be assembled to provide an approximate total. During the early years of the twentieth century, anthropologist James Mooney did precisely that. His estimates, published in 1928, proposed a precontact North American population of approximately 1.1 million. Because Mooney was a respected researcher (and no one before had attempted so systematic an enumeration), his estimate was widely accepted and frequently cited in textbooks and other surveys. A decade later, another well-known anthropologist, Alfred Kroeber, reduced the estimate to 1 million or less. (Mooney's figures were "probably mostly too high rather than too low," Kroeber asserted.)

But if we examine Mooney's original computations (his notes have been preserved at the Smithsonian Institution), a disquieting pattern emerges. Mooney died before he could actually publish his work. For unstated reasons, the editor who published his final figures often reduced these numbers by 5 or 10 percent. In addition, Mooney's notes show that his numbers were not necessarily what he believed to be the true precontact population, but merely a bedrock minimum upon which even the most conservative scholars could agree. In many cases, his preliminary notes show even larger totals, which he cautiously reduced for the final tally.

For example, in 1674, Daniel Gookin, a missionary, tried to calculate the precontact population of New England. To do so, he asked Indian elders to estimate the number of adult males each tribe could have marshaled for a war in the years before whites arrived. When combined, the elders' estimates came to a total of 18,000. Assuming that for every able-bodied male there might be three or four additional women, children, and old men, Gookin estimated a total population anywhere from 72,000 to 90,000. His number was noted by a nineteenth-century historian, John Palfrey, but Palfrey lowered it to about 50,000, for reasons he never stated. Mooney took that figure and conservatively cut it to "about 25,000 or about one-half what the historian Palfrey makes it." Similar reductions were repeated elsewhere in Mooney's notes.

Of course, even a quick look at such calculations shows how difficult it is to arrive at reliable figures. For the Narraganset tribe, the minister Edward Johnson's estimate of 30,000 warriors was six times higher than Gookin's claim of 5,000. Mooney laughed off Johnson's number as ridiculously high and also rejected Gookin's ("his usual exaggeration"), choosing rather to accept a figure of 1,000 warriors, which was Gookin's estimate of the adult male population in his own day, half a century after whites had arrived in New England. Mooney did not explain his reasoning, but we might guess that he decided Gookin's information about his own times was more accurate than numbers supplied by elderly chiefs about bygone days when their tribes were supposed to have been much more powerful.

Perhaps these suppositions are valid. But when such imprecise calculations become a part of the "judgment" involved in adjusting estimates, there is room for unstated assumptions to influence the results. Why was it that Mooney, Kroeber, and older historians like Palfrey always tended to reduce estimates rather than increase them? Could it have been partly because they viewed Indian societies as primitive and therefore unable to support such relatively large populations? Palfrey certainly made no attempt to hide his disdain for Indian culture. "These people held a low place on the scale of humanity," he wrote:

> Even their physical capacities contradicted the promise of their external conformation. Supple and agile, so that it was said they would run eighty or a hundred miles in a day, and back again in the next two, they sank under continuous labor. The lymphatic temperament indicated the same preponderance in them of "vegetative nature" which marked other animals of the same continent.

Alfred Kroeber, who reduced Mooney's calculations even further, shunned the racism evident in Palfrey's remarks. Nevertheless, Kroeber hesitated to accept the high population estimates of many sixteenth- and seventeenth-century observers. Indian societies in general, he explained, were characterized by "insane, unending, continuously attritional" warfare, which would prevent tribes from becoming too large. Kroeber admitted that Indians along the eastern lands of North America grew crops and that the practice of agriculture in Europe and Asia had led to larger populations. But the Indians along the Atlantic were agricultural hunters," not really "farmers," he argued.

> Every man, or his wife, grew food for his household. The population remaining stationary, excess planting was not practiced, nor would it have led to anything in the way of economic or social benefit nor of increase of numbers. Ninety-nine per cent or more of what might have been developed remained virgin.

"The population remaining stationary": Here Kroeber's argument was circular—for of course he possessed no hard information about whether the population was expanding or decreasing. It must have remained stationary, he assumed, because Indians lacked the skills to expand. Therefore no one planted extra food, because it wouldn't be of any use. But we have already seen that in early Virginia, the Indians did plant enough corn to amass surpluses. More than once they gave or sold it to the fledgling Virginia colony, which sorely needed it to stave off starvation. Kroeber simply ignored evidence that did not fit his assumptions.

Indeed, more recent historians have criticized the readiness of many to explain away the large estimates of contemporary observers. The Spanish "found sparse settlements of barbarians," asserted one Scottish observer during the eighteenth century. But "in their surprise at seeing even modest structures, they turned [these sparse settlements] into populous civilized realms with great stone temples and palaces." Early twentieth-century scholars discounted Spanish estimates of 40 to 60 million Indians in Central and South America, suggesting that "all parties were equally interested in exaggerating the flourishing state of the recently discovered nations." Another scholar approvingly quoted an old truism: "To count is a modern practice; the ancient method was to guess; and when numbers are guessed they are always magnified." But those who proposed such hypotheses did not offer any concrete evidence of exaggeration.

By the mid-1970s, many anthropologists had come to believe that conservative population estimates were seriously flawed. In arriving at new ones, especially in Mexico and Spanish California, they developed a number of useful techniques. One, known as *projection*, focused on the detailed study of a smaller region, where population could be determined more accurately. Having established a density for that limited area, anthropologists could project the result over larger regions, making allowances for varying conditions, climates, and patterns of settlement. Anthropologists also used the technique of *cross-checking* to compare the results of different methods of calculation. For example, some Spanish churches recorded the number of Indian children brought to be baptized during their "age of innocence"—that is, age four or younger. By drawing on population studies to determine what percentage of Indians would have been four or under (perhaps 10 percent), it became possible to calculate a rough total population. At the same time, the records sometimes supplied a conquistador's estimate of warriors from the same village. Using the kind of technique we saw applied to Daniel Gookin's figures, a second population estimate could be derived. In addition, if archaeological studies have revealed the number of houses in a particular village, a third calculation might be made. By a cross-check of these different estimates, it is possible to see whether the results reinforce each other, which improves reliability.

By the 1960s and 1970s, enough studies had been done to suggest that older estimates of precontact population were markedly low. Earlier figures had set total population in North and South America at no more than 8 to 14 million; more recent studies suggest anywhere from 57 to 112 million, 5 to 10 million of whom lived north of Mexico. Such figures undermine the stereotype of precontact America as virgin, untamed wilderness. If these figures are correct, when Columbus landed in 1492 on Hispaniola, that island alone was inhabited by as many as 7 or 8 million people, compared with about 6 to 10 million for all of Spain, an area seven times as large. (England's population at the time was only about 5 million.) The Aztec capital of Tenochtitlán, estimated to have held anywhere from 165,000 to 250,000 inhabitants, was larger than the greatest European cities of the day: Constantinople, Naples, Venice, Milan, and Paris. In fact, more people may have been living in the Americas in 1492 than in western Europe.

THE MIGRATION OF MICROBES

It would be natural to expect that figures compiled from existing records might be somewhat inaccurate. But why were such estimates as much as ten times too low? Some hint of the answer can be found in the classic story of the Pilgrims, who arrived in December 1620 on the shores of Cape Cod unsure of how they would survive in a "hideous and desolate wilderness." As they began to explore what they feared would be wild forest, they discovered instead many acres of open fields, ready for crops to be planted. Obviously, the lands had been cleared by Indians, but none were now living there.

What had happened? The Pilgrims learned that not many years earlier, an epidemic had devastated the population, causing the villages in the area to be abandoned. The epidemic, most likely chicken pox, had been brought by fishermen to American shores around 1616 and then raged for three years from Maine to Cape Cod. Devoutly, the Pilgrims thanked God for "sweeping away great multitudes of natives . . . that he might make room for us there."

Even before the Pilgrims had settled down, in other words, Native Americans had been decimated by diseases brought from Europe. Before 1492, Native Americans had never been exposed to smallpox, measles, malaria, or yellow fever. When their ancestors came to America, tens of thousands of years earlier, the process of migration cut them off from the major disease pools of the world. In order to survive, disease-carrying microorganisms need a host population large and dense enough to prevent the disease from gradually running out of new victims. Thus, large cities or any large groups of people (armies, schools) are prime disease pools. The pools need not be human: domestic animals such as cattle and horses are often hosts for infections that periodically spread to their caretakers.

But the first hunters who made their way over the Asian land bridge to America migrated in sparsely populated bands. They did not bring herds of domestic animals, and the cold climates through which they passed served as a barrier to many disease-carrying microorganisms. As a result, Indians were not subjected to cycles of epidemics like those that drastically reduced populations in Europe and Asia. Not that disease was unknown. Chemical analysis of bone samples by physical anthropologists indicates that Indian civilizations with higher population densities experienced significant increases in mortality from tuberculosis and treponemal disease (bacterial infections, including syphilis). The spread of agricultural societies that depended heavily on a diet of corn may also have led to nutritional deficiencies—deficiencies that were magnified with the coming of Europeans after 1492.

Because European and Asian populations were periodically reexposed to diseases like smallpox, a significant portion developed immunities. For some diseases, such as measles, protection was acquired during childhood (when the body is constitutionally better able to build immunity). By the sixteenth century, much of Europe's adult population was protected when outbreaks periodically reappeared. For virgin populations, however, such diseases were deadly. The Indian villages near the Pilgrim settlements had experienced mortality rates as high as 95 percent, and the first European colonists were often astonished to find pile after pile of unburied bones, picked clean by the wolves and bleached by the sun. Similar epidemics struck down Native Americans along the Great Lakes, where French trappers and priests penetrated, while in the southern colonies, smallpox "destroy'd whole Towns, without leaving one *Indian* alive in the Village." Farther south, Cortés was able to conquer the mighty Aztec empire in large part because smallpox ravaged the capital of Tenochtitlán. When the Spanish finally entered the conquered city, "the streets, squares, houses, and courts were filled with bodies, so that it was almost impossible to pass. Even Cortés was sick from the stench in his nostrils."

Anthropologists like Mooney had certainly been aware of the diseases that afflicted Indians. But they had not calculated in any detail how severely such epidemics might have affected total populations. More recently, researchers have attempted to establish depopulation ratios in order to project population trends backward over time. If the records from a region provide two population estimates a number of years apart, a ratio of depopulation can be established. For example, Spanish tax records might indicate that in some villages the Indian population dropped by 50 percent over forty years. Using that ratio, it is possible to project earlier populations for regions that have figures only for the later period. Cross-checking this technique with others, historians have concluded that the population of Mexico dropped from perhaps 25 million in 1500 to only 3 million in 1568—a mortality rate of 88 percent in only two-thirds of a century.

Textbooks have finally begun to take note of these large-scale epidemics, but the focus has centered largely on the depopulation of the sixteenth and seventeenth centuries. Yet as the frontiers of white settlement continued to move across the continent, so did the invisible pioneers. During the eighteenth century, smallpox epidemics broke out in the Northeast as well as the Southwest; along the California coast as well as up and down the Mississippi Valley. During the nineteenth century, as fur traders and pioneers began pushing across the Great Plains and through the Rockies, no less than twenty-seven epidemics decimated the continent: thirteen of smallpox, five of measles, three of cholera, two of influenza and one each of diphtheria, scarlet fever, tularemia, and malaria. These numbers were greater than those recorded for any previous century of contact.

We can perhaps sense the magnitude of the disaster by following the course of only one epidemic. In 1837 the American Fur Company steamer the *St. Peter* left St. Louis carrying supplies and passengers for the trading posts along the upper Missouri. When the boat stopped near Fort Clark on June 18, all seemed well. But by a week later, when it pulled into Fort Union, at least one person on board had broken out with smallpox. The traders, well aware of the disease's effect, tried to protect the Indians at the fort by inoculating them with smallpox pus.[1] Unfortunately, the attempt miscarried and most of the Indians died. At the same time, a band of forty Indians arrived at the fort, eager to barter. The trader in charge refused to admit them, but they kept pounding at the gate, until finally he opened it briefly to exhibit a boy whose face was covered with a mass of smallpox scabs. The Indians retreated, but they took the disease with them. More than half the party died.

Traders tried to keep smallpox from Fort McKenzie, the next stop upstream, by unloading their cargo halfway and sending word to the fort not to come for it until the risk of catching the disease had passed. But the Indians, eager for goods and suspicious of white motives, pressed the chief trader to bring the boat up, and again the epidemic spread.

The map on page 110 shows the depressing progress of the disease. Near Fort Clark, smallpox appeared among the Mandan a month after the *St. Peter* passed through. From there it spread to the Arikara during the summer and to the Sioux by October. The Assiniboin picked up the disease, probably from Fort Union, and soon after, the Crow got it. The Gros Ventres were infected by December. Because the disease often spread far from white posts, its route was not always easy to trace; but by 1838 it had apparently crossed the Rockies to the Cayuse, who blamed missionary Marcus Whitman and attacked his settlement. In 1838 it also moved south, reaching the Pawnee by way of several Sioux prisoners taken that spring. From the Pawnee it spread to the Osage and thence to the Kiowa and other Texas tribes, killing many Apache and Comanche. Moving west into New Mexico, it reached Santa Fe, and from there white traders carried it full circle, back to the frontiers of the United States.

Loss of life ran anywhere from 50 to 95 percent of the populations affected. But horrifying as these numbers are, they fail to tell the whole tale. At stake were not only lives but the viability of entire cultures. The dislocations caused by disease were economic, social, and spiritual.

Economically, many Indian peoples could not carry out even their basic day-to-day work. In part, this was because the epidemics proved most deadly to those between the ages of fifteen and forty. (Scientists are still not sure why, in unexposed populations, this age group seems to be the hardest hit.) Healthy, in the prime of life, these victims were precisely those members of the community who contributed the most economically, as hunters, farmers, or food gatherers. Furthermore, the survivors of an epidemic often fled in terror from their traditional homelands. Resettling, they were obligated to discover anew the best hunting spots, places to gather nuts or berries, or sites with rich soils.

---

1. The technique of variolation, or transferring pus from a smallpox victim to a healthy subject, was often used before vaccination with cowpox became common. Although riskier, variolation often reduced mortality rates significantly.

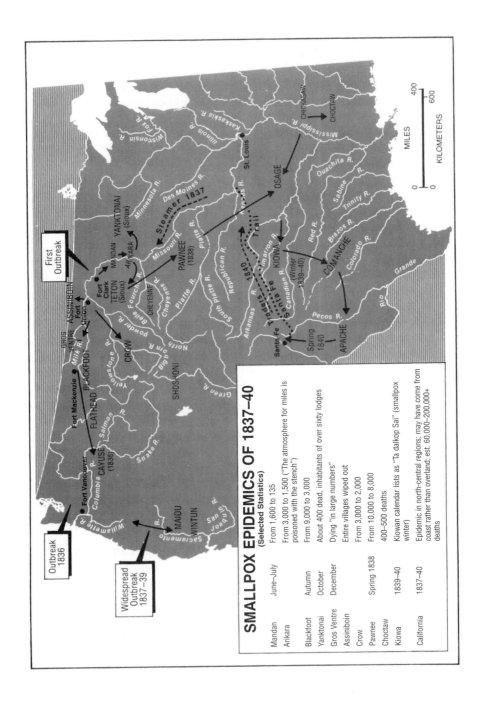

SMALLPOX EPIDEMICS OF 1837–40
(Selected Statistics)

Mandan	June–July	From 1,600 to 135
Arikara		From 3,000 to 1,500 ("The atmosphere for miles is poisoned with the stench")
Blackfoot	Autumn	From 9,000 to 3,000
Yanktonai	October	About 400 dead, inhabitants of over sixty lodges
Gros Ventre	December	Dying "in large numbers"
Assiniboin		Entire villages wiped out
Crow		From 3,000 to 2,000
Pawnee	Spring 1838	From 10,000 to 8,000
Choctaw		400–500 deaths
Kiowa	1839–40	Kiowan calendar lists as "Ta dalkop Sai" (smallpox winter)
California	1837–40	Epidemic in north-central regions; may have come from coast rather than overland; est. 60,000–200,000+ deaths

Socially, the disruptions were equally severe. Because male warriors were among those hit hardest, hostile neighbors, either white or Indian, were more difficult to resist. The plague-stricken Indians of New England had "their courage much abated," reported one colonist; "their countenance is dejected, and they seem as a people affrighted." Near Charleston, South Carolina, an Indian told a settler they had "forgotten most of their traditions since the Establishment of this Colony, they keep their Festivals and can tell but little of the reasons: their Old Men are dead." Farther west, Lewis and Clark traveled up the Missouri only a few years after the smallpox epidemic of 1801–1802. Clark reported that the remnant of the Omaha nation, "haveing no houses no Corn or anything more than the graves of their ansesters to attach them to the old Village," led a much more nomadic existence. "I am told when this fatal malady [smallpox] was among them they Carried their franzey to verry extraordinary length, not only of burning their Village, but they put their wives and children to *Death* with a view of their all going together to some better Countrey."

Even when despair did not lead to suicide, Native Americans were severely challenged by what seemed to be the Europeans' superior gods. Both Indians and whites read supernatural meaning into the epidemics, attributing such outbreaks to divine anger. Yet because the new diseases singled out nonimmune Native Americans and spared Europeans, both peoples tended to credit the superiority of the European deity. When Francis Drake's sailors brought illness to Florida in 1585, "the wilde people . . . died verie fast and said amongst themselves, it was the Inglisshe God that made them die so fast." More cynical whites were not above capitalizing on this dread. In 1812 James McDougall warned the Chinook Indians of the Columbia River not to carry out an attack against the whites:

> You imagine that because we are few you can easily kill us, but it is not so; or if you do you will only bring the greater evils upon yourselves. The medicine of the white man dead is mightier than that of the red man living. . . . You know the smallpox. Listen: I am the smallpox chief. In this bottle I have it confined. All I have to do is to pull the cork, send it forth among you, and you are dead men. But this is for my enemies and not for my friends.

Given that disease did strike Indians more severely than whites, it is no wonder many believed such exhortations. In any case, the result was to severely strain Native Americans' traditional beliefs.

COMPETING ECOLOGICAL SYSTEMS

Undoubtedly, the spread of European microorganisms had an immense effect on the cultural balances of North America. But other ecological pioneers played important roles. Colonists imported plants and animals that were new to America, and the ways settlers made use of them differed markedly from the way Native Americans used their own natural resources.

In large part, the Old World meeting the New became a clash between competing ecological systems. In the ensuing struggle, the European ecologies often prevailed.

Many of the European plants that came to America spread for the same reasons European diseases did. More than a few American plants, having been relatively isolated from competition for thousands of years, yielded quickly to hardier European stocks. Some plants spread so widely that today they are commonly taken to be native. "Kentucky" blue grass originated in Europe. So did the dandelion, the daisy, white clover, ragweed, and plantain. (The last was called "the Englishman's foot" by New England Indians, for it seemed to sprout wherever the new settlers wandered.)

Many of these plants were introduced purely by accident. Seeds might arrive in chests of folded clothes or in clods of mud or dung. But settlers also deliberately imported many plants. On the Oregon trail, several overlanders made a business of carrying trees and fruits across the country. The most successful was an Iowa Quaker, Henderson Welling, who in 1847 hauled 700 trees, vines, and shrubs in his wagons, including such varieties as apple, cherry, pear, plum, black walnut, and quince. His imports helped launch a multi-million-dollar orchard business in California and Oregon.[2]

As for the animal frontier, we have already seen that the horse outran Europeans in crossing the continent. Most Indian peoples took to the horse rapidly; in performance they soon outstripped the Spaniards, who were a horse-loving people to begin with. Male Plains Indians learned to ride bareback, controlling their mounts with a gentle pressure of the knees instead of using reins. This ability left a rider's hands free to use a bow and arrow. A good hunter-warrior could travel at full gallop, drop to one side of his pony for cover, and launch a continuous stream of arrows with such force that a shaft might bury itself entirely in a buffalo. The Comanche men were such accomplished riders that a unit of the U.S. Cavalry was in one contest disgusted to find its finest Kentucky mare beaten by a "miserable sheep of a pony" upon which a Comanche rider was mounted backward, so he could mockingly wave (with "hideous grimaces") for his American rival to "come on a little faster!"

Above all, horses gave those Indians who possessed them immensely greater mobility. Previously, all hunting was done on foot by male members of the tribe; mounted, they searched out the buffalo with comparative ease. In addition, mounted nations were able to drive rivals from long-held territories. By 1826, according to an early fur trader, the Klamath Indians along

---

2. Limitations of space make it impossible to discuss an equally important topic, the migration of American flora and fauna to Europe. Perhaps the most influential Native American contributions to world civilization were agricultural products. Maize corn, unknown in Europe, had been developed by Indians over thousands of years from ears that were originally the size of a finger. The tomato, now so closely linked with Italian cuisine, was an American product; so too was the potato, before it ever reached Ireland. These imports may have contributed significantly to the rise of population in Europe, which began an upward trend in the sixteenth century.

the California-Oregon border had been raided so often by their well-mounted enemies that one village was forced in desperation to relocate on land surrounded by marsh and water, "approachable only by canoes."

While the supply of horses diffused toward the north and east, another frontier—that of guns—moved in the opposite direction, west and south. The Spanish possessed firearms, but their laws forbade selling any to Indians. English and French fur traders of the Northeast, however, operated under no such restraints. The gun and horse frontiers met along the upper Missouri during the first half of the eighteenth century and, in crossing, touched off an extremely unsettled period for Indians of the West. In the late 1700s, the Cree, Assiniboin, and Ojibwa, with their guns, forced the Teton Sioux, Cheyenne, Arapaho, and Crow south across the Missouri River. Agricultural peoples, such as the Mandan and Arikara, found themselves more frequently attacked, while tribes that were originally nomadic became even more so.

Women of nomadic tribes were also affected by the coming of the horse. With mounts available as beasts of burden, women were required to do much less hauling when camps were moved. In some tribes, women were even allowed to own their own horses. Homes, too, became more spacious: in "dog days," teepees had been constructed of five or six skins, small enough to be carried on the dog travois. With horses to carry them, the teepees grew to fifteen or twenty skins. A fur trader in 1805 summed the situation up by noting that while Crow women did "most of the work," they were "not so wretchedly situated as those nations who live in the forests. . . . [and] are indebted solely to their having horses for the ease they enjoy more than their neighbors." Older people may well have benefited too, for nomadic tribes sometimes abandoned or killed those who were too feeble to travel. With horses to carry the infirm, such practices seem to have lessened.

While the horse changed the lives of Plains Indians, it did not radically alter their cultures. It was as "an intensifier of original Plains traits" that the horse presented its strongest claim, noted anthropologist Clark Wissler. The situation was far different once whites themselves reached Native American lands. Their coming set in motion a train of events that fundamentally changed the relationships between the land and the Indians who used it.

Underlying this change was the apparently simple fact that, from the very first, European explorers came to America in search of resources that were scarce in Europe. Invariably, they returned home praising the many precious "commodities" that were available. Spain reaped vast profits from the gold and silver of Central and South America, and the French and English hoped to follow suit. In the end, though, they discovered that the most easily extractable commodities of North America were the animals of the forest: beaver, fox, marten, muskrat, otter.

Native Americans had hunted such animals time out of mind; Europeans merely encouraged them to trap a larger surplus. But the act of creating this surplus, and then linking it to a worldwide economy, meant that trading took on a different aspect for Indians. As William Cronon has pointed out, the fur trade was

While Indian men often road bareback, women such as this Sioux used a saddle with high ends fore and aft to keep from being pitched off. Decorations include brightly colored cloth bordered by porcupine quills and beads. Even the horse has pendants dangling from his ears! Wrote Miller, "To have a good horse and full equipment is the realization of heaven on earth to an Indian girl, never having heard of the Poet's 'Beauty unadorned,' she goes to the other extreme, and piles it on as thick as possible, in the way of ornament; and what with hawk's bells innumerable, and tags of tin fastened to her fringes, the movements of her horse create abundance of noise as she gallops over the prairie." (Walters Art Gallery, Baltimore, Maryland)

far more complicated than a simple exchange of European metal goods for Indian beaver skins. . . . Trade linked these groups with an abstract set of equivalent values measured in pelts, bushels of corn, fathoms of wampum, and price movements in sterling on London markets. The essential lesson for the Indians was that certain things began to have prices that had not had them before. In particular, one could buy personal prestige by killing animals and exchanging their skins for wampum or high-status European goods.

Even by the 1640s, the demand for furs had depleted beaver near the New England coast. By the end of the century, most of the region's streams and forests were trapped out. And the pattern repeated itself as the frontier moved westward. Lewis and Clark's Rocky Mountains, which in 1804 were "richer in beaver and otter than any country on earth," by 1840 were so poor, according to one trapper, "that one would stand a right good chance of starving, if he were obliged to hang up here for seven days. The game is all driven out."

The pressure on resources became even keener once pioneers began to cross the plains. The case of timber provides a good example. Wood is a resource not usually associated with the vast plains and open prairies. Yet precisely because trees were scarce, they played an important part in Indian ecology. Cottonwood, clustered along the richer bottomlands of plains rivers, offered crucial protection during winter blizzards as well as concealment of a village's smoke from its enemies. In lean seasons, horses fed on its bark, which was surprisingly nourishing. And along rivers during spring breakup, men, women, and children could be seen leaping onto the ice floes as they swirled downstream, tying cords to floating deadwood and hauling it ashore. Timber was worth taking big risks to obtain.

The overland migrations of the 1840s and 1850s created severe wood shortages in many areas along the trails. Although most settlers were only passing through, fully a quarter of a million whites made the trip before the Civil War, and the pressure of such numbers soon showed itself. "The road, from morning till night, is crowded like Pearl Street or Broadway," wrote a traveler in 1850. It was not uncommon for several thousand people to pass Fort Laramie in a single day. Such hordes inevitably destroyed many of the best timber stands. "By the Mormon guide we here expected to find the last timber," wrote A. W. Harlan, along the Platte, "but all had been used up by others ahead of us so we must go about 200 miles without any provisions cooked up."

Faced by this procession of wagon trains, many Indian nations responded by demanding payment, usually in provisions, for the privilege of passing through their homelands. Some bands even erected bridges and attempted to collect tolls at strategic stream crossings. In either case, they made it clear that they regarded such fees as compensation for the use of their lands, for the rights to timber, grazing, and the animals shot in their hunting territories. Some emigrants grudgingly paid the fees, but others took matters into their own hands. "When we got to the bridge there was a lot of Indians standing there," wrote one overlander, "and my Partner made a motion to the right & Left but the Indians did not move he made a dive for the nearest one and with his fist knocked him spralling and with his left fist sent another one down and he had 3 of them down in half the time I have been writing it. . . . the[y] got out of the way and we had no further trouble."

The loss of timber or grazing areas was bad enough, but Native Americans had an even more serious complaint—that "the buffalo are wantonly killed and scared off," as one white observer noted, "which renders their only means of subsistence every year more precarious." This complaint was especially grave not only because the bison, like the beaver, became an important commodity in the trading economy but also because white settlers were replacing such wildlife with their own livestock. A large part of Indian life revolved around the hunting of wild creatures: deer, moose, buffalo, antelope. Over time, the land occupied by these animals came to be seen by whites as desirable for cattle, sheep, or pigs. The resulting competition for grazing lands spelled the death knell for Native American ways. Next to the

The flood of wagon trains onto the plains was often wider than the procession in this photograph. Aerial photographs of old wagon routes show them spreading as much as thirty times wider than modern paved roads nearby. It was not so much the people as the animals that came with them—oxen, mules, horses, cattle, sheep—that damaged the plains environment. In 1853 there were about eleven animals for every human along the Platte River route. (©The New York Historical Society)

invisible pioneers of disease, the "emigrants" that most threatened Indian cultures were European domestic animals.

In the precontact era, Native Americans had only a few domesticated animals—in North America, primarily the dog. Wild animals, on the other hand, were viewed as property only after they had been killed. This attitude differed from the European notion that a person might raise and own animals as a source of food. Even if such stock was allowed to roam free, it was still owned by individuals, as the brand on a cow's flank or the cut on a sheep's ear signified. Domestic animals like oxen also allowed Europeans to use plows on a widespread scale, which meant more fields could be cultivated and their surpluses sold in an expanding capitalist economy. All these customs—central to the way Europeans managed their resources—were foreign to Native Americans.

In Mexico, agriculture played a crucial role in feeding large native populations. There, the Spanish ranchers who turned corn and bean fields into grazing lands upset a pivotal Indian resource. The first viceroy of New Spain, Antonio de Mendoza, recognized the problem and wrote the king, warning "May your Lordship realize that if cattle are allowed, the Indians will be destroyed." Spanish pigs also spread quickly, as both domestic animals and wild. To cite only one example, Hernando DeSoto brought 13 pigs to Florida in 1539; these pigs multiplied in only three years to more than 700.

On the Great Plains, domestic cattle and sheep replaced bison and antelope, just as cattle, swine, and sheep had replaced deer in the East. Although the cowboy came into his own only after the Civil War, livestock drives were common along the overland trails in the 1850s. Perhaps a half million cattle and another half million sheep made the trek. At first, such drives did not destroy the traditional plains ecology. In California, early ranching even seemed to help some wildlife temporarily, like the grizzly, who gorged on the corpses of stock skinned for their hides. Sheep, too, fell as easy prey to coyotes. But hunting pressure on the bison steadily increased. In the 1850s a traveler was already writing that "the valley of the Platte for 200 miles presents the aspect of the vicinity of a slaughter yard; dotted all over with skeletons of buffalos." By the 1860s wagon trains could no longer count on hunting food on the way across; grocery stores had sprung up instead.

But pressure on the bison herds came not only from white emigrants. As European settlement pressed westward toward the open prairies and plains, Indians were either driven or moved out onto the plains ahead of white settlement. Historians estimate that the Indian population of central plains grew from perhaps 8,000 Indians in 1820 to as many as 20,000 in the 1850s, despite the periodic toll of epidemic disease. For a time, increased competition for hunting grounds actually helped protect the bison. The contested borderlands between rival tribes served in effect as refuges, since hunting could be conducted only sporadically in these buffer zones. But after 1840 Indian diplomacy brought relative peace to the plains. Under such conditions hunting pressures mounted, with Indian hunters especially setting their sights on two- to five-year-old bison cows for their tender meat and their thinner, more easily processed hides. Because these cows were the most fertile members of the herd, their deaths sharply reduced the number of new births.

Once the transcontinental railroad was completed, the slaughter of the herds accelerated. "Buffalo Bill" Cody gained prominence as a hunter for the train crews of the Kansas Pacific. Sportsmen riding the rails took potshots from the passing cars or, seeking better yields, tracked down the big herds and opened fire with such abandon that their gun barrels overheated after a time. A single hunter could kill more than a hundred animals in an hour. By the early 1870s the demand for buffalo robes had risen sharply in the East,

As the Indian population of the Great Plains increased sharply in the three decades after 1820, natural resources were stretched by Indians as well as white newcomers. A Cheyenne encampment like this one held forty or so people who needed to be fed. But equally important, the tribe required pasturage for the several hundred horses who were a part of the camp. The crucial time for survival came not during the summer months, when most white wagon trains passed through, but in winter. Then, Indians flocked to sheltered river valleys like those of the South Platte River. In 1848 one white traveler there encountered a string of Lakota and Cheyenne villages with thousands of horses strung out for nearly eighty miles. (Denver Public Library, Western History Department, Colorado)

so commercial companies hauled out perhaps as many as 10 million hides. A decade later the herds were nearly gone, their lands being swiftly occupied by cattle, sheep, cowpunchers, and sodbusters.

America had been transformed. The land of 1890 was vastly different from the precontact world of 1490, in large part because of the series of ecological frontiers that had crossed the continent. Beyond doubt, the most important was the frontier of disease, which provided Europeans with nothing less than the opportunity to remake the Americas in their own image. Today, having lived so long with the outcome, we tend to take the results as a foregone conclusion. We assume that European success in America was due to superior technology and efficient social and economic organization. No doubt these elements played a role. But during the same era Spain, England, France, and Portugal were also expanding eastward with markedly different results. In China and India, where diseases did not decimate the local populations, Asian cultural and political traditions remained strong, regardless of "superior" European technology. European merchants and settlers were confined to trading stations and coastal enclaves. Even where Western elites came to rule a country, as the British did in India, they remained only the upper stratum of a colonial system. In the twentieth century, when nationalist movements ejected the colonial powers, Asian cultures played a renewed and revitalized role.

But in the Americas? The Aztecs and Incas had complex civilizations and, if they had not been decimated by disease, they too might have kept the Spanish pinned down along the coast. Farther north, the English found it difficult enough as it was to establish colonies. They might have been even less successful if the full complement of Native Americans had survived to resist them. But with 50 to 90 percent of the population wiped out within a century, not only peoples but cultures suffered. And hard upon the heels of disease came a host of other European "pioneers"—horses, pigs, and cattle—led by masters who employed these new beasts to organize society in foreign ways.

Even after the frontier passed into history, ecological constraints continued to influence American development. Newcomers to the plains soon found that natural limits forced them to change their ways. Barbed wire and sod huts replaced the wood traditionally used for fences and homes. Dry farming techniques were needed to make the land yield adequate harvests. Windmills used the ample resource of the wind to secure the much scarcer resource of water. But these stories belong to a later era; even in this chapter, seven-league boots have their limits. What remains clear is that, on both sides of the frontier, American history has been shaped and altered by ecological factors that historians have too often lightly passed over.

➣ ➣ ➣ ADDITIONAL READING ⬿ ⬿ ⬿

The subject of this chapter (not to mention its chronological span) is so vast that we can only make the briefest attempt at a bibliography. Almost every topic discussed—the effect of the horse on Native American cultures, of human-caused fires on the environment, of epidemic disease on native populations—has produced a sizable literature.

For an introduction to ecology, especially as it relates to history, see John W. Bennett, *The Ecological Transition: Cultural Anthropology and Human Adaptation* (New York, 1976). William L. Thomas, ed., *Man's Role in Changing the Face of the Earth* (Chicago, 1956) is a wide-ranging collection of papers, including some on the Indians' use of fire and the effect of domestic livestock on the grasslands of the plains. For information on the history of ecology, see Donald Worster, *Nature's Economy* (San Francisco, 1977) and Ronald C. Tobey, *Saving the Prairies: The Life Cycle of the Founding School of American Plant Ecology, 1895–1955* (Berkeley, Calif., 1981). Alfred W. Crosby Jr. provides excellent overviews of ecological frontiers in *The Columbian Exchange:*

Biological and Cultural Consequences of 1492 (Westport, Conn., 1972) and *Ecological Imperialism: The Biological Expansion of Europe, 900–1900* (Cambridge, 1986). For a model of how ecology and history may be united in the study of one region, it would be hard to surpass William Cronon's *Changes in the Land: Indians, Colonists, and the Ecology of New England* (New York, 1983), a work that has been most helpful to us.

The abundance of flora and fauna of precontact North America may be inferred from the descriptions left by early white visitors. Among many travelers' accounts worth consulting, Peter Kalm's *Travels in North America* (New York, 1964) provides material for the mid-eighteenth century. For the early nineteenth century, Lewis and Clark's journals, available in a number of editions, are informative, as is Paul Cutright's *Lewis and Clark: Pioneering Naturalists* (Urbana, Ill., 1969).

For an introduction to the difficulties of estimating precontact populations, see Russell Thornton, *American Indian Holocaust and Survival: A Population History since 1492* (Norman, Okla., 1987). The move toward sharply higher estimates received impetus from Henry F. Dobyns, "Estimating Aboriginal Population: An Appraisal of Techniques with a New Hemispheric Estimate," *Current Anthropology* 7 (1966): 395–416. Dobyns raised his earlier estimate of 10 million Indians in precontact North America to 18 million in *Their Number Become Thinned: Native American Population Dynamics in Eastern North America* (Knoxville, Tenn., 1983), but scholars have been much more wary of these calculations. The most sophisticated treatment of the effect of epidemics on precontact populations is John W. Verano and Douglas H. Ubelaker, eds., *Disease and Demography in the Americas* (Washington, D.C., 1992). Francis Jennings explores some of the racist assumptions underlying earlier population estimates in *The Invasion of America* (Chapel Hill, N.C., 1975). For a survey of other hemispheric studies, see William M. Denevan, ed., *The Native Population of the Americas in 1492* (Madison, Wis., 1976), which includes a discussion of James Mooney's estimates.

William McNeill's superb *Plagues and Peoples* (Garden City, N.Y., 1976) is the starting point for understanding the effects of disease in history. Alfred Crosby discusses "Virgin Soil Epidemics as a Factor in the Aboriginal Depopulation in America" in *William and Mary Quarterly* 33 (April 1976): 289–99. For a sense of how archaeological evidence may be used to substantiate depopulation estimates, see the papers in Verano and Ubelaker. One essay by Michael K. Trimble reviews the 1837 smallpox epidemic on the upper Missouri (pp. 257–64). For a discussion of smallpox, see E. Wagner Stearn and Allen E. Stearn, *The Effect of Smallpox on the Destiny of the Amerindian* (Boston, 1945).

Of the innumerable works on Indian-white relations, we list here only a handful whose ecological perspective we have found helpful. Cronon covers early New England, while the southeastern frontier is surveyed by James H. Merrell, *The Indians' New World: Catawbas and Their World from European Contact through the Era of Removal* (Chapel Hill, N.C., 1989). The work of John Ewers, always lively and astute, can be sampled in *Indian Life of the Up-*

per Missouri (Norman, Okla., 1968); he is the source of Weasel Tail's account of how the Blackfeet discovered horses.

For animal frontiers, see the exhaustive (and sometimes exhausting) Frank Gilbert Roe, *The North American Buffalo: A Critical Study of the Species in Its Wild State* (Toronto, 1970). With equal pertinacity, Roe has surveyed *The Indian and the Horse* (Norman, Okla., 1955). Frank R. Secoy traces how the horse and gun frontiers affected Indian life in *Changing Military Patterns on the Great Plains: 17th Century through Early 19th Century* (Locust Valley, N.Y., 1953). Our own chapter has given only scant attention to the important effects of the fur trade on Native American life. For one ecologically sensitive introduction, see David J. Wishart, *The Fur Trade of the American West, 1807–1840: A Geographical Synthesis* (Lincoln, Nebr., 1979). Calvin Martin's *Keepers of the Game* (Berkeley, Calif., 1978) is a controversial attempt to see Indian overtrapping as a consequence of the newly introduced epidemics; for a response, see Shepard Krech III, ed., *Indians, Animals, and the Fur Trade* (Athens, Ga., 1981). Eric Wolf adopts a global perspective in *Europe and the People without History* (Berkeley, Calif., 1982).

For the traditional frontier of the overland trail, John D. Unruh, *The Plains Across: Overland Emigrants and the Trans-Mississippi West, 1840–60* (Urbana, Ill., 1982) dispels the myth of the lonely trail. Although not focused on ecological aspects of the frontier, Unruh is sensitive to the movement of livestock and the effect of whites' grazing and hunting on Indian lands. The demise of the bison is covered in a pathbreaking article by Dan Flores, "Bison Ecology and Bison Diplomacy: The Southern Plains from 1800 to 1840," *Journal of American History* (September 1991): 465–85. Flores shows that the traditional explanation, that white hunters decimated the herd in the 1870s, is only a partial explanation. Elliott West has come to similar conclusions about the central plains in his eminently readable *The Way to the West: Essays on the Central Plains* (Albuquerque, N.M., 1995). See also his more recent work, *The Contested Plains: Indians, Goldseekers, and the Rush to Colorado* (Lincoln, Nebr., 1998).

✣ ✢ SIX ✣ ✢

The Madness
of John Brown

For more than two months the twenty-one men hid in the cramped attic. They were mostly idealistic young men in their twenties, bound together during the tedious waiting by a common hatred of slavery. Now, on October 16, 1859, their leader, Old John Brown, revealed to them his final plan. The group comprised five blacks and sixteen whites, including three of the old man's sons, Owen, Oliver, and Watson. For years Brown had nurtured the idea of striking a blow against the southern citadel of slavery. Tomorrow he explained, they would move into Harpers Ferry, Virginia, and capture the town and its federal arsenal. As they gathered arms, slaves would pour in from the surrounding countryside to join their army. Before the local militia had time to organize, Brown's forces would escape to the nearby hills. From there, they would fight a guerilla war until the curse of slavery had been exorcised and all slaves freed from bondage. No one among them questioned Brown or his plan.

An autumn chill filled the air, and a light rain fell as the war party made its way down the dark road toward Harpers Ferry. Three men had remained behind to handle supplies and arm slaves who took up the fight. A sleepy stillness covered the small town nestled in the hills where the Shenandoah joined the Potomac sixty miles from Washington, D.C. It was a region of small farms and relatively few slaves. Most likely, the presence of the arsenal and an armory explain why Brown chose to begin his campaign there.

The attack began without a hitch. Two raiders cut telegraph lines running east and west from the town. The others seized a rifle works, the armory, and three hostages, including a local planter descended from the Washington family. Soon the sounds of gunfire drew the townspeople from their beds. Amid the confusion, the church bell pealed the alarm dreaded throughout the South—slave insurrection! By late morning the hastily joined militia and armed farmers had trapped Brown and his men in the engine house of the Baltimore and Ohio Railroad. One son had been killed and another lay dying at his father's side. Drunken crowds thronged the streets crying for blood and revenge. When news of the raid reached Washington, President Buchanan dispatched federal troops under Colonel Robert E. Lee to put down the insurrection.

Thirty-six hours after the first shot, John Brown's war on slavery ended. By any calculation the raid had been a total failure. Not a single slave had risen to join Brown's army. Ten of the raiders lay dead or dying; the rest had been scattered or captured. Though himself wounded, Brown had miraculously escaped death. The commander of the assault force had tried to kill him with his dress sword, but it merely bent double from the force of the blow. Seven other people had been killed and nine more wounded during the raid.

Most historians would agree that the Harpers Ferry raid was to the Civil War what the Boston Massacre had been to the American Revolution: an incendiary event. In an atmosphere of aroused passions, profound suspicions, and irreconcilable differences, Brown and his men put a match to the fuse. Once their deed had been done and blood had been shed, there seemed to be no drawing back for either North or South. The shouts of angry men overwhelmed the voices of compromise.

From pulpits and public platforms across the North leading abolitionists leapt to Brown's defense. No less a spokesman than Ralph Waldo Emerson pronounced the raider a "saint . . . whose martyrdom, if it shall be perfected, will make the gallows as glorious as the cross." Newspaper editor Horace Greeley called the raid "the work of a madman" for which he had nothing but the highest admiration. At the same time the defenders of national union

John Brown, man of action: After the Pottawatomie Massacre, Brown grew a beard to disguise his appearance. His eastern backers were impressed with the aura he radiated as a western man of action. The image was not hurt by the fact that Brown hinted darkly of vigorous actions soon to be taken, or that he carried a bowie knife in his boot and regularly barricaded himself nights in his hotel rooms as a precaution against proslavery agents. (Library of Congress)

and of law and order generally condemned Brown and his violent tactics. Such northern political leaders as Abraham Lincoln, Stephen Douglas, and William Seward spoke out against Brown. The Republican party in 1860 went so far as to adopt a platform censuring the Harpers Ferry raid.

Moderate northern voices were lost, however, on southern fire-eaters, to whom all abolitionists and Republicans were potential John Browns. Across the South angry mobs attacked northerners regardless of their views on the slave question. Everywhere the specter of slave insurrection fed fears, and the uproar strengthened the hand of secessionists who argued that the South's salvation lay in expunging all traces of northern influence.

THE MOTIVES OF A FANATIC

And what of the man who triggered all those passions? Had John Brown foreseen that his quixotic crusade would reap such a whirlwind of violence? On that issue both his contemporaries and historians have been sharply divided. Brown himself left a confusing and often contradictory record of his objectives. To his men, and to Frederick Douglass, the former slave and black abolitionist, Brown made clear he intended nothing less than to provoke a general slave insurrection. His preparations all pointed to that goal. He went to Harpers Ferry armed for such a task, and the choice of the armory as the raid's target left little doubt he intended to equip a slave army. But throughout the months of preparation, Brown had consistently warned the coconspirators financing his scheme that the raid might fail. In that event, he told them, he still hoped the gesture would so divide the nation that a sectional crisis would ensue, leading to the destruction of slavery.

From his jail cell and at his trial Brown offered a decidedly contradictory explanation. Ignoring the weapons he had accumulated, he suggested that the raid was intended as an extension of the underground railroad work he had previously done. He repeatedly denied any intention to commit violence or instigate a slave rebellion. "I claim to be here in carrying out a measure I believe perfectly justifiable," he told a skeptical newspaper reporter, "and not to act the part of an incendiary or ruffian, but to aid those [slaves] suffering great wrong." To Congressman Clement Vallandigham of Ohio, who asked Brown if he expected a slave uprising, the old man replied, "No sir; nor did I wish it. I expected to gather them up from time to time and set them free." In court with his life hanging in the balance, Brown once again denied any violent intent. He sought only to expand his campaign for the liberation of slaves.

Brown's contradictory testimony has provoked much speculation over the man and his motives. Was he being quite rational and calculating in abruptly changing his story after capture? Certainly Brown knew how much his martyrdom would enhance the abolitionist movement. His execution, he wrote his wife, would "do vastly more toward advancing the cause I have earnestly endeavored to promote, than all I have done in my life before." On the other hand, perhaps Brown was so imbued with his own righeousness that he deceived himself into believing he had not acted the part of "incendiary or ruffian," but only meant to aid those slaves "suffering great wrong." "Poor old man!" commented Republican presidential hopeful Salmon Chase. "How sadly misled by his own imaginations!"

Yet for every American who saw Brown as either a calculating insurrectionist or a genuine if somewhat self-deluded martyr, there were those who thought him insane. How else could they explain the hopeless assault of eighteen men against a federal arsenal and the state of Virginia—where slaves were "not abundant" and where "no Abolitionists were ever known to peep"? Who but a "madman" (to quote Greeley) could have concocted, much less attempted, such a wild scheme?

Nor was the issue of John Brown's sanity laid to rest by his execution on December 2, 1859. Brown had become a symbol, for both North and South,

John Brown, the impractical idealist: "The old idiot—the quicker they hang him and get him out of the way, the better." So wrote the editor of a Chicago paper to Abraham Lincoln. Many contemporaries shared the view of the cartoon reprinted here, that Brown was a foolish dreamer. Yet Brown had other ideas. "I think you are fanatical!" exclaimed one southern bystander after Brown had been captured. "And I think you are fanatical," Brown retorted. "'Whom the Gods would destroy they first made mad,' and you are mad." (Library of Congress)

of the dimensions of the sectional struggle, condensing the issues of the larger conflict in his own actions. Inevitably, the question of personal motivation becomes inextricably bound to historians' interpretations of the root causes of sectional and social conflict. Was Brown a heroic martyr—a white man in a racist society with the courage to lay down his life on behalf of his black brothers and the principles of the Declaration? Or was he an emotionally unbalanced fanatic whose propensity for wanton violence propelled the nation toward avoidable tragedy?

During the middle years of the twentieth century the view of Brown as an emotional fanatic gained ground. John Garraty, in a popular college survey text, described Brown as so "deranged" that rather than hang him for his "dreadful act. . . . It would have been far wiser and more just to have committed him to an asylum." Allen Nevins defined a middle ground when he argued that on all questions except slavery, Brown could act coherently and rationally. "But on this special question of the readiness of slavery to crumble at a blow," Nevins thought, "his monomania . . . or his paranoia as a modern alienist [psychoanalyst] would define it, rendered him irresponsible."

Brown's most recent academic biographer, Stephen Oates, while recognizing in Brown much that was in no sense "normal," rejected the idea that insanity could either be adequately demonstrated or used in any substantive way to explain Brown's actions. That Brown had an "excitable temperament" and a single-minded obsession with slavery Oates conceded. He concluded, too, that Brown was egotistical, an overbearing father, an often inept man worn down by disease and suffering, and a revolutionary who believed himself called to his mission by God.

But having said all that, Oates demanded that before they dismissed Brown as insane, historians must consider the context of Brown's actions. To call him insane, Oates argued, "is to ignore the tremendous sympathy he felt for the black man in America." And, he added, "to label him a 'maniac' out of touch with 'reality' is to ignore the piercing insight he had into what his raid—whether it succeeded or whether it failed—would do to sectional tensions."

Given such conflicting views on the question of John Brown's sanity, it makes sense to examine more closely the evidence of his mental state. The most readily available material, and the most promising at first glance, was presented after the original trial by Brown's attorney, George Hoyt. As a last-minute stratagem, Hoyt submitted nineteen affidavits from Brown's friends and acquaintances, purporting to demonstrate Brown's instability.

Two major themes appear in those affidavits. First, a number of people testified to a pronounced pattern of insanity in the Brown family, particularly on his mother's side. In addition to his maternal grandmother and numerous uncles, aunts, and cousins, Brown's sister, his brother Salmon, his first wife, Dianthe, and his sons Frederick and John Jr. were all said to have shown evidence of mental disorders. Second, some respondents described certain patterns of instability they saw in Brown himself. Almost everyone agreed he was profoundly religious and that he became agitated over the slavery question. A few traced Brown's insanity back through his years of

John Brown, martyr of freedom:

John Brown of Ossawatomie, they led him out to die;
And lo! a poor slave-mother with her little child pressed nigh,
Then the bold, blue eye grew tender, and the harsh face grew mild,
And he stooped between the jeering ranks and kissed the Negro's child!

John Greenleaf Whittier based this incident in his poem, "Brown of Ossawatomie" (December 1859), on an erroneous newspaper report. Apparently Brown did kiss the child of a white jailor he had befriended. Brown also remarked to the same jailer that "he would prefer to be surrounded in his last moments by a poor weeping slave mother with her children," noting that this "would make the picture at the gallows complete." (Library of Congress) repeated business failures. The "wild and desperate" nature of those business schemes and the rigidity with which he pursued them persuaded several friends of his "unsound" mind and "monomania."

Many old acquaintances thought that Brown's controversial experiences in Kansas had unhinged the man. There, in May 1856, proslavery forces had attacked the antislavery town of Lawrence. In retaliation, Brown led a band of seven men (including four of his sons) in a midnight raid on some of his proslavery neighbors at Pottawatomie Creek. Although the Pottawatomie residents had taken no part in the attack on faraway Lawrence, Brown's men, under his orders, took their broadswords and hacked to death five neighbors. That grisly act horrified free state and proslavery advocates alike. John Jr., one of Brown's sons who had not participated in the raid, suffered a nervous breakdown from his own personal torment and from the abuse he received after being thrown into prison. Another of Brown's sons, Frederick, was murdered a few months later in the civil war that swiftly erupted in Kansas.

Thus a number of acquaintances testified in 1859 that from the time of the Pottawatomie killings onward, Brown had been mentally deranged. E. N. Sill, an acquaintance of both Brown and his father, admitted that he had once had considerable sympathy for Brown's plan to defend antislavery families in Kansas. "But from his peculiarities," Sill recalled, "I thought Brown an unsafe man to be commissioned with such a matter." It was Sill who suggested the idea, which Allen Nevins later adopted, that on the slav-

John Brown, the terrorist:
Mahala Doyle, the wife of James P. Doyle, one of the men Brown killed at Pottawatomie, testified of Brown, "He said if a man stood between him and what he considered right, he would take his life as cooly as he would eat his breakfast. His actions show what he is. Always restless, he seems never to sleep. With an eye like a snake, he looks like a demon." (Library of Congress)

ery question alone Brown was insane. "I have no confidence in his judgment in matters appertaining to slavery," he asserted. "I have no doubt that, upon this subject . . . he is surely as monomaniac as any inmate in any lunatic asylum in the country." David King, who talked to Brown after his Kansas experience, observed that "on the subject of slavery he was crazy" and that Brown saw himself as "an instrument in the hands of God to free slaves."

Such testimony seems to support the view that Harpers Ferry was the outcome of insanity. Yet even then and ever since many people have rejected that conclusion. Confronted with the affidavits, Governor Henry Wise of Virginia thought to have Brown examined by the head of the state's insane asylums. Upon reflection he changed his mind. Wise believed Brown perfectly sane and had even come to admire begrudgingly the old man's "indomitable" spirit. Wise once described Brown as "the gamest man I ever saw."

For what it is worth, Brown himself rejected any intimation that he was anything but sane. He refused to plead insanity at his trial and instead adopted the posture of the self-sacrificing revolutionary idealist. For him, slavery constituted an unethical and unconstitutional assault of one class of citizens against another. Under that assault acts that society deemed unlawful—dishonesty, murder, theft, or treason—could be justified in the name of a higher morality.

Furthermore, Oates and other historians have attacked the affidavits persented by Hoyt as patently unreliable. Many people had good reason to have Brown declared insane. Among those signing the affidavits were friends and relatives who hoped Governor Wise would spare Brown's life. Might they not have exaggerated the instances of mental disorders in his family to make their case more convincing? Most had not taken Brown's fanaticism seriously until his raid on Harpers Ferry. That event, as much as earlier observation, had shaped their opinions. Just as important, none of them had any medical training or experience that would qualify them to determine with any expertise whether Brown or any member of his family could be judged insane. Only one affidavit came from a doctor, and, like most physicians of the day, he had no particular competence in psychological observation.

Though it would be foolish to suggest that we in the twentieth century are better judges of character than our forebears, it is fair to say that at least we have a better clinical understanding of mental disorders. Many symptoms that in the nineteenth century were lumped together under the term *insanity* have since been identified as a variety of very different diseases, each with its own distinct causes. Among those "crazy" Brown relatives were those who, based on the descriptions in the affidavits, may have suffered from senility, epilepsy, Addison's disease, or brain tumors. Thus the "preponderance" of insanity in Brown's family could well have been a series of unrelated disorders. Even if the disorders were related, psychologists today still hotly debate the extent to which psychological disorders are inheritable.

The insanity defense also had considerable appeal to political leaders. Moderates from both North and South, seeking to preserve the Union, needed an argument to soften the divisive impact of Harpers Ferry. Were Brown declared insane, northern abolitionists could not so easily portray him as a martyr. Southern secessionists could not treat Brown as typical of all northern abolitionists. As a result, their argument that the South would be safe only outside the Union would have far less force. Even antislavery Republicans tried to dissociate themselves from Brown's more radical tactics. During the 1859 Congressional elections, the Democrats tried to persuade voters that Harpers Ferry resulted inevitably from the Republicans' appeal to the doctrine of "irresistible conflict" and "higher law" abolitionism. To blunt such attacks, leading Republicans regularly attributed the raid to Brown's insanity.

Clearly, the affidavits provide only the flimsiest basis for judging the condition of Brown's mental health. But some historians have argued that the larger pattern of Brown's life demonstrated his imbalance. Indeed, even the most generous biographers must admit that Brown botched miserably much that he attempted to do. In the years before moving to Kansas, Brown had tried his hand at tanning, sheepherding, surveying, cattle-driving, and wool-merchandising—all with disastrous results. By 1852 he had suffered fifteen business failures in four different states. Creditors were continually hounding him. "Over the years before his Kansas escapade," John Garraty concluded, "Brown had been a drifter, horse thief and swindler, several times a bankrupt, a failure in everything he attempted."

But this evidence, too, must be considered with circumspection. During the period Brown applied himself in business, the American economy went through repeated cycles of boom and bust. Many hardworking entrepreneurs lost their shirts in business despite their best efforts. Brown's failures over the years may only suggest that he did not have an aptitude for business. His schemes were usually ill-conceived, and he was too inflexible to adapt to the rapidly changing business climate. But to show that Brown was a poor businessman and that much of his life he pursued the wrong career hardly proves him insane. Under those terms, much of the adult population in the United States would belong in asylums.

To call Brown a drifter is once again to condemn most Americans. Physical mobility has been such a salient trait of this nation that one respected historian has used it to distinguish the national character. During some periods of American history as much as 20 percent of the population has moved *each year*. In the 1840s and 1850s, a whole generation of Americans shared Brown's dream of remaking their fortunes in a new place. Many like him found the lure of new frontiers irresistible. And just as many failed along the way, only to pack up and try again.

The accusation that Brown was a swindler, while containing a measure of truth, convicts him on arbitrary evidence. After several of his many business disasters, creditors hounded him in the courts. A few accused him of fraud. Yet Simon Perkins, an Ohio businessman who lost more money to Brown and who was more familiar with his business practices than anyone else, never accused Brown of swindling, even when the two dissolved their partnership in 1854. Again, it was poor business sense rather than a desire to swindle that led Brown into his difficulties.

The horse thievery charge hinges on the observer's point of view. During the years of fighting in Kansas, Brown occasionally "confiscated" horses from proslavery forces. Those who supported his cause treated the thefts as legitimate acts of war. Brown's enemies never believed he was sincere in his convictions. They accused him of exploiting the tensions in Kansas to act like a brigand. But in any case, it is far from clear that Brown ever stole for personal gain. Whatever money he raised, save for small sums he sent his wife, went toward organizing his crusade against slavery. Besides, it is one thing to establish Brown's behavior as antisocial and quite another to find him insane.

From the point of view of the "facts of the case," the question of insanity cannot be easily resolved. The issue becomes further muddled when we consider its theoretical aspects. Theory, as we saw when examining Andrew Jackson, will inevitably affect any judgment in the case. The question, "Was John Brown insane?" frames our inquiry and determines the kind of evidence being sought. And in this case, the question is particularly controversial because it remains unclear just exactly what we are asking. What does it mean, after all, to be "insane"?

Modern psychologists and psychiatrists have given up using the concept of insanity diagnostically because it is a catchall term and too unspecific to have definite meaning. The only major attempt to define the concept more precisely has been in the legal world. In civil law insanity refers to the inability of individuals to maintain contractual or other legal obligations. Thus, to void a will, an injured party might try to demonstrate that at the time of composition its author was not "of sound mind"—that is, not responsible for his or her actions. Insanity is considered sufficient grounds to commit an individual to a mental hospital. But since it involves such a curtailment of rights and freedom, it is extremely difficult to prove and generally requires the corroboration of several disinterested professionals.

Insanity has been widely used as a defense in criminal cases. By demonstrating that at the time of the crime a client could not distinguish right from wrong or was incapable of determining the nature of the act committed, a lawyer can protect the accused from some of the legal consequences of the act. To find Brown insane, as attorney Hoyt attempted to have the court do, would have been to assert Brown's inability to understand the consequences of his actions at Harpers Ferry. The raid would represent the irrational anger of a deranged man, deserving pity rather than hatred or admiration.

In the legal sense, then, Brown would have to be considered fit to stand trial. He may have been unrealistic in estimating his chance of success at Harpers Ferry, but he repeatedly demonstrated that he knew the consequences of his actions: that he would be arrested and punished if caught; that large portions of American society would condemn him; that, nevertheless, he believed himself in the right. In the legal sense, Brown was quite sane and clearheaded about his actions.

The Turbulent Currents
of Psychohistory

Yet the court's judgment, accurate as it may have been, is likely to leave us uneasy. To have Brown pronounced sane or insane, in addition to guilty or not guilty, does little to explain, deep down, why the man acted as he did. The verdict leaves us with the same emptiness that impelled psychologists to reject the whole concept of insanity. What drove John Brown to crusade against slavery? to execute in cold blood five men along a Kansas creek? to lead twenty-one men to Harpers Ferry? Other northerners abhorred the institution of slavery. Yet only John Brown acted with such vehemence. In that sense he was far from being a normal American; far, even, from being a normal abolitionist. How can we begin to understand the intensity of his deeds?

Here we approach the limits of explanations based on rational motives. To describe John Brown simply by referring to his professed and undoubtedly sincere antislavery ideology is to leave unexplored the fire in the man. Such an approach assumes too easily that consciously expressed motives can be taken at face value. Yet we have already seen, in the case of the bewitched at Salem, that unconscious motivations often play important roles in human behavior. If we are willing to grant that apparently "normal" people sometimes act for reasons beyond those they consciously express, how much more likely is it that we must go beyond rational motives in understanding Brown? It seems only logical that historians should bring to bear the tools of modern psychology to assess the man's personality.

Indeed, a subbranch of history has applied such methods to a wide variety of historical problems. Known as psychohistory, this approach has most often drawn on the discipline of psychoanalysis pioneered by Sigmund Freud, an Austrian physician who propounded his theories during the early twentieth century. Freud assumed that every individual experiences intensely personal conflicts in life that are extremely difficult to resolve. When a person resists coming to terms with such situations in an open and direct manner, that person represses the conflict; that is, he or she is *unable* to think about it consciously. Under such conditions the conflict does not go away; it is merely forced to express itself indirectly. The surface manifestations are disguised in neurotic symptoms such as obsessions, nervous tics, or hysterical behaviors.

By exploring a patient's life history through a process of free association about memories, dreams, and fantasies, the psychoanalyst takes the fragments of evidence presented by the patient and guides him or her toward a recognition of the unconscious forces that have shaped the personality. Thus the analyst seeks to explore the territory of the unconscious much as the historian seeks to make sense out of the jumble of documentary evidence.

What sort of map to the unconscious does Freudian analysis supply? Freud called special attention to two areas he believed were the source of much tension and conflict: instinctual sexual drives and the formative experiences of infancy and childhood. Consider two examples. Every infant receives its first nourishment of mother's milk from the nipple. (More recently, of course, the baby bottle has sometimes served as a substitute.) Freud suggested that every baby experiences a crisis when the mother weans the child from her breast. The infant, Freud argued, has become accustomed to this constant gratification from the mother and experiences rage when the breast is withheld.

Even more famous among Freudian concepts is the notion of an oedipal conflict in young boys. The concept draws its name from Sophocles' *Oedipus Rex*, a Greek tragedy in which Oedipus unknowingly commits incest with his mother. For this "crime" he suffers blindness and exile. Freud contended that somewhere between the ages of three and six, every boy normally passes through an "oedipal phase," during which his consciousness of erotic gratification intensifies. The natural object of attraction is the woman closest to the boy—his mother. Yet the child is aware that this love object is forbidden; it belongs to his father, and therefore the child fears his father's imagined jealous rage.

Many of Freud's concepts—and these examples are only two, sketched in briefest outline—strike laypeople as not only counterintuitive but plain farfetched. Yet Freud's psychological principles received increasing respect and attention in the first three decades of the twentieth century, both in the medical community and among the broader public. Psychoanalysts were (and still are) trained in his methods, and patients undergo therapy that often lasts for years.

Although controversial among historians, psychoanalytic theory came to be used by an increasing minority of them. In Chapter 4 for example, we noted that Michael Rogin, writing in the 1970s, analyzed Andrew Jackson from the point of view of his role in removing Indians from the Old Southwest. But Rogin also argued that to explain Indian removal, historians could not rely merely on the motives of simple land hunger and material greed. Using Freudian theory, he pointed out that white-Indian relations during the Jacksonian era were fraught with parent-child symbolism. White treaty negotiators constantly urged Indians to make peace with their "white father," the President of the United States. If friendly tribes did not conclude treaties, Jackson once warned, "We may then be under the necessity of raising the hatchet against our own friends and brothers. Your father the President wishes to avoid this unnatural state of things."

Pursuing the Freudian focus on childhood, Rogin suggested that Jackson's well-known temper as an adult might be connected to the kinds of infant rages posited by Freud. Did the death of Jackson's father before he was born affect Jackson's mother during his infancy? Rogin wondered. "Problems in infancy, involving feeding, weaning, or holding the child, often intensify infantile rage and accentuate later difficulties in the struggle of the child to break securely free of the mother." Rogin quoted Jefferson's description of Jackson "choking with rage" on the Senate floor; and noted that according to eyewitnesses, Jackson often slobbered and spoke incoherently when excited or angry. "Jackson's slobbering," argued Rogin, "suggests early problems with speech, mouth, and aggression. Speech difficulties often indicate a problematic oral relationship."

In the 1980s and 1990s, however, Freudian theory came under broad attack. Medicine, which for many years had been an art as much as a science, increasingly demanded that hypotheses be rigorously tested and confirmed by replicable experiments. By their very nature Freudian theories about the unconscious dealt with propositions that were either unverifiable or extremely difficult to confirm. In addition, as more of Freud's letters and papers became public (for years many had been available only to scholars sympathetic to psychoanalysis), they shed doubts on the methods of the master. Freud established his psychoanalytic method, for example, when treating thirteen young women who he said recounted tales of being seduced when they were children. In fact, Freud's papers reveal that the girls had no such recollections until *after* his analysis was in full swing. Even after Freud used, in his own words, the "strongest compulsion" to "induce" his patients to free-associate or fantasize such stories, he admitted that "they have no feeling of remembering the scenes." This revelation goes to the heart of the evidentiary problem. If such memories are not part of the patient's recollection until an analyst strongly induces them, how can we decide whether the memories truly spring from the unconscious rather than merely from the suggestive comments of the analyst?

Given the strong challenges to Freudian theory, its value for analyzing *any* person seems at the very least in serious doubt—let alone for analyzing a historical figure like John Brown, who cannot be subjected to a process of lengthy psychoanalysis on the couch. Must we throw up our hands at the possibility of understanding the inner workings of Brown's deepest motivations? It seems to us that the historian still has options.

Even Frederick Crews, one of Freud's most vocal literary critics, has suggested that it is possible to "dissent" from the rigid orthodoxy of psychoanalytic theory "without forsaking the most promising aspects of psychoanalysis—its attentiveness to signs of conflict, its hospitality to multiple significance, its ideas of ambivalence, identification, repression, and projection." Freud wished his patients to free-associate about childhood experiences in part because he recognized that unexpected patterns often emerged from these memories: recurring images, fears, preoccupations. Psychologists—whether they are strict Freudians or not—have learned to pay close attention to such patterns.

THE MOTIVES OF A SON—AND A FATHER

Although John Brown never underwent a psychological examination about his childhood, he has provided us, as it happens, with the means of conducting one ourselves. At the age of fifty-seven, Brown wrote a long letter addressed to a thirteen-year-old boy named Harry Stearns. Harry was the son of one of Brown's wealthiest financial patrons. In the letter, Brown told the story of "a certain boy of my acquaintance" who, "for convenience," he called John. This name was especially convenient because the boy was none other than Brown himself. The letter is one of the few suriving sources of information about Brown's childhood. It is reprinted here with only a few omissions of routine biographical data.

I can not tell you of anything in the first Four years of John's life worth mentioning save that at that *early age* he was tempted by Three large Brass Pins belonging to a girl who lived in the family & *stole them.* In this he was detected by his Mother; & after having a full day to think of the wrong; received from her a thorough whipping. When he was Five years old his Father moved to Ohio; then a wilderness filled with wild beasts, & Indians. During the long journey, which was performed in part or mostly with an *ox-team;* he was called on by turns to assist a boy Five years older (who had been adopted by his Father & Mother) & learned to think he could accomplish *smart things* by driving the Cows; & riding the horses. Sometimes he met with Rattle Snakes which were very large; & which some of the company generally managed to kill. After getting to Ohio in 1805 he was for some time rather afraid of the Indians, & of their Rifles; but this soon wore off: & he used to hang about them quite as much as was consistent with good manners; & learned a trifle of their talk. His father learned to dress Deer Skins, & at 6 years old John was installed a young Buck Skin. He was perhaps rather observing as he ever after remembered the entire process of Deer Skin *dressing;* so that he could at any time dress his own leather such as Squirel, Raccoon, Cat, Wolf and Dog Skins, and also learned to make Whip Lashes, which brought him some change at times, & was of considerable service in many ways. At Six years old he began to be a rambler in the wild new country finding birds and squirrels and sometimes a wild Turkey's nest. But about this period he was placed in the school of *adversity;* which my young friend was a most necessary part of his early training. You may *laugh* when you come to read about it; but these were *sore trials* to John: whose earthly treasures were very *few & small.* These were the beginning of a severe but *much needed course* of discipline which he afterwards was to pass through; & which it is to be hoped has learned him before this time that the Heavenly Father sees it best to take all the little things out of his hands which he has ever placed in them. When John was in his Sixth year a poor *Indian boy* gave him a Yellow Marble the first he had ever seen. This he thought a great deal of; & kept it a good while; but at last *he lost it* beyond recovery. *It took years to heal the wound* & I *think* he cried at times about it. About Five months after this he caught a young Squirrel tearing off his tail in doing it; & getting severely bitten at the same time himself. He however held on *to the little bob tail Squirrel;* & finally got him perfectly tamed, so that he almost idolized his pet. *This too he lost;* by its wandering away; or by getting killed; & for a year or two John was *in mourning;* and looking at all the Squirrels he could see to try & discover Bobtail, *if possible*. I must not neglect to tell you of a verry *bad and foolish* habbit to which John was somewhat addicted. I mean *telling lies*; generally to screen himself from blame; or from punishment. He could not well endure to be reproached; & I now think had he been oftener encouraged to be entirely frank; *by making frankness a kind of atonement* for some of his faults; he would not have been so often guilty of this fault; nor have been (in after life) obliged to struggle *so long* with *so mean* a habit.

John was never *quarelsome*; but was *excessively* fond of the *hardest & roughest* kind of plays; & could *never get enough* [of] them. Indeed when for a short time he was sometimes sent to School the opportunity it afforded to wrestle & Snow ball & run & jump & knock off old seedy Wool hats; offered to him almost the only compensation for the confinement, & restraints of school. I need not tell you that with such a feeling & but little chance of going to school *at all:* he did not become much of a schollar. He would always choose to stay at home & work hard rather than be sent to school; & during the warm season might generally be seen *barefooted & bareheaded:* with Buck skin Breeches suspended often with one leather strap over his shoulder but sometimes with Two. To be sent off through the wilderness alone to very considerable distances was particularly his delight; & in this he was often indulged so that by the time he was Twelve years old he was sent off more than a Hundred Miles with companies of cattle; & he would have thought his character much injured had he been obliged to be helped in any such job. This was a boyish kind of feeling but characteristic however.

At Eight years old, John was left a Motherless boy which loss was complete and pearmanent for notwithstanding his Father again married to a sensible, intelligent, and on many accounts a very estimable woman; yet he never *adopted her in feeling*; but continued to pine after his own Mother for years. This opperated very unfavorably upon him; as he was both naturally fond of females; &, withall, extremely diffident; & deprived him of a suitable connecting link between the different sexes; the want of which might under some circumstances, have proved his ruin. . . .

During the war with England [in 1812] a circumstance occured that in the end made him a most *determined Abolitionist*: & led him to declare, or *Swear: Eternal war* with Slavery. He was staying for a short time with a very gentlemanly landlord since a United States Marshall who held a slave boy near his own age very active, inteligent and good feeling; & to whom John was under considerable obligation for numerous little acts of kindness. *The master* made a great pet of John: brought him to table with his first company; & friends; called their attention to every little smart thing he *said or did:* & to the fact of his being more than a hundred miles from home with a company of cattle alone; while the *negro boy* (who was fully if not more than his equal) was badly clothed, poorly fed; *& lodged in cold weather*; & beaten before his eyes with Iron Shovels or any other thing that came first to hand. This brought John to reflect on the wretched, hopeless condition, of *Fatherless & Motherless* slave *children:* for such children have neither Fathers or Mothers to protect, & provide for them. He sometimes would raise the question *is God their Father?* . . .

I had like to have forgotten to tell you of one of John's misfortunes which set rather hard on him while a young boy. He had by some means *perhaps* by gift of his father become the owner of a little Ewe Lamb which did finely till it was about Two Thirds grown; & then sickened & died. This brought another protracted *mourning season:* not that he felt the pecuniary loss so much: for that was never his disposition; but so strong & earnest were his attachments.

John had been taught from earliest childhood to "fear God and keep his commandments;" & though quite skeptical he had always by turns felt much serious doubt as to his future well being; & about this time became to some extent a convert to Christianity & ever after a firm believer in the divine authenticity of the Bible. With this book he became very familiar, & possessed a most unusual memory of its entire contents.

Now some of the things I have been *telling of;* were just such as I would recommend to you: & I would like to know that you had selected these out; & adopted them as part of your own plan of life; & I wish you to have some *deffinite plan.* Many seem to have none; & others never stick to any that they do form. This was not the case with John. He followed up with *tenacity* whatever he set about so long as it answered his general purpose; & hence he rarely failed in some good degree to effect the things he undertook. This was so much the case that he *habitually expected to succeed* in his undertakings. With this feeling *should be coupled;* the consciousness that our plans are right in themselves.

During the period I have named, John had acquired a kind of ownership to certain animals of some little value but as he had come to understand that the *title of minors* might be a little imperfect: he had recourse to various means in order to secure a more *independent;* & perfect right of property. One of those means was to exchange with his Father for something of far less value. Another was by trading with others persons for something his Father had never owned. Older persons have some times found difficulty with *titles.*

From Fifteen to Twenty years old, he spent most of his time working at the Tanner & Currier's trade keeping Bachelors hall; & he officiating as Cook; & for most of the time as foreman of the establishment under his Father. During this period he found much trouble with some of the bad habits I have mentioned & with some that I have not told you off: his conscience urging him forward with great power in this matter: but his close attention to *business;* & success in its management, together with the way he got along with a company of men, & boys; made him quite a favorite with the serious & more inteligent portion of older persons. This was so much the case; & secured for him so many little notices from those he esteemed; that his vanity was very much fed by it: & he came forward to manhood quite full of self-conceit; & self-confident; notwithstanding his *extreme* bashfulness. A younger brother used sometimes to remind him of this: & to repeat to him *this expression* which you may somewhere find, "A King against whom there is no rising up." The habit so early formed of being obeyed rendered him in after life too much disposed to speak in an imperious or dictating way. From Fifteen years & upward he felt a good deal of anxiety to learn; but could only read & studdy a little; both for want of time; & on account of inflammation of the eyes. He however managed by the help of books to make himself tolerably well acquainted with common arithmetic; & Surveying; which he practiced more or less after he was Twenty years old.

Before exploring the letter's deeper psychological significance, it may be worth reminding ourselves what a straightforward reading of the document provides. Attention would naturally center on Brown's striking tale of how, as a twelve-year-old, he was first roused to oppose slavery. Shocked by the cruel treatment of his young black friend, John was further incensed by the unfair and contrasting treatment he benefited from simply because he was white. This vivid, emotional experience seems to go a good way toward explaining why the evil of slavery weighed so heavily on Brown's mind. In an article on the motivations behind the raid at Harpers Ferry, this anecdote is quite clearly the one piece of evidence worth extracting from the long letter. The additional material on Brown's childhood, which often seems to ramble incoherently, might be included in a book-length biography of Brown, but hardly seems relevant to an article that must quickly get to the heart of the man's involvement with abolition.

Yet when we look more closely, Brown's story of the mistreated young slave does not go very far toward explaining Brown's motives. In a land where slavery was central to the culture, hundreds, even thousands, of young white boys must have had experiences in which black playmates were unfairly whipped, degraded, and treated as inferiors. Nonetheless, many of those boys went on to become slaveholders. Furthermore, although some undoubtedly developed a strong dislike of slavery (Abraham Lincoln among them[1]), none felt compelled to mount the kind of campaigns Brown did in Kansas and at Harpers Ferry. Why did Brown's rather commonplace experience make such a strong impression on him?

The answer to that question may be learned if we do not dismiss the other portions of Brown's childhood experiences as irrelevant but instead examine them for clues to his psychological development. So let us turn, for a moment, from a direct examination of Brown's abolitionism to the other elements of the letter to Harry Stearns. In doing so we must consider each of Brown's stories, illustrations, and comments with care, keeping in mind Freud's stress on unconscious motivations. In previous chapters we have seen that historians must always treat primary sources skeptically, identifying the personal perspectives and biases that may influence the writer. Psychoanalytic theory requires us to take that skepticism one step further, assuming not only that the evidence may be influenced by unstated motivations (such as Brown's wishing to impress Harry Stearns's father with his virtue) but also that some, even the most powerful of Brown's motivations, may be unconscious—hidden even from Brown himself.

At first glance the narrative appears to recount fairly ordinary events in a child's life. Who, after all, has not cried one time or another at the loss of a

---

1. As a young man, Lincoln was reputed to have been strongly moved by the sight of slaves being auctioned in New Orleans.

pet, or has not been proud of accomplishments like driving cows and riding horses? Yet we must remember that these events are only a few selected from among thousands in Brown's childhood; events meaningful enough to him that he has remembered and related them more than fifty years later. Why did Brown retain these memories rather than others? What suggestive images and themes recur? Because psychoanalytic theory emphasizes the importance of parental relationships, we may begin by examining Brown's relationship with his mother and father.

Of the two parents, John's mother is the most visible in this letter, and it is clear that Brown loved her dearly. Notice the language describing his mother's death. John "was left a Motherless boy," he writes—not the simpler and less revealing, "John's mother died," which places the emphasis on the mother rather than on the loss incurred by the "Motherless boy." Furthermore, the loss was "complete & pearmanent." Brown never grew to love his new mother and "continued to pine after his own Mother for years." The phrase, "pine after" (which the Oxford English Dictionary defines as being "consumed with longing," or languishing "with intense desire") has erotic overtones, which are made even more manifest by the sentence that follows. Brown moves directly from his love for his mother to the erotic temptations young women had for him, implicitly linking the two: "This opperated very unfavourably uppon him; as he was both naturally fond of females; & withall extremely diffident; & deprived him of a suitable connecting link between the different sexes; the want of which might under some circumstances have proved his ruin."

John's father, at first glance, appears to have taken a less prominent role in the letter, either positively or negatively. True, Owen Brown does teach John the art of dressing skins (and also, John takes care to note, of making "Whip Lashes"); but the attention centers not on the father's devoted teaching so much as John's remarkable ability to learn by watching his father only once. Perhaps most revealing, however, is an ambiguous passage in which Brown's father does *not* appear, yet plays a substantial, hidden role. The relevant paragraph begins by noting that John had "acquired a kind of ownership to certain animals of some little value." From earlier parts of the letter, we are aware how much these pets meant to him—the loss of the squirrel "Bobtail" (which he "almost idolized") and later the ewe lamb (which he had *"perhaps"* by gift of his father become the owner). Now, Brown indicates that he had owned other animals, but apparently not completely. He is curiously circumspect about explaining why: the ownership, he says, was incomplete because "the *title of minors*" was "a little imperfect." Apparently, animals that he thought he owned were taken away from him, on the grounds that he did not have "title" to them as a minor. So John, being extremely strong-willed despite his bashfulness, determinedly set out to "secure a more independent; & perfect right of property." Significantly, this question of ownership appears to have occurred more than once, for Brown noted that he devised "various means" to deal with it.

What is happening here? Brown's evasive language makes the situation difficult to reconstruct, but certain outlines emerge. The only logical person who might repeatedly prevent John from obtaining full "title" to his pets was his father, Owen. Why Owen objected is never stated, but several ideas suggest themselves. Conceivably the elder Brown needed one of John's "pet" sheep or cows to feed the family or to sell for income. Furthermore, in a frontier settlement where unfenced woodlands merged with small farms, wild or stray domestic animals might have roamed onto the Brown farm from time to time. If young John Brown found them, he would likely have claimed them as pets, only to discover that the animal was on father Owen's land—and duly appropriated for food or income.

Whatever the specific situations, young Brown repeatedly attempted to secure his property through one of two means. "One of those means was to exchange with his Father for something of far less value." The implication is that in some cases Owen Brown allowed John to treat animals as pets if they were formally "purchased" from his father for a token fee ("something of far less value"). In such cases, Owen Brown acted kindly toward his son, though rigorously insisting that the formalities of "property" and "title" be observed. But on other occasions John apparently could not convince his father to spare such pets, for the letter indicates that another means of obtaining them "was by trading with others persons for something his Father had never owned." If Owen would not give him pets, John would be able to get them from more willing neighbors.

The conflict of ownership between father and son obviously left a strong imprint. More than forty years later, Brown still vividly remembered how Owen confiscated his pets, as well as the means he worked out to satisfy, or in some cases, actually to evade his father's authority. Even more important, the evasive language in the passage demonstrates that Brown remained unable to acknowledge his anger openly. In effect, the paragraph reveals a concealed hostility that Brown was still carrying toward his father. The last sentence amounts to a condemnation, but the son could only express his anger indirectly, through use of a generality: "Older persons have some times found difficulty with *titles.*"

Unconsciously, Brown may have been applying the last phrase to himself as well. For the crucial message of the passage is not Brown's hostility toward his father, but the issues through which the hostility is expressed, that is to say, title and ownership. Indeed, a psychoanalytic interpretation of Brown's childhood suggests that throughout his life, Brown never fully resolved the question of "titles" of his own identity. The more the letter is probed, the more it reveals a patterned obsession with property and title. Brown continually describes himself as finding some piece of "property," forming strong attachments to it, and then losing it and severely mourning the loss.

What, after all, is the very first experience in Brown's life that he can recall? Before the age of four, John steals three brass pins, discovers that his title to them is imperfect, has them taken away, and is severely whipped. At six, John receives a treasured yellow marble, loses it, and mourns for "years." Soon afterward, John catches a squirrel, pulling its tail off in the process; then tames and idolizes it; then loses it and mourns another year or two. At eight, John loses another precious possession—his mother—and pines after her for years.

Then comes the story of the lamb; and later, his conflicts with his father over the ownership of other pets. The religious moral drawn from these lessons ("a severe but *much needed course* of discipline") was that "the Heavenly Father sees it best to take all the little things out of his hands which he has ever placed in them." Clearly, the process of becoming an independent adult was for John Brown a continuing effort to reconcile his guilt and anger over losing property with his fierce desire to become truly independent, to possess clear title to his own pets, to become a "propertied" father like Owen and—dare we say it?—even like God the father himself. Paradoxically, only when Brown internalized and accepted the authority of his fathers could he then act the part of a stern, loving parent himself. Submission to his father's authority made it possible for him to accept as legitimate his authority over his own "pets."

The pattern of Brown's struggle for autonomy is reflected in the role he played as father to his own children. Owen Brown had been a stern disciplinarian, in part because he had felt the lack of a strong hand in his own childhood. John internalized and emulated this severe approach early on. When his younger brother, Salmon, had been pardoned for some misdeed by a boarding-school teacher, John went to the teacher and told him that "if Salmon had done this thing at home, father would have punished him. I know he would expect you to punish him now for doing this—and if you don't, I shall." When the schoolmaster persisted in his lenience, John was reported to have given Salmon a "severe flogging." As a parent, Brown's discipline was equally harsh. When his three-year-old son Jason claimed that a certain dream actually had occurred, Brown felt obliged to whip the boy for

John Brown, the kindly father: Brown's daughter Ruth remembered the following incident from her childhood: "When I first began to go to school, I found a piece of calico one day behind one of the benches,—it was not large, but seemed quite a treasure to me, and I did not show it to any one until I got home. Father heard me then telling about it, and said, 'Don't you know what girl lost it?' I told him I did not. 'Well, when you go to school tomorrow take it with you, and find out if you can who lost it. It is a trifling thing, but always remember that if you should lose anything *you* valued, no matter how small, you would want the person that found it to give it back to you." (Library of Congress)

lying. The father's immense ambivalence in such a situation was evidenced by the tears that welled up in his eyes as he performed the whipping.

For Brown, even sins took on an aspect of property. The father kept a detailed account book of his son John Jr.'s transgressions, along with the number of whiplashes each sin deserved. Recalled the son:

> On a certain Sunday morning he invited me to accompany him from the house to the tannery, saying that he had concluded it was time for a settlement. We went into the upper or finishing room, and after a long and tearful talk over my faults, he again showed me my account, which exhibited a fearful footing up of *debits*. . . . I then paid about one-third of the debt, reckoned in strokes from a nicely-prepared blue-beech switch, laid on 'masterly.' Then, to my utter astonishment, father stripped off his shirt, and, seating himself on a block, gave me the whip and bade me 'lay it on' to his bare back. I dared not refuse to obey, but at first I did not strike hard. 'Harder!' he said; 'harder, harder!' until he received the *balance of the account*. Small drops of blood showed on his back where the tip end of the tingling beech cut through. Thus ended the account and settlement, which was also my first practical illustration of the Doctrine of Atonement.

In this astonishing tableau, Brown's personal conflicts are vividly reflected. The father punishes the son as justice demands; yet Brown also plays the wayward son himself. And as John Brown Jr. recognized only later, his father was consciously assuming the mantle of Christ, whom the heavenly father had permitted humankind to crucify and punish, in order that other children's sins would be forgiven.

The upshot of such discipline was that Brown's sons harbored a similar ambivalence toward their father—an intense feeling of loyalty and submission countered by a strong desire for independence. The contradiction of such training became apparent to one of Brown's sons, Watson, during the raid on Harpers Ferry. "The trouble is," Watson remarked to his father, "you want your boys to be brave as tigers, and still afraid of you." "And that was perfectly true," agreed Salmon Brown, another son.

Psychoanalytic insight has thus helped to reveal some of John Brown's most intense personal conflicts: his ambivalence toward his father's strict discipline; the paradox of his struggle to internalize and accept his father's authority in order to become independent himself; and his excessive concern with property and "pets" as a means of defining his independence. Having exposed these themes, let us now return to the starting point of our original analysis of the letter—the anecdote about Brown and the young slave. Suddenly, what had seemed a straightforward tale is filled with immensely suggestive vocabulary, whose overtones reveal a great deal. The passage is worth reading once again:

> During the war with England a circumstance occurred that in the end made him a most *determined Abolitionist:* & led him to declare, or *Swear: Eternal war with Slavery.* He was staying for a short time with a very gentlemanly landlord since a United States Marshall who held a slave boy near his own age very active, inteligent and good feeling; & to whom John was under considerable obligation for numerous little acts of kindness. *The master* made a great pet of

John Brown, the stern father: Brown was influenced in his harsh discipline by his father, Owen (left), and in turn influenced his own son, John Jr. (right). Father John kept a detailed account book of young John's sinful acts, along with the number of whiplashes each sin deserved. Even sins, it seemed, were carefully enumerated as property. (Library of Congress)

John: brought him to table with his first company; & friends; called their attention to every little smart thing he *said or did*; & to the fact of his being more than a hundred miles from home with a company of cattle alone; while the *negro boy* (who was fully if not more than his equal) was badly clothed, poorly fed; *& lodged in cold weather*; & beaten before his eyes with Iron Shovels or any other thing that came first to hand. This brought John to reflect on the wretched, hopeless condition, of *Fatherless & Motherless* slave *children*: for such children have neither Fathers or Mothers to protect, & provide for them. He sometimes would raise the question *is God their Father?*

Upon this second reading, it becomes evident that Brown's language and metaphors here are full of references to parental relationships, dependence, and authority. John stayed with a "very gentlemanly landlord" who "made a great pet of John," treating the boy just as John treated his own pets. At the same time, however, this gentlemanly father acted like no father at all to the negro boy, beating him unmercifully. This led John to reflect "on the wretched, hopeless condition, of *Fatherless & Motherless* slave *children*." "*Is God their Father?*" he asked himself.

The situation confronted young Brown with two starkly contrasting models of a father, corresponding with the boy's own ambivalent feelings toward Owen. Naturally, John wanted his own father to discipline him less harshly. He wanted to be treated as a "pet"; as his own animals were treated; as this gentleman treated him. Similarly, he identified with the negro boy, an innocent lad who was being punished just as Owen Brown punished John. Yet like all boys, he also identified with his own father. He desired as well as hated the power that Owen wielded over him and that this gentleman wielded over the negro boy. He thus felt the tug of two conflicting loyalties. To use the religious imagery so familiar to that age, John Brown wanted to grow up and act both as God the merciful Father and as God the righteous Judge.

This ambivalent father-son relationship suggests that Brown's intense lifelong identification with black slaves might well have sprung from the struggle he experienced with paternal discipline. Helping slaves was ultimately a means of helping himself without consciously recognizing the source of his emotions and convictions. He could channel the repressed hostility toward his father into a more acceptable form—hatred of the slaveholders, another class of paternalistic oppressors who cruelly whipped their charges. In attacking the planters, Brown relieved the sense of guilt he harbored for secretly wishing to destroy his father. After all, God the implacable Father and Judge was using Brown as his instrument for bringing justice to the world. At the same time, by protecting and defending the helpless slaves, Brown carried out God's will as a merciful father. In liberating the black nation, he could free himself. In some indirect yet significant way, the raid at Harpers Ferry involved the working out of psychological turmoil that had troubled Brown since childhood.

Does all this speculation lead us then to assume that childhood neuroses rather than moral conviction dictated Brown's actions? Few historians would go that far. A full explanation of any person's actions and beliefs must, in the end, be multicausal if it is to reflect the complexity of real life. We cannot minimize the sincerity—nor the nobility—of Brown's belief in the brotherhood of black people and white people. Yet the stirrings of deeply rooted unconscious forces can be neglected no more than the more rational components of behavior can.

This psychological interpretation, then, is not offered as a definitive or an exclusive one. And our brief exposition of one letter constitutes only one small part of what should properly be a much larger analysis of Brown's personality and career. But the exposition is ample enough to suggest how fruitful a broadly psychoanalytical approach can be. As Michael Rogin suggested in the case of Andrew Jackson, psychohistory provides historians with a theory that sensitizes them to profitable themes, motifs, and vocabularies. An awareness of recurring tensions stemming from Brown's childhood makes it possible to appreciate how his personal sufferings incorporated the larger events of the period.

At the moment Brown transcended his life of failure, he forced his generation to identify either positively or negatively with the action he took to liberate black Americans. His act of violence was appropriate to what Oates described as "the violent, irrational, and paradoxical times in which he lived." Given Brown's profoundly religious nature and commitment to human liberty and equality, he could not be at peace until his society recognized the contradiction between its religious and political ideals and the existence of slavery.

In the end, John Brown turned the tables on society. His raid on Harpers Ferry pressed his fellow Americans to consider whether it was not actually their values, and society's, that were immoral and "abnormal." The outbreak of civil war, after all, demonstrated that American society was so maladjusted and so divided that it could not remain a "normal," integrated whole without violently purging itself. If Brown's raid was an isolated act of a disturbed man, why did it drive an entire generation to the brink of war? Why did Brown's generation find it impossible to agree about the meaning of Harpers Ferry? As C. Vann Woodward concluded, the importance lay not so much in the man or event, but in the use made of them by northern and southern partisans. For every Emerson or Thoreau who pronounced the raid the work of a saint, a southern fire-eater condemned the venture as the villainy of all northerners.

None of these actors in the historical drama paid much attention to evidence. A crisis mentality thwarted any attempts at understanding or reconciliation. In the fury of mutual recrimination, both sides lost sight of the man who had provoked the public outcry and propelled the nation toward war. In such times it will always be, as abolitionist Wendell Phillips remarked, "hard to tell who's mad."

❯❯ ❯❯ ❯❯ ADDITIONAL READING ❮❮ ❮❮ ❮❮

The best of modern biographies on John Brown is Stephen Oates, *To Purge This Land with Blood* (New York, 1970). Oates's treatment is evenhanded, scholarly, and stirring in its narrative. (Other modern biographies include studies by Jules C. Abels and Richard O. Boyer, both published during the 1970s.) Oswald Garrison Villard, *John Brown, 1800–1859: A Biography Fifty Years After* (Boston, 1910), is an older work worth reading. It draws on and excerpts many primary sources. C. Vann Woodward, "John Brown's Private War," is one of the best short interpretive essays available on the raid and can be found in his *Burden of Southern History* (Baton Rouge, La., 1968). For a detailed account of Brown's earlier doings in Kansas, see James C. Malin, *John Brown and the Legacy of Fifty-Six* (Philadelphia, 1942). Brown's relationship with his conspirators is grippingly told in Edward J. Renehan Jr., *The Secret Six: The True Tale of the Men Who Conspired with John Brown* (New York, 1995). Franklin B. Sanborn, *The Life and Letters of John Brown* (Boston, 1891), an older biography unabashedly sympathetic to Brown, contains many valuable personal letters. The fullest collection of materials on the raid and trial is *The Life, Trial, and Execution of John Brown* (New York, 1859).

The debate over John Brown's mental state continues. For additional perspectives see Paul Finkelman, ed., *His Soul Goes Marching On: Responses to John Brown and the Harpers Ferry Raid* (Charlottesville, Va., 1995), in particular the essays by Bertram Wyatt-Brown (pp. 10–40) and Robert E. McGlone, who discusses the political considerations of contemporaries' debates about Brown's sanity (pp. 213–52). McGlone's forthcoming *Apocalyptic Visions: John Brown's Witness against Slavery* will argue that Brown suffered from a bipolar depressive condition.

With so little space available in this chapter, we chose to avoid the intricacies of the debates over the present state of Freudian psychology. Readers who would like a biography of Sigmund Freud should turn to Peter Gay's sympathetic *Freud: A Life for Our Time* (New York, 1988). For a good introduction to Freudian theory, see Charles Brenner, *An Elementary Textbook of Psychoanalysis* (New York, 1974). In 1998, the Library of Congress (which holds many of Freud's papers, some of them still restricted in access) mounted an exhibition on Freud. The accompanying book provides a number of useful perspectives: Michael S. Roth, ed., *Freud: Conflict and Culture— Essays on His Life, Work, and Legacy* (New York, 1998). The assault on Freud and his methods receives the best brief treatment in Frederick Crews, ed., *Unauthorized Freud: Doubters Confront a Legend* (New York, 1998). One of the weightiest challenges to the scientific validity of Freudian theory came from Adolf Grünbaum, *The Foundations of Psychoanalysis* (Berkeley, Calif., 1984). Other critical works include another voluminous study, Malcolm Macmillan's *Freud Evaluated: The Completed Arc* (Cambridge, Mass., 1997), and the more succinct analysis by Allen Esterson, *Seductive Mirage: An Exploration of the Work of Sigmund Freud* (Chicago, 1993).

Like psychoanalysis itself, psychohistory has always been a tempestuous field. It was formally acknowledged when historian William L. Langer used his presidential address to the American Historical Association to call for increased use of psychoanalytic techniques. "The Next Assignment," Langer's address, appears in the *American Historical Review* 63 (January 1958): 283–304. But Freud himself had dabbled in historical waters, with disastrous results, in (among other studies) a psychobiography coauthored with William Bullitt entitled *Thomas Woodrow Wilson* (Boston, reprinted 1968). More responsible efforts include Erik Erikson's biographies, *Young Man Luther* (New York, 1958) and *Gandhi's Truth* (New York, 1969). The methods of psychohistory are discussed in Robert J. Lifton, ed., *Explorations in Psychohistory* (New York, 1974). Also useful is George M. Kren and Leon H. Rappoport, eds., *Varieties of Psychohistory* (New York, 1976) and Robert J. Brugger, ed., *Our Selves/Our Past: Psychological Approaches to American History* (Baltimore, 1981). For recent examples of the discipline, see current issues of *The Journal of Psychohistory*. David E. Stannard applies the Freudian critique to the problems of psychohistory in *Shrinking History* (New York, 1980). Peter Gay's brief for the defense, *Freud for Historians* (New York, 1985) strikes us as disappointing, and Stannard provides a scathing commentary in "Grand Illusions," *Reviews in American History* 14:2 (June 1986): 289–308.

As professed amateurs in the psychoanalytic field, we would like to thank Dr. David Musto, able psychiatrist and historian, for a fine introduction to the territory in his graduate seminars at Yale University. In evaluating John Brown, we also consulted with two practicing psychiatrists, both aware of the possibilities and limitations of their discipline: Dr. Geoff Linburn of the M.I.T. mental health staff and Dr. Eric Berger of Yale psychiatric faculty. Finally, our friend Dr. John Rugge brought into focus Brown's striking concern for property and ownership.

❧ ❧ SEVEN ❧ ❧

The View from the Bottom Rail

Thunder. From across the swamps and salt marshes of the Carolina coast came the distant, repetitive pounding. Thunder out of a clear blue sky. Down at the slave quarters, young Sam Mitchell heard the noise and wondered. In Beaufort, the nearby village, planter John Chaplin heard too, and dashed for his carriage. The drive back to his plantation was as quick as Chaplin could make it. Once home, he ordered his wife and children to pack; then looked for his slaves. The flatboat must be made ready, he told them; the family was going to Charleston. He needed eight men at the oars. One of the slaves, Sam Mitchell's father, brought the news to his wife and son at the slave quarters. "You ain't gonna row no boat to Charleston," the wife snapped, "you go out dat back door and keep agoing." Young Sam was mystified by all the commotion. How could it thunder without a cloud in the sky? "Son, dat ain't no t'under," explained the mother, "dat Yankee come to gib you freedom."

The pounding of the guns came relatively quickly to Beaufort—November of 1861, only seven months after the first hostilities at Fort Sumter. Yet it was only a matter of time before the thunder of freedom rolled across the rest of the south, from the bayous and deltas of Louisiana in 1862 to the farms around Richmond in 1865. And as the guns of the Union spoke, thousands of Sam Mitchells experienced their own unforgettable moments. Freedom was coming to a nation of four million slaves.

To most slaves, the men in the blue coats were foreigners. As foreigners, they were sometimes suspect. Many southern masters painted the prospect of northern invasion in deliberately lurid colors. Union soldiers, one Tennessee slave was told, "got long horns on their heads, and tushes in their mouths, and eyes sticking out like a cow! They're mean old things." A fearful Mississippi slave refused to come down out of a tree until the Union soldier below her took off his cap and demonstrated he had no horns. Many slaves, however, took such tales with more than a grain of salt. "We all hear 'bout dem Yankees," a Carolina slave told his overseer. "Folks tell we they has horns and a tail . . . Wen I see dem coming I shall run like all possess." But as soon as the overseer fled, leaving the plantation in the slaves' care, the tune changed: "Good-by, ole man, good-by. That's right. Skedaddle as fast as you kin. . . . We's gwine to run sure enough; but we knows the Yankees, an' we runs that way."

This slave family lived on a plantation at Beaufort, South Carolina, not far from the plantation where Sam Mitchell heard the thunder of northern guns in 1861. The photograph was taken after northern forces had occupied the Sea Islands area. (Library of Congress)

For some slaves, the habit of long years, the bond of loyalty, or the fear of alternatives led them to side with their masters. Faithful slaves hid valuable silver, persuaded Yankees that their departed masters were actually Union sympathizers, or feigned contagious illness in order to scare off marauding soldiers. One slave even led Yankees right to the plantation beehives. "De Yankees forgot all about de meat an' things dey done stole," she noted with satisfaction; "they took off down de road at a run." But in many cases, the conflict between loyalty and freedom caused confusion and anguish. A Georgia couple, both more than sixty years old, greeted the advance of Sherman's soldiers calmly and with apparent lack of interest. They seemed entirely content to remain under the care of their master instead of joining the mass of slaves flocking along behind Sherman's troops. As the soldiers prepared to leave, however, the old woman suddenly stood up, a "fierce, almost devilish" look in her eyes, and turned to her husband. "What you sit dar for?" she asked vehemently. "You s'pose I wait sixty years for nutten? Don't yer see de door open? I'se follow my child; I not stay. Yes, anudder day I goes 'long wid dese people; yes, sar, I walks till I drop in my tracks."

Other slaves felt no hesitation about choosing freedom; indeed, they found it difficult to contain their joy. One woman, who overheard the news of emancipation just before she was to serve her master's dinner, asked to be excused because she had to get water from a nearby spring. Once she had reached the seclusion of the spring, she allowed her feelings free rein.

> I jump up and scream, "Glory, glory hallelujah to Jesus! I'se free! I'se free! Glory to God, you come down an' free us; no big man could do it." An' I got sort o' scared, afeared somebody hear me, an' I takes another good look, an' fall on de goun' an' roll over, an' kiss de gound' fo' de Lord's sake, I's so full o' praise to Masser Jesus.

To the newly freed slaves, it seemed as if the world had been turned upside down. Rich and powerful masters were fleeing before Yankees, while freed slaves were left with the run of the plantation. The situation was summed up succinctly by one black soldier who was surprised—and delighted—to find his former master among the prisoners he was guarding. "Hello, massa!" he said cheerfully, "bottom rail top dis time!"

RECOVERING THE FREEDPEOPLE'S POINT OF VIEW

The freeing of four million black slaves surely ranks as one of the major events in American history. Yet the story has not been an easy one to tell. To understand the personal trials and triumphs of the newly liberated slaves, or freedpeople as they have come to be called,[1] historians must draw on the personal experiences of those at the center of the drama. They must re-create the freedpeople's point of view. But slaves had occupied the lowest level of America's social and economic scale. They sat, as the black soldier correctly noted, on the bottom rail of the fence. For several reasons, that social reality has made it more difficult for historians to recover the freedpeople's point of view.

In the first place, most traditional histories have suffered from a natural "top-rail" bias. They have most often taken as their subjects members of the higher social classes. Histories cannot be written without the aid of documentary raw material, and by and large, those on the top rails of society have produced the most voluminous records. Having been privileged to receive an education, members of the middle and upper classes are more apt to publish memoirs, keep diaries, or write letters. As leaders of society who make decisions, they are the subjects of official minutes and records. They are more often written about and commented on by their contemporaries.

---

1. White contemporaries of the newly freed slaves referred to them as freedmen. More recently historians have preferred the gender neutral term *freedpeople*, which we will use here except when quoting primary sources.

At the other end of the social spectrum, ordinary folk lead lives that are often less documented. While political leaders involve themselves in what appears to be one momentous issue after another, the work of farmers and laborers is often repetitive and appears to have little effect on the course of history. The decade of the 1970s, however, saw an increasing interest by historians in the writing of social histories that would shed greater light on the lives of ordinary people. In Chapter 1, for example, we saw that a knowledge of the social and economic position of the serving class was essential to understanding the volatile society of early Virginia. Similarly, we turned to the social tensions of ordinary farmers in order to explore the alliances behind the witchcraft controversy at Salem.

Although social historians have found it challenging to piece together the lives of any anonymous class of Americans, reconstructing the perspective of enslaved African Americans has proved particularly challenging. In the years before the Civil War, not only were slaves discouraged from learning to read and write, southern legislatures passed slave codes that flatly forbade whites to teach them. The laws were not entirely effective. A few blacks employed as drivers on large plantations learned to read and correspond so that their absent masters might send them instructions. Some black preachers were also literate. Still, most reading remained a clandestine affair, done out of sight of the master or other whites. During the war, a literate slave named Squires Jackson was eagerly scanning a newspaper for word of northern victories when his master unexpectedly entered the room and demanded to know what the slave was doing. The surprised reader deftly turned the newspaper upside down, put on a foolish grin, and said, "Confederates done won the war!" The master laughed and went about his business.

Even though most slaves never wrote letters, kept diaries, or left other written records, it might at first seem easy enough to learn about slave life from accounts written by white contemporaries. Any number of letters, books, travelers' accounts, and diaries survive, after all—full of descriptions of life under slavery and of the experiences of freedpeople after the war. Yet the question of perspective raises serious problems. The vantage point of white Americans observing slavery was emphatically not that of slaves who lived under the "peculiar institution" nor of those freedpeople forced to cope with their dramatically changed circumstances. The marked differences between the social and psychological positions of blacks and whites make it extremely difficult to reconstruct the black point of view solely from white accounts.

Consider, first, the observations of those white people who associated most often and most closely with black slaves: their masters. The relation between master and slave was inherently unequal. Slaves could be whipped for trifling offenses; they could be sold or separated from their families and closest friends; even under "kind" masters, they were bound to labor as ordered if they wanted their ration of food and clothing. With slaves so dependent on the master's authority, they were hardly likely to reveal their true feelings; the dangerous consequences of such indiscretion were too great.

In fact, we have already encountered an example in which a slave deceived his master: the case of Squires Jackson and his newspaper. Think for a moment about the source of that story. Even without a footnote to indicate where the information came from, readers of this chapter can deduce that it was left in the historical record by Jackson, not the planter. (The planter, after all, went away convinced Jackson could not read.) And indeed, Jackson is the source of the story. But imagine how much different our impression would be if the only surviving record of Jackson's conduct was the planter's diary. No such diary has survived, but if it had, we might have read an entry something like the following:

> A humorous incident occurred today. While entering the woodshed to attend some business, I came upon my slave Squires. His large eyes were fixed with intense interest upon an old copy of a newspaper he had come upon, which alarmed me some until I discovered the rascal was reading its contents upside down. "Why Squires," I said innocently. "What is the latest news?" He looked up at me with a big grin and said, "Massa, de 'Federates jes' won de war!" It made me laugh to see the darkey's simple confidence. I wish I could share his optimism.

This entry is fictional, but having Jackson's version of the story serves to cast suspicion on similar entries in real planter diaries. One Louisiana slaveowner, for instance, marveled that his field hands went on with their Christmas party apparently unaware that Yankee raiding parties had pillaged a nearby town. "We have been watching the negroes dancing for the last two hours. . . . They are having a merry time, thoughtless creatures, they think not of the morrow." It apparently never occurred to the planter that the "thoughtless" merriment may have been especially great because of the northern troops nearby.[2]

The harsh realities of the war caused many southerners to realize for the first time just how little they really knew about their slaves. In areas where Union troops were near, slaves ran for freedom—often the very servants that masters had deemed most loyal. Mary Chesnut, whose house was not far from Fort Sumter, sought in vain to penetrate the blank expressions of her slaves. "Not by one word or look can we detect any change in the demeanor of these Negro servants. . . . You could not tell that they even hear the awful noise that is going on in the bay [at Fort Sumter], though it is dinning in their ears night and day. . . . Are they stolidly stupid, or wiser than we are, silent and strong, biding their time?"

---

2. Readers who review the opening narrative of this chapter will discover that they have already encountered quite a few other examples of deception arising out of the social situations in which the actors found themselves. In fact, except for the black soldier's comment about the bottom rail being top, every example of white-black relations cited in the opening section has some element of concealment or deception. It may be worth noting that we did not select the opening incidents with that fact in mind. The preponderance of deception was noted only when we reviewed the draft several days after it had been written.

"They are having a merry time, thoughtless creatures, they think not of the morrow." This scene of a Christmas party, similar to the one described by the Louisiana planter, appeared with an article written by a northern correspondent for *Frank Leslie's Illustrated Newspaper* in 1857. The picture, reflecting the popular stereotype of slaves as cheerful and ignorantly content with their lot, suggests that the social constraints of the times made it as difficult for southern African Americans to be completely candid with their northern liberators as it had been to be candid with their southern masters. (Library of Congress)

It is tempting to suppose that white northerners who helped liberate slaves might provide more sympathetic or accurate accounts of freedpeople's attitudes. But that assumption is dangerous. Although virtually all northern slaves had been freed by 1820, race prejudice remained overwhelmingly evident. Antislavery forces often combined a vehement dislike of slavery with an equally vehement desire to keep the freedpeople out of the North. For African Americans who did live there, most housing and transportation facilities were segregated. Whites and blacks had much less contact than that afforded by the easy, if unequal, familiarity common in the South.

Consequently, while some Union soldiers went out of their way to be kind to the slaves they encountered, many more looked upon African Americans with distaste and open hostility. Many Yankees strongly believed that they were fighting a war to save the Union, not to free the "cursed Nigger," as one recruit put it. Even white officers who commanded black regiments could be remarkably unsympathetic. "Any one listening to your shouting and singing can see how grotesquely ignorant you are," one officer lectured his troops when they refused to accept less than the pay promised them on enlistment. Even missionaries and other sympathetic northerners who came to occupied territory had preconceptions to overcome. "I saw some very low-looking women who answered very intelligently, contrary to my expectations," noted Philadelphia missionary Laura Towne. Another female missionary, much less sympathetic than Laura Towne, bridled when a black child greeted her with too much familiarity. "I say good-mornin' to my young missus," recounted the child to a friend, "and she say, 'I slap your mouth for your impudence, you nigger.'" Such callousness underlines the need for caution when reviewing northern accounts.

Indeed, perceptive northern whites recognized that black people would continue to be circumspect around white people. Just as the slave had been dependent on his southern masters, so freedpeople found themselves similarly vulnerable to the new class of conquerors. "One of these blacks, fresh from slavery, will most adroitly tell you precisely what you want to hear," noted northerner Charles Nordhoff.

> To cross-examine such a creature is a task of the most delicate nature; if you chance to put a leading question he will answer to its spirit as closely as the compass needle answers to the magnetic pole. Ask if the enemy had fifty thousand men, and he will be sure that they had at least that many; express your belief that they had not five thousand, and he will laugh at the idea of their having more than forty-five hundred.

Samuel Gridley Howe, a wartime commissioner investigating the freedpeople's condition, saw the situation clearly. "The negro, like other men, naturally desires to live in the light of truth," he argued, "but he hides in the shadow of falsehood, more or less deeply, according as his safety or welfare seems to require it. Other things equal, the freer a people, the more truthful; and only the perfectly free and fearless are perfectly truthful."

Even sympathetic northerners were at a disadvantage in recounting the freedpeople's point of view, simply because the culture of southern African Americans was so unfamiliar to them. The first hurdle was simple communication, given the wide variety of accents and dialects spoken by northerners and southerners. Charles Nordhoff noted that often he had the feeling that he was "speaking with foreigners." The slaves' phrase "I go shum" puzzled him until he discovered it to be a contraction of "I'll go see about it." Another missionary was "teaching the little darkies gymnastics and what various things were for, eyes, etc. He asked what ears were made for, and when they said, 'To yer with,' he could not understand them at all."

If black dialect was difficult to understand, black culture and religion could appear even more unfathomable. Although most slaves nominally shared with northerners a belief in Christianity, black methods of worship shocked more than one staid Unitarian. After church meetings, slaves often participated in a singing and dancing session known as a "shout," in which the leader would sing out a line of song and the chorus would respond, dancing in rhythm to the music. As the night proceeded, the music became more vocal and the dancing more vigorous. "Tonight I have been to a 'shout'," reported Laura Towne, "which seems to me certainly the remains of some old idol worship . . . I never saw anything so savage." Another missionary noted, "It was the most hideous and at the same time the most pitiful sight I ever witnessed."

Thus, as sympathetic as many northerners wished to be, significant obstacles prevented them from fully appreciating the freedpeople's point of view. The nature of slave society and the persistence of race prejudice made it virtually impossible for blacks and whites to deal with one another in open, candid ways.

The Freedpeople Speak

Given the scarcity of first-person African American accounts, how can we fully recover the freedpeople's point of view? From the very beginning, some observers recognized the value of the former slaves' perspective. If few black people could write, their stories could be written down by others and made public. Oral testimony, transcribed by literate editors, would allow black Americans to speak out on issues that affected them most.

The tradition of oral evidence began even before the slaves were freed. Abolitionists recognized the value of firsthand testimony against the slave system. They took down the stories of fugitive slaves who had made their way North, and they published the accounts. During the war Congress also established the Freedman's Inquiry Commission, which collected information that might aid the government in formulating policies toward the newly freed slaves.

In the half-century following Reconstruction, however, interest in preserving black history generally languished. An occasional journalist or historian traveled through the South to interview former slaves. Educators at black schools, such as the Hampton Institute, published recollections. But a relatively small number of subjects were interviewed. Often the interviews were published in daily newspapers whose standards of accuracy were not high and where the interviews were severely edited to fit limited space.

Furthermore, the vast majority of professional historians writing about Reconstruction ignored these interviews, as well as the freedpeople's perspective in general. Historians most often relied on white accounts, which, not unexpectedly, painted a rather partial picture. William A. Dunning, a historian at Columbia University, was perhaps the most influential advocate of the prevailing viewpoint. He painted the freedpeople as childish, happy-go-lucky creatures who failed to appreciate the responsibilities of their new status. "As the full meaning of [emancipation] was grasped by the freedmen," Dunning wrote, "great numbers of them abandoned their old homes, and, regardless of crops to be cultivated, stock to be cared for, or food to be provided, gave themselves up to testing their freedom. They wandered aimlessly but happy through the country." At the same time Dunning asserted that Confederate soldiers and other southern whites had "devoted themselves with desperate energy to the procurement of what must sustain the life of both themselves and their former slaves." Such were the conclusions deduced without the aid of the freedpeople's perspectives.

Only in the twentieth century were systematic efforts made to question blacks about their experiences as slaves and freedpeople. Interest in the African American heritage rose markedly during the 1920s, in great part spurred by the efforts of black scholars like W. E. B. Du Bois, Charles Johnson, and Carter Woodson, the editor and founder of the *Journal of Negro History*. Those scholars labored diligently to overturn the Reconstruction stereotypes promoted by the Dunning school. Moreover, the growth of both sociology and anthropology departments at American universities encouraged scholars to analyze Southern culture using the tools of the new social sciences. By the beginning of the 1930s, historians at Fisk and Southern universities had instituted projects to collect oral evidence.

Ironically, the economic adversity of the Depression sparked the greatest single effort to gather oral testimony from the freedpeople. One of the many alphabet-soup agencies chartered by the Roosevelt administration was the Federal Writers' Project (FWP). The project's primary goal was to compile cultural guides to each of the forty-eight states, using unemployed writers and journalists to collect and edit the information. But under the direction of folklorist John Lomax, the FWP also organized staffs in many states to interview former slaves.

Although Lomax's project placed greatest emphasis on collecting black folklore and songs, the FWP's directive to interviewers included a long list of historical questions that interviewers were encouraged to ask. The following sampling gives an indication of the project's interests:

> What work did you do in slavery days? Did you ever earn any money?
> What did you eat and how was it cooked? Any possums? Rabbits? Fish?
> Was there a jail for slaves? Did you ever see any slaves sold or auctioned off?
>   How and for what causes were the slaves punished? Tell what you saw.
> What do you remember about the war that brought you your freedom? When
>   the Yankees came what did they do or say?
> What did the slaves do after the war? What did they receive generally? What
>   do they think about the reconstruction period?

The results of these interviews are remarkable, even in terms of sheer bulk. More than 2,300 were recorded and edited in state FWP offices and then sent to Washington, assembled in 1941, and published in typescript. A facsimile edition, issued during the 1970s, takes up nineteen volumes. Supplementary materials, including hundreds of interviews never forwarded to Washington during the project's life, comprise another twenty-two volumes. Benjamin Botkin, the series' original editor, recognized the collection's importance:

> These life histories, taken down as far as possible in the narrator's words, constitute an invaluable body of unconscious evidence or indirect source material, which scholars and writers dealing with the South, especially, social

psychologists and cultural anthropologists, cannot afford to reckon without. For the first and last time, a large number of surviving slaves (many of whom have since died) have been permitted to tell their own story, in their own way.

At first glance, the slave narrative collection would appear to fulfill admirably the need for a guide to the freedpeople's point of view. But even Botkin, for all his enthusiasm, recognized that the narratives could not simply be taken at face value. Like other primary source materials, they need to be viewed in terms of the context in which they originated.

To begin with, no matter how massive the nineteen volumes of interviews may appear on the library shelf, they still constitute a small sampling of the original four million freedpeople. What sort of selection bias might exist? Geographic imbalance comes quickly to mind. Are the slave interviews drawn from a broad cross section of southern states? Counting the number of slaves interviewed from each state, we discover only 155 interviews from African Americans living in Virginia, Missouri, Maryland, Delaware, and Kentucky—about 6 percent of the total number of interviews published. Yet in 1860, 23 percent of the southern slave population lived in those states. Thus the upper South is underrepresented in the collection.

What about age? Because the interviews took place primarily between 1936 and 1938, former slaves were fairly old: fully two-thirds of them were more than eighty years of age. The predominance of elderly interviewees raises several questions, most obviously, how sharp were the informants' memories? The Civil War was already seventy years in the past. Ability to recall accurately varies from person to person, but common sense suggests that the further away from an event, the less detailed a person's memory is likely to be. In addition, age may have biased the type of recollections as well as their accuracy. Historian John Blassingame has noted that the average life expectancy of a slave in 1850 was less than fifty years. Those who lived to a ripe old age might well have survived because they were treated better than the average slave. If so, their accounts would reflect some of the milder experiences of slaves.

Also, if those interviewed were predominantly old in 1936, they were predominantly young during the Civil War. Almost half (43 percent) were less than ten years old in 1865. Sixty-seven percent were under age fifteen, and 83 percent were under age twenty. Thus, many interviewers remembered slavery as it would have been experienced by a child. Since the conditions of bondage were relatively less harsh for a child than for an adult slave, once again the FWP narratives may be somewhat skewed toward an optimistic view of slavery. (On the other hand, it might be argued that because children are so impressionable, memories both good and bad might have been vividly magnified.)

Other possible sampling biases come to mind—the sex of the subjects or the kinds of labor they performed as slaves. But distortions may be introduced into the slave narratives in ways more serious than sample bias. Interviewers, simply by choosing their questions, define the kinds of information a subject will volunteer. We have already seen that sensitive observers, such as Charles Nordhoff, recognized how important it was not to ask leading questions. But even Nordhoff may not have realized how many unconscious cues the most innocent questions carry.

Social scientists specializing in interviewing have pointed out that even the grammatical form of a question will influence a subject's response. Take, for example, the following questions:

> Where did you hear about this job opening?
> How did you hear about this job opening?
> So you saw our want ad for this job?

Each question is directed at the same information, yet each suggests to the subject a different response. The first version ("Where did you hear . . .") implies that the interviewer wants a specific, limited answer ("Down at the employment center."). The second question, by substituting "how" for "where," invites the subject to offer a longer response ("Well, I'd been looking around for a job for several weeks, and I was over at the employment office when . . ."). The final question signals that the interviewer wants only a yes or no confirmation to a question whose answer is believed to be already known.

Interviewers, in other words, constantly communicate to their subjects the kinds of evidence they want, the length of the answers, and even the manner in which answers ought to be offered. If such interviewing cues influence routine conversations, they prove even more crucial when a subject as controversial as slavery is involved, and where relations between blacks and whites continue to be strained. In fact, the most important cue an interviewer was likely to have given was one presented before any conversation took place. Was the interviewer white or black? William Ferris, a sociologist obtaining oral folklore in the Mississippi Delta region in 1968, discussed the problem. "It was not possible to maintain rapport with both Whites and Blacks in the same community," he noted,

> for the confidence and cooperation of each was based on their belief that I was "with them" in my convictions about racial taboos of Delta society. Thus when I was "presented" to Blacks by a white member of the community, the informants regarded me as a member of the white caste and therefore limited their lore to noncontroversial topics.

Such tensions were even more prevalent throughout the South during the 1930s. In hundreds of ways, black people were made aware that they were still considered inferior to white people, and that they were to remain within strictly segregated and subordinate bounds. From 1931 to 1935, more than seventy African Americans were lynched in the South, often for minor or nonexistent crimes. Black prisoners found themselves forced to negotiate grossly unfavorable labor contracts if they wished to be released. Many sharecroppers and other poor farmers were constantly in debt to white property owners.

Smaller matters of etiquette reflected the larger state of affairs. A white southerner would commonly address black adults by their first names, or as "boy," "auntie," "uncle," regardless of the black person's status and even if the white person knew the black person's full name. Black people were required to address white people as "ma'am" or "mister." Such distinctions were maintained even on the telephone. If an African American placed a long-distance call for "Mr. Smith" in a neighboring town, the white operator would ask, "Is he colored?" The answer being yes, her reply would be, "Don't you say 'Mister' to me. He ain't 'Mister' to me." Conversely, an operator would refuse to place a call by a black caller who did not address her as "Ma'am."

In such circumstances, most African Americans were naturally reticent about volunteering information to white FWP interviewers. "Lots of old slaves closes the door before they tell the truth about their days of slavery," noted one black Texan to an interviewer. "When the door is open, they tell how kind their masters was how rosy it all was." Samuel S. Taylor, a skilled black interviewer in Arkansas, found that he had to reassure informants that the information they were giving would not be used against them. "I've told you too much," one subject concluded. "How come they want all this stuff from the colored people anyway? Do you take any stories from the white people? They know all about it. They know more about it than I do. They don't need me to tell it to them."

Often the whites who interviewed blacks lived in the same town and were long acquaintances. "I 'members when you was barefoot at de bottom," one black interviewee told his white (and balding) interviewer; "now I see you a settin' dere, gittin' bare at de top, as bare as de palm of my hand." Another black man revealed an even closer relationship when he noted that his wife, Ellen, " 'joy herself, have a good time nussin' [nursing] white folks chillun. Nussed you; she tell me 'bout it many time." In such circumstances African Americans could hardly be expected to speak frankly. One older woman summed up the situation quite cheerfully. "Oh, I know your father en your granfather en all of dem. Bless Mercy, child, I don't want to tell you nothin' but what to please you."

The methods used to set down FWP interviews raise additional problems. With only a few exceptions (see our bibliography at the end of the chapter), audio tape recorders were not used. Instead, interviewers took written notes of their conversations, from which they later reconstructed their interview. In the process, interviewers often edited their material. Sometimes changes were made simply to improve the flow, so that the interview did not jump jarringly from topic to topic. Other interviewers edited out material they believed to be irrelevant or objectionable.

Furthermore, no protocol existed for transcribing African American dialect onto the written page. A few interviewers took great pains to render their accounts in correct English, so that regional accents and dialect disappeared. ("Fo' " became "for," "dem" became "them," and so forth.) But most interviewers tried to provide a flavor of black dialect, with wildly varying success. In some cases the end result sounded more like the stereotypical

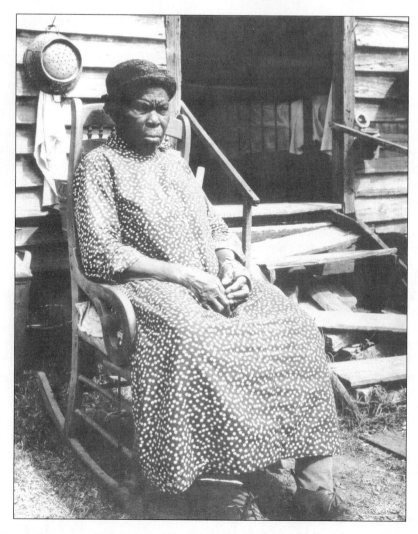

"I've told you too much. How come they want all this stuff from the colored people anyway? Do you take any stories from the white people? They don't need me to tell it to them." This Georgia woman, like many of the subjects interviewed for the Federal Writers' Project, was still living in the 1930s on the plantation where she had grown up as a slave child. The plantation was still owned by descendants of her former master. Under such conditions suspicion toward FWP interviewers was a predictable reaction, even if the interviewer was black; doubly so if he or she was white and a resident of the community. (National Archives)

"darky dialect" popular with whites of the period. "I wuz comin' frum de back uv de stable," an interviewer might quote his subject as saying—a colloquial approach that, to some readers, might at first seem unobjectionable. Yet few of the same interviewers would have thought it necessary to render, with similar offbeat spelling, the accents of a white "southun plantuh," whose speech might seem equally exotic to an American from another region of the United States. For that matter, consider the spellings used in "I wuz comin' frum de back uv de stable." In fact, there is no difference in pronunciation between "was" and "wuz;" or "frum" and "from;" or "uv" and "of." In effect, those transcriptions are simply cultural markers conveying the unspoken message that, in the eyes of the interviewer, the speaker comes from a different (read: less cultured and less educated) social class. Eventually the FWP sent its interviewers a list of "Approved Dialect Expressions:" "dem," "dose," and "gwine" were among the permitted transcriptions; "wuz," "ovah," and "uv" were not allowed.

By understanding the difficulties of gathering oral evidence, researchers are able to proceed more carefully in evaluating the slave narrative collection. Even so, readers new to this field may find it difficult to appreciate the varying responses that different interviewers might elicit. In order to bring the point home, it may be helpful to analyze material that we came across during our own research in the slave narrative collection. The first interview is with Susan Hamlin, a black woman who lived in Charleston, and we reprint it below exactly as it appears in typescript.

Interview With Ex-Slave

On July 6th, I interviewed Susan Hamlin, ex-slave, at 17 Henrietta street, Charleston, S. C. She was sitting just inside of the front door, on a step leading up to the porch, and upon hearing me inquire for her she assumed that I was from the Welfare office, from which she had received aid prior to its closing. I did not correct this impression, and at no time did she suspect that the object of my visit was to get the story of her experience as a slave. During our conversation she mentioned her age. "Why that's very interesting, Susan," I told her, "If you are that old you probably remember the Civil War and slavery days." "Yes, Ma'am, I been a slave myself," she said, and told me the following story:

"I kin remember some things like it was yesterday, but I is 104 years old now, and age is starting to get me, I can't remember everything like I use to. I getting old, old. You know I is old when I been a grown woman when the Civil War broke out. I was hired out then, to a Mr. McDonald, who lived on Atlantic Street, and I remembers when de first shot was fired, and the shells went right over de city. I got seven dollars a month for looking after children, not taking them out, you understand, just minding them. I did not got the money, Mausa got it." "Don't you think that was fair?" I asked. "If you were fed and clothed by him, shouldn't he be paid for your work?" Course it been fair," she answered, "I belong to him and he got to get something to take care of me."

"My name before I was married was Susan Calder, but I married a man named Hamlin. I belonged to Mr. Edward Fuller, he was president of the First National Bank. He was a good man to his people till de Lord took him. Mr. Fuller got his slaves by marriage. He married Miss Mikell, a lady what lived on Edisto Island, who was a slave owner, and we lived on Edisto on a plantation. I don't remember de name cause when Mr. Fuller got to be president of de bank we come to Charleston to live. He sell out the plantation and say them (the slaves) that want to come to Charleston with him could come and them what wants to stay can stay on the island with his wife's people. We had our choice. Some is come and some is stay, but my ma and us children come with Mr. Fuller.

We lived on St. Philip street. The house still there, good as ever. I go 'round there to see it all de time; the cistern still there too, where we used to sit 'round and drink the cold water, and eat, and talk and laugh. Mr. Fuller have lots of servants and the ones he didn't need hisself he hired out. The slaves had rooms in the back, the ones with children had two rooms and them that didn't have any children had one room, not to cook in but to sleep in. They all cooked and ate downstairs in the hall that they had for the colored people. I don't know about slavery but I know all the slavery I know about, the people was good to me. Mr. Fuller was a good man and his wife's people been grand people, all good to their slaves. Seem like Mr. Fuller just git his slaves so he could be good to dem. He made all the little colored chillen love him. If you don't believe they loved him what they all cry, and scream, and holler for when dey hear he dead? 'Oh, Mausa dead my Mausa dead, what I going to do, my Mausa dead.' Dey tell dem t'aint no use to cry, dat can't bring him back, but de chillen keep on crying. We used to call him Mausa Eddie but he named Mr. Edward Fuller, and he sure was a good man.

"A man come here about a month ago, say he from de Government, and dey send him to find out 'bout slavery. I give him most a book, and what he give me? A dime. He ask me all kind of questions. He ask me dis and he ask me dat, didn't de white people do dis and did dey do dat but Mr. Fuller was a good man, he was sure good to me and all his people, dey all like him, God bless him, he in de ground now but I ain't going to let nobody lie on him. You know he good when even the little chillen cry and holler when he dead. I tell you dey couldn't jsut fix us up any kind of way when we going to Sunday School. We had to be dressed nice, if you pass him and you ain't dress to suit him he send you right back and say tell your ma to see dat you dress right. Dey couldn't send you out in de cold barefoot neither. I 'member one day my ma want to send me wid some milk for her sister-in-law what lived 'round de corner. I fuss cause it cold and say 'how you going to send me out wid no shoe, and it cold?' Mausa hear how I talkin and turn he back and laugh, den he call to my ma to gone in de house and find shoe to put on my feet and don't let him see me barefoot again in cold weather.

When de war start going good and de shell fly over Charleston he take all us up to Aiken for protection. Talk 'bout marching through Georgia, dey sure march through Aiken, soldiers was everywhere.

"My ma had six children, three boys and three girls, but I de only one left, all my white people and all de colored people gone, not a soul left but me. I ain't been sick in 25 years. I is near my church and I don't miss service any Sunday, night or morning. I kin walk wherever I please, I kin walk to de Battery if I want to. The Welfare use to help me but dey shut down now, I can't find out if dey going to open again or not. Miss (Mrs.) Buist and Miss Pringle, dey help me when I can go there but all my own dead."

"Were most of the masters kind?" I asked. "Well you know," she answered, "times den was just like dey is now, some was kind and some was mean; heaps of wickedness went on just de same as now. All my people was good people. I see some wickedness and I hear 'bout all kinds of t'ings but you don't know whether it was lie or not. Mr Fuller been a Christian man."

"Do you think it would have been better if the Negroes had never left Africa?" was the next question I asked. "No Ma'am, (emphatically) dem heathen didn't have no religion. I tell you how I t'ink it is. The Lord made t'ree nations, the white, the red and the black, and put dem in different places on de earth where dey was to stay. Dose black ignoramuses in Africa forgot God, and didn't have no religion and God blessed and prospered the white people dat did remember Him and sent dem to teach de black people even if dey have to grab dem and bring dem into bondage till dey learned some sense. The Indians forgot God and dey had to be taught better so dey land was taken away from dem. God sure bless and prosper de white people and He put de red and de black people under dem so dey could teach dem and bring dem into sense wid God. Dey had to get dere brains right, and honor God, and learn uprightness wid God cause ain't He make you, and ain't His Son redeem you and save you wid His Precious blood. You kin plan all de wickedness you want and pull hard as you choose but when the Lord mek up His mind you is to change, He can change you dat quick (snapping her fingers) and easy. You got to believe on Him if it tek bondage to bring you to your knees.

You know I is got converted. I been in Big Bethel (church) on my knees praying under one of de preachers. I see a great, big, dark pack on my back, and it had me all bent over and my shoulders drawn down, all hunch up. I look up and I see de glory, I see a big beautiful light, a great light, and in de middle is de Sabior, hanging so (extending her arms) just like He died. Den I gone to praying good, and I can feel de sheckles (shackles) loose up and moving and de pack fall off. I don't know where it went to, I see de angels in de Heaven, and hear dem say 'Your sins are forgiven.' I scream and fell off so. (Swoon.) When I come to dey has laid me out straight and I know I is converted cause you can't see no such sight and go on like you is before. I know I is still a sinner but I believe in de power of God and I trust his Holy name. Den dey put me wid de seekers but I know I is already saved."

"Did they take good care of the slaves when their babies were born?" she was asked. "If you want chickens for fat (to fatten) you got to feed dem," she said with a smile, "and if you want people to work dey got to be strong, you got to feed dem and take care of dem too. If dey can't work it come out of your pocket. Lots of wickedness gone on in dem days, just as it do now, some good, some mean, black and white, it just dere nature, if dey good dey going to be kind to everybody, if dey mean dey going to be mean to everybody. Sometimes chillen was sold away from dey parents. De Mausa would come and say "Where Jennie," tell um to put clothes on dat baby, I want um. He sell de baby and de ma scream and holler, you know how dey carry on. Geneally (generally) dey sold it when de ma wasn't dere. Mr. Fuller didn't sell none of us, we stay wid our ma's till we grown, I stay wid my ma till she dead.

"You know I is mix blood, my grandfather bin a white man and my grandmother a mulatto. She been marry to a black so dat how I get fix like I is. I got both blood, so how I going to quarrel wid either side?"

SOURCE: Interview with Susan Hamlin, 17 Henrietta Street

NOTE * Susan lives with a mulatto family of the better type. The name is Hamlin not Hamilton, and her name prior to her marriage was Calder not Collins. I paid particular attention to this and had them spell the names for me. I would judge Susan to be in the late nineties but she is wonderfully well preserved. She now claims to be 104 years old.

From the beginning, the circumstances of this conversation arouse suspicion. The white interviewer, Jessie Butler, mentions that she allowed Hamlin to think she was from the welfare office. Evidently, Butler thought Hamlin would speak more freely if the real purpose of the visit was hidden. But surely the deception had the opposite effect. Hamlin, like most of the black people interviewed, was elderly, unable to work, and dependent on charity. If Butler appeared to be from the welfare office, Hamlin would likely have done whatever she could to ingratiate herself. Many black interviewees consistently assumed that their white interviewers had influence with the welfare office. "You through wid me now, boss? I sho' is glad of dat," concluded one subject. "Help all you kin to get me dat pension befo' I die and de Lord will bless you, honey. . . . Has you got a dime to give dis old nigger, boss?"

Furthermore, Butler's questioning was hardly subtle. When Hamlin noted that she had to give her master the money she made from looking after children, Butler asked, "Don't you think that was fair?" "Course it been fair," came the quick response. Hamlin knew very well what was expected, especially since Butler had already answered the question herself: "If you were fed and clothed by him, shouldn't he be paid for your work?"

Not surprisingly, then, the interview paints slavery in relatively mild colors. Hamlin describes in great detail how good her master was and how she had shoes in the winter. When asked whether most masters were kind, Hamlin appears eminently "fair"—"some was kind and some was mean." She admits hearing "all kinds of t'ings but you don't know whether it was lie or not." She does note that slave children could be sold away from parents and that black mothers protested; but she talks as if that were only to be expected. ("De ma scream and holler, you know how dey carry on.")

Equally flattering is the picture Hamlin paints of relations between the races. "Black ignoramuses" in Africa had forgotten about God, she explains, just as the Indians had; but "God sure bless and prosper de white people."

So Africans and the Indians are placed under white supervision, "to get dere brains right, and honor God, and learn uprightness." Those words were not exactly the ones proslavery apologists would have used to describe the situation, but they were the same sentiments. Defenders of slavery constantly stressed that Europeans served as benevolent models ("parents," Andrew Jackson might have said) leading Africans and Indians on the slow upward road to civilization.

All these aspects of the interview led us to be suspicious about its content. Moreover, several additional clues in the document puzzled us. Hamlin had mentioned a man who visited her "about a month ago, say he from de Government, and dey send him to find out 'bout slavery." Apparently her interview with Jessie Butler was the second she had given. Butler, for her part, made a fuss at the end of the transcript over the spelling of Hamlin's name. ("I paid particular attention to this.") It was "Hamlin not Hamilton" and her maiden name was "Calder not Collins." The phrasing indicates that somewhere else Butler had seen Hamlin referred to as "Susan Hamilton." If someone had interviewed Hamlin earlier, we wondered, could Hamilton have been the name on that original report?

We found the answer when we continued on through the narrative collection. The interview following Butler's was conducted by a man named Augustus Ladson, with a slave named "Susan Hamilton." When compared with Jessie Butler's interview, Augustus Ladson's makes absorbing reading. Here it is, printed exactly as it appears in the collection:

Ex-Slave 101 Years of Age

Has Never Shaken Hands Since 1863

Was on Knees Scrubbing when Freedom Gun Fired

I'm a hund'ed an' one years old now, son. De only one livin' in my crowd frum de days I wuz a slave. Mr. Fuller, my master, who was president of the Firs' National Bank, owned the fambly of us except my father. There were eight men an' women with five girls an' six boys workin' for him. Most o' them wus hired out. De house in which we stayed is still dere with de sisterns an' slave quarters. I always go to see de old home which is on St. Phillip Street.

My ma had t'ree boys an' t'ree girls who did well at their work. Hope Mikell, my eldest brodder, an' James wus de shoemaker. William Fuller, son of our Master, wus de bricklayer. Margurite an' Catharine wus de maids an' look as de children.

My pa b'long to a man on Edisto Island. Frum what he said, his master was very mean. Pa real name wus Adam Collins but he took his master' name; he wus de coachman. Pa did supin one day en his master whipped him. De next day which wus Monday, pa carry him 'bout four miles frum home in de woods an' give him de same 'mount of lickin' he wus given on Sunday. He tied him to a tree an' unhitched de horse so it couldn't git tie-up an' kill e self. Pa den gone to de landin' an' cetch a boat dat wus comin' to Charleston wood fa'm products. He (was) permitted by his master to go to town on errands, which helped him to go on de boat without bein' question'. W'en he got here he gone on de water-front an' ax for a job on a ship so he could git to de North. He got de job an' sail' wood de ship. Dey search de island up an' down for him wood houndogs en w'en it wus t'ought he wus drowned, 'cause dey track him to de river, did dey give up. One of his master' friend gone to New York en went in a store w'ere pas wus employed as a clerk. He reconize' pa is easy is pa reconize' him. He gone back home an' tell pa master who know den dat pa wusn't comin' back an' before he died he sign' papers dat pa wus free. Pa' ma wus dead an' he come down to bury her by de permission of his master' son who had promised no ha'm would come to him, but dey wus' fixin' plans to keep him, so he went to de Work House an' ax to be sold 'cause any slave could sell e self if e could git to de Work House. But it wus on record down dere so dey couldn't sell 'im an' told him his master' people couldn't hold him a slave.

People den use to do de same t'ings dey do now. Some marry an' some live together jus' like now. One t'ing, no minister nebber say in readin' de matrimony "let no man put asounder" 'cause a couple would be married tonight an' tomorrow one would be taken away en be sold. All slaves wus married in dere master house, in de livin' room where slaves an' dere missus an' mossa wus to witness de ceremony. Brides use to wear some of de finest dress an' if dey could afford it, have de best kind of furniture. Your master nor your missus objected to good t'ings.

I'll always 'member Clory, de washer. She wus very high-tempered. She was a mulatto with beautiful hair she could sit on; Clory didn't take foolishness frum anybody. One day our missus gone in de laundry an' find fault with de clothes. Clory didn't do a t'ing but pick her up bodily an' throw 'er out de door. Dey had to sen' fur a doctor 'cause she pregnant an' less than two hours de baby wus bo'n. Afta dat she begged to be sold fur she didn't [want] to kill missus, but our master ain't nebber want to sell his slaves. But dat didn't keep Clory frum gittin' a brutal whippin'. Dey whip' 'er until dere wusn't a white spot on her body. Dat wus de worst I ebber see a human bein' got such a beatin'. I t'ought she wus goin' to die, but she got well an' didn't get any better but meaner until our master decide it wus bes' to rent her out. She willingly agree' since she wusn't 'round missus. She hated an' detest' both of them an' all de fambly.

W'en any slave wus whipped all de other slaves wus made to watch. I see women hung frum de ceilin' of buildin's an' whipped with only supin tied 'round her lower part of de body, until w'en dey wus taken down, dere wusn't breath in de body. I had some terribly bad experiences.

Yankees use to come t'rough de streets, especially de Big Market, huntin' those who want to go to de "free country" as dey call' it. Men an' women wus always missin' an' nobody could give 'count of dere disappearance. De men wus train' up North fur sojus.

De white race is so brazen. Dey come here an' run de Indians frum dere own lan', but dey couldn't make dem slaves 'cause dey wouldn't stan' for it. Indians use to git up in trees an' shoot dem with poison arrow. W'en dey couldn't make dem slaves den dey gone to Africa an' bring dere black brother an' sister. Dey say 'mong themselves, "we gwine mix dem up en make ourselves king. Dats d only way we'd git even with de Indians."

All time, night an' day, you could hear men an' women screamin' to de tip of dere voices as either ma, pa, sister, or brother wus take without any warnin' an' sell. Some time mother who had only one chile wus separated fur life. People wus always dyin' frum a broken heart.

One night a couple married an' de next mornin' de boss sell de wife. De gal ma got in in de street an' cursed de white woman fur all she could find. She said: "dat damn white, pale-face bastard sell my daughter who jus' married las' night," an' other t'ings. The white man tresten' her to call de police if she didn't stop, but de collud woman said: "hit me or call de police. I redder die dan to stan' dis any longer." De police took her to de Work House by de white woman orders an' what became of 'er, I never hear.

W'en de war began we wus taken to Aiken, South Ca'lina were we stay' until de Yankees come t'rough. We could see balls sailin' t'rough de air w'en Sherman wus comin'. Bumbs hit trees in our yard. W'en de freedom gun wus fired, I wus on my 'nees scrubbin'. Dey tell me I wus free but I didn't b'lieve it.

In de days of slavory woman wus jus' given time 'nough to deliver dere babies. Dey deliver de baby 'bout eight in de mornin' an' twelve had to be back to work.

I wus a member of Emmanuel African Methodist Episcopal Church for 67 years. Big Zion, across de street wus my church before den an' before Old Bethel w'en I lived on de other end of town.

Sence Lincoln shook hands with his assasin who at de same time shoot him, frum dat day I stop shakin' hands, even in de church, an' you know how long dat wus. I don't b'lieve in kissin' neider fur all carry dere meannesses. De Master wus betrayed by one of his bosom frien' with a kiss.

SOURCE: Interview with (Mrs.) Susan Hamilton, 17 Henrietta Street, who claims to be 101 years of age. She has never been sick for twenty years and walks as though just 40. She was hired out by her master for seven dollars a month which had to be given her master.

Susan Hamlin and Susan Hamilton are obviously one and the same, yet by the end of Ladson's interview, we are wondering if we have been listening to the same person! Kindness of the masters? We hear no tales about old Mr. Fuller; only vivid recollections of whippings so harsh "dere wusn't a white spot on her body." To Butler, Hamlin had mentioned only cruelties that she had heard about secondhand ("you don't know whether it was lie or not"); to Ladson, she recounts firsthand experiences ("I see women hung from de ceilin' of buildin's an' whipped with only supin tied 'round her lower part of de body.").

Discussions of happy family relations? Instead of tales about shoes in the winter, we hear of Hamlin's father, whipped so severely, he rebels and flees. We hear of family separations, not downplayed with a "you know how dey carry on," but with all the bitterness of mothers whose children had been taken "without any warnin'." We hear of a couple married one night, then

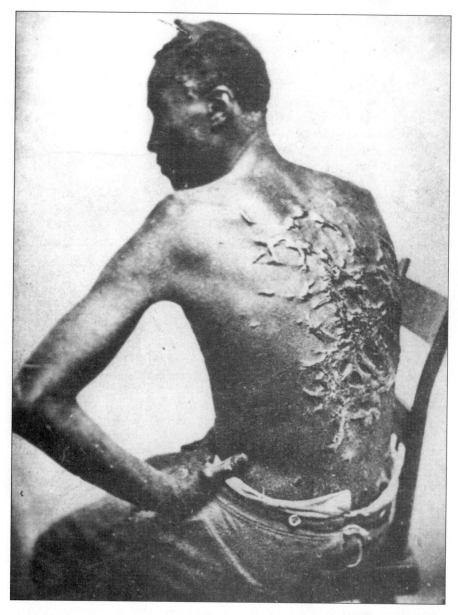

"W'en any slave wus whipped all de other slaves was made to watch. . . . I had some terribly bad experiences." The scars from whippings on this slave's back were recorded in 1863 by an unknown photographer traveling with the Union army. (National Archives)

callously separated and sold the next day. In the Butler account, slave babies are fed well, treated nicely; in the Ladson account, the recollection is of mothers who were given only a few hours away from the fields in order to deliver their children.

Benevolent white paternalism? This time Hamlin's tale of three races draws a different moral. The white race is "brazen," running the Indians off their land. With a touch of admiration, she notes that the Indians "wouldn't stan' for" being made slaves. White motives are seen not as religious but as exploitative and vengeful: "Dey say 'mong themselves, 'we gwine mix dem up and make ourselves king. Dats de only way we'll git even with de Indians.'" The difference between the two interviews, both in tone and substance, is astonishing.

How do we account for this difference? Nowhere in the South Carolina narratives is the race of Augustus Ladson mentioned, but internal evidence would indicate he is black. In a culture in which blacks usually addressed whites respectfully with a "sir," "ma'am," or "boss," it seems doubtful that Susan Hamlin would address a white man as "son." ("I'm a hund'ed an' one years old now, son.") Furthermore, the content of the interview is just too consistently critical of whites. Hamlin would never have remarked, "De white race is so brazen," if Ladson had been white, especially given the reticence demonstrated in her interview with Butler. Nor would she have been so specific about the angry mother's curses ("damn white, pale-face bastard"). It would be difficult to conceive of a more strikingly dramatic demonstration of how an interviewer can affect the responses of a subject.

FREEDOM AND DECEPTION

The slave narrative collection, then, is not the direct, unfiltered perspective that it first appears to be. In fact, interviews like the ones with Susan Hamlin seem to suggest that the search for the "true" perspectives of the freed-people is bound to end in failure and frustration. We have seen, first, that information from planters and other white sources must be treated with extreme skepticism; second, that northern white sources deserve similar caution. Finally, it appears that even the oral testimony of African Americans themselves must be questioned, given the circumstances under which much of it was gathered. It is as if a detective discovered that all the clues so carefully pieced together were hopelessly biased, leading the investigation down the wrong path.

The seriousness of the problem should not be underestimated. It is fundamental. We can try to ease out of the dilemma by noting that differing degrees of bias undoubtedly exist—that some accounts, relatively speaking, are likely to be less deceptive than others. It can be argued, for instance, that Susan Hamlin's interview with Ladson is a more accurate portrayal of her feelings than the interview with Butler. In large measure that assumption is probably true. But does that mean we must reject all of the Butler interview? Presumably, Susan Hamlin's master did give her a pair of shoes one cold winter day. Are we to assume, because of Ladson's interview, that the young child felt no gratitude or obligation to "kind old" Mr. Fuller? or that the old woman did not look back on those years with some ambivalence? For all her life, both slave and free, Susan Hamlin lived in a world where she was required to "feel" one set of emotions when dealing with some people and a different set when dealing with other people. Can we rest completely confident in concluding that the emotions she expressed to Ladson were her "real" feelings, while the ones to Jessie Butler were her "false" feelings? How can we possibly arrive at an objective conclusion about "real" feelings in any social situation in which such severe strains existed?

Yet putting the question in this light offers at least a partial way out of the dilemma. If so many clues in the investigation are hopelessly "biased"—that is, distorted by the social situation in which they are set—then the very pervasiveness of the distortion may serve as a key to understanding the situation. The evidence in the case is warped precisely because it accurately reflects a distortion in the society itself. The elements of racism and slavery determined a culture in which personal relations were necessarily grounded in mistrust and deception; in which slaves could survive only if they remained acutely conscious of the need to adapt their feelings to the situation. The distortion in the evidence, in other words, speaks eloquently of the hurt inflicted in a society in which personal behavior routinely operated under an economy of deception.

The deception was mutual—practiced by both sides on each other. Susan Hamlin was adapting the story of her past to the needs of the moment at the same time that Jessie Butler was letting Hamlin believe her to be a welfare agent. White masters painted lurid stories of Yankee devils with horns while slaves, playing roles they were expected to play, rolled their eyes in fear until they had the chance to run straight for Union lines. The deceptions fed on each other and were compounded, becoming an inextricable part of daily life.

It would be tempting, given our awareness of this situation, simply to turn previous historical interpretations on their heads. Whereas William Dunning and his disciples took most of their primary sources at face value and thus saw only cheerful, childlike Sambos, an enlightened history would read the documents upside down, so to speak, stripping away the camouflage to reveal slaves who, quite rationally, went about the daily business of "puttin' on ole massa." And of course we have already seen abundant evidence that slaves did use calculated deception in order to protect themselves.

But simply to replace one set of feelings with another is to ignore the intricate and tense relationships between them. It drastically underestimates the strains that arose out of an economy of deception. The longer and more consistently that masters and slaves were compelled to live false or inauthentic lives, the easier it must have been for them to mislead themselves as well as others. Where white and black people alike engaged in daily dissimulation, some of the deception was inevitably directed inward, simply to preserve the fiction of living in a tolerable, normally functioning society.

When the war came, shattering that fiction, whites and blacks were exposed in concrete and vivid ways to the deception that had been so much a part of their lives. For white slaveholders, the revelation usually came when Union troops entered a region and slaves deserted the plantations in droves. Especially demoralizing was the flight of slaves whom planters had believed most loyal. "He was about my age and I had always treated him more as a companion than a slave," noted one planter of the first defector from his ranks. Mary Chesnut, the woman near Fort Sumter who had tried to penetrate the blank expressions of her slaves, discovered how impossible the task had been. "Jonathan, whom we trusted, betrayed us," she lamented, while "Claiborne, that black rascal who was suspected by all the world," faithfully protected the plantation.

Many slaveholders, when faced with the truth, refused to recognize the role that deception had played in their lives, thereby deceiving themselves further. "The poor negroes don't do us any harm except when they are put up to it," concluded one Georgia woman. A Richmond newspaper editor demanded that a slave who had denounced Jefferson Davis "be whipped every day until he confesses what white man put these notions in his head." Yet the war brought painful insight to others. "We were all laboring under a delusion," confessed one South Carolina planter. "I believed that these people were content, happy, and attached to their masters. But events and reflection have caused me to change these opinions. . . . If they were content, happy and attached to their masters, why did they desert him in the moment of his need and flock to an enemy, whom they did not know?"

For slaves, the news of emancipation brought an entirely different reaction, but still one conditioned by the old habits. We have already seen how one old Georgia slave couple remained impassive as Sherman's troops passed through, until finally the wife could restrain herself no longer. Even the servant who eloquently shouted the praises of freedom at a secluded brook instinctively remembered the need for caution: "I got sort o' scared, afeared somebody hear me, an' I takes another good look." Although emancipation promised a society founded on equal treatment and open relations, slaves could not help wondering whether the new order would fully replace the old. That transformation would occur only if freedpeople could forge relationships that were no longer based on the customs of deception nor rooted in the central fiction of slavery—that blacks were morally and intellectually incapable of assuming a place in free society.

As historians increasingly came to recognize the value of the slave narrative collection, they drew upon its evidence, along with the standard range of primary sources, to re-create the perspectives of freedpeople as they sought the real meaning of their new freedom. Certainly that meaning was by no means evident once the first excitement of liberation had passed. James Lucas, a slave of Jefferson Davis, recalled the inevitable confusion: "Dey all had diffe'nt ways o' thinkin' 'bout it. Mos'ly though dey was jus' lak me, dey didn' know jus' zackly what it meant. It was jus' somp'n dat de white folks an' slaves all de time talk 'bout. Dat's all. Folks dat ain' never been free don' rightly know de feel of bein' free. Dey don' know de meanin' of it." But former slaves were not long in taking their first steps toward defining freedom. On the surface, many of these steps seemed small. But however limited, they served to distance the freedpeople in significant ways from the old habits of bondage.

The taking of new names was one such step. As slaves, African Americans often had no surname or took the name of their master. Equally demeaning, given names were often casually assigned by their owners. Cicero, Pompey, and other Latin or Biblical names were commonly bestowed in jest. And whether or not slaves had a surname, they were always addressed familiarly, by their given names. Such customs were part of the symbolic language of deception, promoting the illusion that black people were helpless and even laughable dependents of the planter's family.

Thus many freedpeople took for themselves new names, severing the symbolic tie with their old masters. "A heap of people say they was going to name their selves over," recalled one freedman. "They named their selves big names. . . . Some of the names was Abraham an' some called their selves Lincum. Any big name 'ceptin' their master's name. It was the fashion." Even former slaves who remained loyal to their masters recognized the significance of the change. "When you'all had de power you was good to me," an older freedman told his master, "an I'll protect you now. No niggers nor Yankees shall touch you. If you want anything, call for Sambo. I mean, call for Mr. Samuel—that's my name now."

Just as freedpeople took new names to symbolize their new status, so also many husbands and wives reaffirmed their marriages in formal ceremonies. Under slavery, many marriages and family ties had been ignored through the convenient fiction that Africans were morally inferior. Black affections, the planters argued, were dominated by impulse and the physical desires of the moment. Such self-deception eased many a master's conscience when slave families were separated and sold. Similarly, many planters married slaves only informally, with a few words sufficing to join the couple. "Don't mean nuthin' less you say, "What God done jined, cain't no man pull asunder," noted one Virginia freedman. "But dey never would say dat. Jus' say, 'Now you married.' " For obvious reasons of human dignity, black couples moved to solemnize their marriage vows. There were practical reasons for an official ceremony too: it might qualify families for military pensions or the division of lands that was widely rumored to be coming.

Equally symbolic for most former slaves was the freedom to travel where they wished. As we have seen, historian William Dunning recognized this fact, but interpreted it from the viewpoint of his southern white sources as "aimless but happy" wandering. Black accounts make abundantly clear how travel helped freedpeople to rid themselves of the role they had been forced to play during their bondage. Richard Edwards, a preacher in Florida, explicitly described the symbolic nature of such a move:

You ain't, none o' you, gwinter feel rale free till you shakes de dus' ob de Old Plantashun offen yore feet an' goes ter a new place whey you kin live out o' sight o' de gret house. So long ez de shadder ob de gret house falls acrost you, you ain't gwine ter feel lak no free man, an' you ain't gwine ter feel lak no free 'oman. You mus' all move—you mus' move clar away from de ole places what you knows, ter de new places what you don't know, whey you kin raise up yore head douten no fear o' Marse Dis ur Marse Tudder.

And so, in the spring and summer of 1865, southern roads were filled with black people, hiving off "like bees trying to find a setting place," as one former slave recalled. Most freedpeople preferred to remain within the general locale of family and friends, merely leaving one plantation in search of work at another. But a sizable minority traveled farther, to settle in cities, move west, or try their fortunes at new occupations.

Many former slaves traveled in order to reunite families separated through previous sales. Freedpeople "had a passion, not so much for wandering, as for getting together," a Freedman's Bureau agent observed; "and every mother's son among them seemed to be in search of his mother; every mother in search of her children." Often, relatives had only scanty information; in other cases, so much time had passed that kin could hardly recognize each other, especially when young children had grown up separated from their parents.

A change of name or location, the formalization of marriages, reunion with relatives—all these acts demonstrated that freedpeople wanted no part of the old constraints and deceptions of slavery. But as much as these acts defined black freedom, larger issues remained. How much would emancipation broaden economic avenues open to African Americans? Would freedom provide an opportunity to rise on the social ladder? The freedpeople looked anxiously for signs of significant changes.

Perhaps the most commonly perceived avenue to success was through education. Slavery had been rationalized, in part, through the fiction that blacks were incapable of profiting from an education. The myth of intellectual inferiority stood side by side with that of moral inferiority. Especially in areas where masters had energetically prevented slaves from acquiring skills in reading, writing, and arithmetic, the freedpeople's hunger for learning was intense. When northerners occupied the Carolina Sea Islands during the war, Yankee plantation superintendents found that the most effective way to force unwilling laborers to work was to threaten to take away their schoolbooks. "The Negroes . . . will do anything for us, if we will only teach them," noted one missionary stationed on the islands.

After the war, when the Freedman's Bureau sent hundreds of northern schoolteachers into the South, black students flocked enthusiastically to the makeshift schoolhouses. Often, classes could be held only at night, but the freedpeople were willing. "We work all day, but we'll come to you in the evening for learning," Georgia freedpeople told their teacher. Some white plantation owners discovered that if they wished to keep their field hands, they would have to provide a schoolhouse and teacher.

"My Lord, ma'am, what a great thing larning is!" a freedman exclaimed to a white teacher. Many white people were surprised by the intensity of the ex-slaves' desire for an education. To say that the freedpeople were "anxious to learn" was not strong enough, one Virginia school official noted; "they are *crazy* to learn." These schoolboys were from South Carolina.

Important as education was, the freedpeople were preoccupied even more with their relation to the lands they had worked for so many years. The vast majority of slaves were field hands. The agricultural life was the one they had grown up with, and as freedpeople, they wanted the chance to own and cultivate their own property. Independent ownership would lay to rest the lie that black people were incapable of managing their own affairs; but without land, the idea of freedom would be just another deception. "Gib us our own land and we take care of ourselves; but widout land, de ole massas can hire us or starve us, as dey please," noted one freedman. In the heady enthusiasm at the close of the war, many former slaves were convinced that the Union would divide up confiscated Confederate plantations. Each family, so the persistent rumor went, would receive forty acres and a mule. "This was no slight error, no trifling idea," reported one white observer, "but a fixed and earnest conviction as strong as any belief a man can ever have." Slaves had worked their masters' lands for so long without significant compensation, it seemed only fair that recompense should finally be made. Further, the liberated had more than hopes to rely on. Ever since southern planters had fled from invading Union troops, some black workers had been allowed to cultivate the abandoned fields.

The largest of such occupied regions was the Sea Islands along the Carolina coast, where young Sam Mitchell had first heard the northern guns. As early as March 1863, freedpeople were purchasing confiscated lands from the government. Then in January 1865, after General William Sherman completed his devastating march to the sea, he extended the area that was open to confiscation. In his Special Field Order No. 15, Sherman decreed that a long strip of abandoned lands, stretching from Charleston on the north to Jacksonville on the south, would be reserved for the freedpeople. The lands would be subdivided into forty-acre tracts, which could be rented for a nominal fee. After three years, the freedpeople had the option to purchase the land outright.

Sherman's order was essentially a tactical maneuver, designed to deal with the overwhelming problem of refugees in his path. But black workers widely perceived this order and other promises by enthusiastic northerners as a foretaste of Reconstruction policy. Consequently, when white planters returned to their plantations, they often found blacks who no longer bowed obsequiously and tipped their hats. Thomas Pinckney of South Carolina, having called his former slaves together, asked them if they would continue to work for him. "O yes, we gwi wuk! we gwi wuk all right," came the angry response. "We gwi wuk fuh ourse'ves. We ain' gwi wuk fuh no white man." Where would they go to work, Pinckney asked—seeing as they had no land? "We ain't gwine nowhar," they replied defiantly. "We gwi wuk right here on de lan' whar we wuz bo'n an' whar belongs tuh us."

Despite the defiance, Pinckney prevailed, as did the vast majority of southern planters. Redistribution of southern lands was an idea strongly supported only by more radical northerners. Thaddeus Stevens introduced a confiscation bill in Congress, but it was swamped by debate and never passed. President Johnson, whose conciliatory policies pleased southern planters, determined to settle the issue as quickly as possible. He summoned General O. O. Howard, head of the Freedman's Bureau, and instructed Howard to reach a solution "mutually satisfactory" to both blacks and planters. Howard, though sympathetic to the freedpeople, could not mistake the true meaning of the President's order.

Regretfully, the general returned to the Sea Islands in October and assembled a group of freedpeople on Edisto Island. The audience, suspecting the bad news, was restless and unruly. Howard tried vainly to speak and made "no progress" until a woman in the crowd began singing, "Nobody knows the trouble I've seen." The crowd joined, then was silent while Howard told them they must give up their lands. Bitter cries of "No! No!" came from the audience. "Why, General Howard, why do you take away our lands?" called one burly man. "You take them from us who have always been true, always true to the Government! You give them to our all-time enemies! That is not right!"

Reluctantly, and sometimes only after forcible resistance, African Americans lost the lands to returning planters. Whatever else freedom might mean, it was not to signify compensation for previous labor. In the years to come Reconstruction would offer freedom of another sort, through the political process. By the beginning of 1866, the radicals in Congress had charted a plan that gave African Americans basic civil rights and political power. Yet even that avenue of opportunity was quickly sealed off. In the decades that followed the first thunder of emancipation, black people would look back on their early experiences almost as if they were part of another, vanished world. The traditions of racial oppression and the daily deceptions that went with them were too strong to be thoroughly overturned by the war.

"I was right smart bit by de freedom bug for awhile," Charlie Davenport of Mississippi recalled.

> It sounded pow'ful nice to be tol: "You don't have to chop cotton no more. You can th'ow dat hoe down an' go fishin' whensoever de notion strikes you. An' you can roam 'roun' at night an' court gals jus' as you please. Aint no marster gwine a-say to you, 'Charlie, you's got to be back when de clock strikes nine.'"
> I was fool 'nough to b'lieve all dat kin' o' stuff.

Both perceptions—the first flush of the "freedom bug" as well as Davenport's later disillusionment—accurately reflect the black experience. Freedom had come to a nation of four million slaves, and it changed their lives in deep and important ways. But for many years after the war put an end to human bondage, too many freedpeople still had to settle for a view from the bottom rail.

❧ ❧ ❧ ADDITIONAL READING ❧ ❧ ❧

Leon Litwack's superb *Been in the Storm So Long: The Aftermath of Slavery* (New York, 1979) was a seminal work incorporating the evidence from the slave narrative collections into a reevaluation of the Reconstruction era. It serves as an excellent starting point for background on the freedpeople's experience after the war. For an overview of Reconstruction, the definitive account is Eric Foner, *Reconstruction: America's Unfinished Revolution* (New York, 1988). Foner places the contributions of African Americans at the center of his account. Herbert Gutman, *The Black Family in Slavery and Freedom, 1750–1925* (New York, 1976) is another influential work.

African American experiences can be traced in a host of state histories, where more attention is given to grassroots effects of the new freedom. For Maryland, see Barbara Jeanne Fields, *Slavery and Freedom on the Middle Ground* (New Haven, 1985); for Virginia, Lynda J. Morgan, *Emancipation in Virginia's Tobacco Belt, 1850–1870* (Athens, Ga., 1992); for Georgia, Joseph P. Reidy, *From Slavery to Agrarian Capitalism in the Cotton Plantation South* (Chapel Hill, N.C., 1992) and Jonathan M. Bryant, *How Curious a Land* (Chapel Hill, N.C., 1996); for South Carolina, Julie Saville, *The Work of Reconstruction* (New York, 1996) and Joel Williamson, *After Slavery* (Chapel Hill, N.C., 1965); for Alabama, Peter Kolchin, *First Freedom* (Westport, Conn., 1972); for Mississippi, William C. Harris, *Day of the Carpetbagger* (Baton Rouge, La.,1979).

A pioneering work on the experiences of black women is Jacqueline Jones, *Labor of Love, Labor of Sorrow: Black Women, Work, and the Family, from Slavery to the Present* (New York, 1985). More recent treatments include Tera W. Hunter, *To 'Joy My Freedom: Southern Black Women's Lives and Labors after the Civil War* (Cambridge, Mass., 1997) and Leslie A. Schwalm, *A Hard Fight For We: Women's Transition from Slavery to Freedom in South Carolina* (Urbana, Ill., 1997). Willie Lee Rose, *Rehearsal for Reconstruction: The Port Royal Experiment* (Indianapolis, 1964), tells the story of the Union occupation of the Carolina Sea Islands, where the North first attempted to forge a coherent Reconstruction policy. For the Freedmen's Bureau, see William O. McFeely's biography of its leader, General O. O. Howard, *Yankee Stepfather* (New Haven, 1968) and Donald Nieman, *To Set the Law in Motion: The Freedmen's Bureau and the Legal Rights of Blacks* (Millwood, N.Y., 1979).

Although oral history has provided one crucial means of recapturing the experiences of the freedpeople, the past two decades have witnessed a complementary revolution in unearthing manuscript primary sources for the period. The leaders of this movement are the scholars working on the Freedmen and Southern Society Project, based at the University of Maryland and overseen by Ira Berlin and Leslie Rowland. To date, the project has issued four volumes of documentary evidence—letters, surveys, court depositions, military reports—gathered from twenty-five collections in the bureaucratic recesses of the National Archives: *Freedom: A Documentary History of Emancipation, 1861–1867* (New York, 1982–) More volumes are promised. The editors have also issued two briefer, easier-to-manage selections from the collection: Ira Berlin et. al., eds., *Free at Last: A Documentary History of Slavery, Freedom, and the Civil War* (New York, 1992) and *Families and Freedom: A Documentary History of African-American Kinship in the Civil War Era* (New York, 1997). The editors discuss these documents in Ira Berlin, Barbara J. Fields, Steven F. Miller, and Leslie S. Rowland, *Slaves No More: Three Essays on Emancipation and the Civil War* (New York, 1992). Other sources for the freedpeople's perspective include Octavia V. Rogers Albert, *The House of Bondage* (New York, 1891); Orland K. Armstrong, *Old Massa's People* (Indianapolis, Ind., 1931); M. F. Armstrong and Helen W. Ludlow, *Hampton and Its Students* (New York, 1875); and Laura Haviland, *A Woman's Life Work* (Cincinnati, Ohio, 1881).

A selection of oral interviews from the Federal Writers' Project (again, edited by Ira Berlin and his associates) appears in *Remembering Slavery: African Americans Talk about Their Personal Experiences of Slavery and Freedom* (New York, 1998). But the highlight of this collection is an audiocassette containing more than a dozen of the only known original recordings of former slaves. For the full collection of interviews, see George P. Rawick, *The American Slave: A Composite Autobiography*, 19 vols. & supplements (Westport, Conn., 1972–). The collection invites use in many ways. Intriguing material is available on the relations between African Americans and Indians, for example, especially in the Oklahoma narratives. Because one interviewer often submitted many interviews, readers may wish to analyze strengths and weaknesses of particular interviewers. The Library of Congress, under Benjamin Botkin's direction, began such an analysis; its records can be examined at the National Archives, cataloged under Correspondence Pertaining to Ex-Slave Studies, Records of the Federal Writers' Project, Records Group 69, Works Progress Administration.

Further information on the slave narratives may be found in Norman Yetman, "The Background of the Slave Narrative Collection," *American Quarterly* 19 (fall 1967): 534–53 and John Blassingame, "Using the Testimony of Ex-slaves: Approaches and Problems," *Journal of Southern History* 41 (November 1975): 473–92, available in expanded form in the introduction to his *Slave Testimony* (Baton Rouge, La., 1977). Paul D. Escott, *Slavery Remembered: A Record of Twentieth-Century Slave Narratives* (Chapel Hill, N.C., 1979) provides a quantitative analysis, including the percentage of interviews with field hands, house servants, and artisans; the occupations they took up as freedpeople, and the destinations of those who migrated.

Finally, those wishing to try their hand at oral history should consult David K. Dunaway and Willa K. Baum, eds., *Oral History: An Interdisciplinary Anthology* (2d ed., Walnut Creek, Calif., 1996). The volume balances good discussions of methodology and technique with more wide-ranging explorations of the ethical questions involved in interviewing as well as international perspectives. Additional nuts-and-bolts information can be found in James Hoopes's excellent *Oral History: An Introduction for Students* (Chapel Hill, N.C., 1979). See also Cullom Davis et al., *Oral History: From Tape to Type* (Chicago, Ill., 1977) and Ramon I. Harris et al., *The Practice of Oral History* (Glen Rock, N.J., 1975).

INDEX